Public Key Infrastructure
Implementation and Design

Public Key Infrastructure Implementation and Design

Suranjan Choudhury, Kartik Bhatnagar,

and Wasim Haque

M&T Books
An imprint of Hungry Minds, Inc.

New York, NY • Cleveland, OH • Indianapolis, IN

Public Key Infrastructure Implementation and Design

Published by
M&T Books
An imprint of Hungry Minds, Inc.
909 Third Avenue
New York, NY 10022
www.hungryminds.com

Library of Congress Control Number: 2001093596

ISBN: 9780764548796

10 9 8 7 6 5 4 3 2 1

1O/SQ/QS/QS/IN

Distributed in the United States by Hungry Minds, Inc.

Distributed by CDG Books Canada Inc. for Canada; by Transworld Publishers Limited in the United Kingdom; by IDG Norge Books for Norway; by IDG Sweden Books for Sweden; by IDG Books Australia Publishing Corporation Pty. Ltd. for Australia and New Zealand; by TransQuest Publishers Pte Ltd. for Singapore, Malaysia, Thailand, Indonesia, and Hong Kong; by Gotop Information Inc. for Taiwan; by ICG Muse, Inc. for Japan; by Intersoft for South Africa; by Eyrolles for France; by International Thomson Publishing for Germany, Austria, and Switzerland; by Distribuidora Cuspide for Argentina; by LR International for Brazil; by Galileo Libros for Chile; by Ediciones ZETA S.C.R. Ltda. for Peru; by WS Computer Publishing Corporation, Inc., for the Philippines; by Contemporanea de Ediciones for Venezuela; by Express Computer Distributors for the Caribbean and West Indies; by Micronesia Media Distributor, Inc. for Micronesia; by Chips Computadoras S.A. de C.V. for Mexico; by Editorial Norma de Panama S.A. for Panama; by American Bookshops for Finland.

For general information on Hungry Minds' books in the U.S., please call our Consumer Customer Service department at 800-762-2974. For reseller information, including discounts and premium sales, please call our Reseller Customer Service department at 800-434-3422.

For information on where to purchase Hungry Minds' books outside the U.S., please contact our International Sales department at 317-572-3993 or fax 317-572-4002.

For consumer information on foreign language translations, please contact our Customer Service department at 800-434-3422, fax 317-572-4002, or e-mail rights@idgbooks.com.

For information on licensing foreign or domestic rights, please phone +1-650-653-7098.

For sales inquiries and special prices for bulk quantities, please contact our Order Services department at 800-434-3422 or write to the address above.

For information on using Hungry Minds' books in the classroom or for ordering examination copies, please contact our Educational Sales department at 800-434-2086 or fax 317-572-4005.

For press review copies, author interviews, or other publicity information, please contact our Public Relations department at 650-653-7000 or fax 650-653-7500.

For authorization to photocopy items for corporate, personal, or educational use, please contact Copyright Clearance Center, 222 Rosewood Drive, Danvers, MA 01923, or fax 978-750-4470.

 is a trademark of Hungry Minds, Inc.

 is a trademark of Hungry Minds, Inc.

Credits

ACQUISITIONS EDITOR
Katie Feltman

PROJECT EDITORS
Kenyon Brown
Kyle Looper

TECHNICAL EDITOR
Tim Crothers

COPY EDITOR
Kenyon Brown

PROJECT COORDINATOR
Nancee Reeves

GRAPHICS AND PRODUCTION SPECIALISTS
Beth Brooks
Sean Decker
Melanie DesJardins
Joyce Haughey
LeAndra Johnson
Laurie Petrone
Betty Schulte
Jeremey Unger

QUALITY CONTROL TECHNICIANS
Andy Hollandbeck
Angel Perez
Carl Pierce

PROOFREADING AND INDEXING
TECHBOOKS Production Services

About the Authors

Suranjan Choudhury, MCSE, CACP, CADC, Sun, is a network security specialist for NIIT, a global training and software organization. He has developed security policies and overseen implementation of secure Web sites and messaging systems (using PKI, firewall, portal, and VPN technologies) for GE, Amro Band, NALCO, and the Indian Ministry of Defense, and other organizations.

Kartik Bhatnagar has an MBA in systems, and is currently employed as a Development Executive with NIIT. His work involves design, development, testing, and implementation of instructor-led training courses and textbooks. To date he has developed several instructor-led training courses on Mac OS 9.0, Cisco security, and Windows 2000 server. He has completed extensive research and implementation of Cisco security, Windows 2000 security, and Oracle applications. He has also written chapters for the *Cisco Security Bible* and *Oracle Applications Performance-Tuning.*

Wasim Haque has over 7 years of experience in Information Technology with expertise in analysis, design, and implementation of enterprise-wide networks using Cisco Router, Alcatel, 3 Com Switches, Cabletron Switches with Frame Relay, Leased Lines, and various security solutions for the enterprise. He holds certifications in Cisco Certified Network Professional Stream (Routing 2.0), Cisco Certified Network Associate, BrainBench Certification CISCO Network Implementation Specialist, and BrainBench Certification Master WAN Technologies Specialist.

Preface

Today we are in the midst of an electronic business revolution. The growth of the Internet and e-commerce has presented businesses with an opportunity to forge new links with customers and partners by transcending borders and removing geographical barriers. Electronic information exchange and networking poses a greater threat than ever before because of fraud, e-mail eavesdropping, and data theft that affect both companies and individuals. Consequently, information security is a major issue today for any company or individual who conducts business electronically.

It is of utmost importance that mechanisms are set up to ensure information and data security. Organizations have recognized the need to balance the concern for protecting information and data with the desire to leverage the electronic medium for competitive advantage. Public Key Infrastructure (PKI) is a step toward providing a secure electronic business environment. With the rapid growth of e-business, PKI is destined to become in the future so commonplace that organizations will issue digital certificates and smart cards as part of their normal business practices.

What the Book Is About

PKI combines hardware and software products with policies and procedures of e-businesses. It provides the mechanism to process secure electronic transactions using a system of digital certificates and certificate authorities. This book provides an in-depth coverage of the important issues that need to be taken into account while implementing PKI in the electronic business environment. It discusses cryptography concepts and details the components of a PKI. It also discusses how to evaluate and deploy a PKI solution. In addition, this book

- ◆ Is structured to facilitate accessibility of concepts that are related to PKI.

- ◆ Provides a scenario-based explanation of concepts. Using scenarios facilitates relating technical concepts to real-life situations.

- ◆ Provides notes and tips on various key concepts.

- ◆ Includes "check your understanding" questions to facilitate learning.

This book teaches you how you can actually implement a PKI solution. No other book that is available in the market teaches the practical implementation of PKI, such as issuing a certificate and implementing SSL, IPSec, and S/MIME. The book

- ◆ Focuses on the skills you need to design and implement a PKI solution for small- to medium-sized networks.

- ◆ Provides a strong foundation to help you build your analytical skills, and guides you through network designing techniques using practice questions.

Problem solving techniques are explained using the stages of planning, implementation, and verification.

◆ Provides explanations of concepts by using diagrams and illustrations to help you visualize the scenarios and understand more effectively.

After reading this book, you will be able to demonstrate proficiency in designing and implementing secure electronic business networks using PKI.

Who Should Read the Book

This book is meant for all experienced network administrators and security specialists who want to evaluate PKI design and implementation, and who want to implement the right PKI solution for their organization.

This book targets network administrators and architects in any industry around the world, namely:

◆ Network Administrators

◆ Networking Consultants

◆ Network Architects

◆ Systems Engineers

◆ Network Engineers

◆ Technical Support Engineers

This book would be ideal for network administrators and security specialists who are familiar with Internet e-commerce.

How This Book Is Organized

The book is organized in 12 chapters, 4 appendixes, and a glossary. The first few chapters discuss the basics of cryptography and PKI. After reviewing the basics, the book moves on to discussing the application of PKI. The information explains how to implement a PKI solution and other PKI-enabled services. We have also included a case study at the end of the book to help you to understand the implementation of PKI based on a real-life scenario.

CHAPTER 1: CRYPTOGRAPHY BASICS

This chapter introduces you to the world of cryptography. It includes two types of cryptographic techniques, namely symmetric cryptography and asymmetric cryptography. This chapter also covers the various applications of cryptography, including Message encryption, Message Authentication Code, and Hash functions. Finally, it discusses the role and use of digital signatures in modern encryption/decryption mechanisms.

CHAPTER 2: PUBLIC KEY INFRASTRUCTURE BASICS

This chapter examines the basics of PKI. It is divided into three sections. The first section examines the roles of different authorities in PKI, namely Certification Authority and Registration Authority. The second section discusses the components of PKI. It introduces you to the concept of certificates, which form the basis of implementing a PKI solution. Finally, the third section discusses the various processes that are typically carried out in PKI.

CHAPTER 3: PKI ARCHITECTURE

This chapter details the various PKI architectures available and advantages and disadvantages of each architecture. It introduces the three primary PKI architectures in use today, which can be used according to the needs of the organization. These three PKI architectures are: Single CA Architecture, Enterprise PKI Architecture, and Hybrid PKI Architecture.

CHAPTER 4: CA FUNCTIONS

This chapter gives you an overview of the various functions carried out by CA. It discusses the process of issuing certificates and the basics of certification revocation. This chapter introduces the concept of certificate policy, which defines the use of certificates in specific applications and situations and of a Certification Practice Statement (CPS) that implements these policies. Finally, this chapter discusses how certificate users access certificate policies and CPS through Policy Object Identifiers and the role of CA certificates.

CHAPTER 5: CERTIFICATE MANAGEMENT

This chapter describes the process of certificate enrollment. It introduces you to Registration Authority (RA) that registers the certificate requests of the users. Then, it discusses the process of key backups, certificate expiry and archiving, and certificate retrieval and validation. It also introduces you to the basics of CRLs, their different versions, CRL extensions, and finally, the CRL distribution process.

CHAPTER 6: PKI MANAGEMENT PROTOCOLS AND STANDARDS

This chapter discusses the working of various PKI management protocols and their evaluation criteria. The PKI management protocols obtain the information needed by CAs to issue or revoke certificates. The most commonly used PKI management protocols are PKCS#10, PKCS#7, Certificate Management Protocol (CMP), Certificate Management using CMS (CMC), and Simple Certificate Enrollment Protocol (SCEP).

CHAPTER 7: PKI-ENABLED SERVICES

This chapter discusses the applications that are supported by PKI, such as SSL/TLS, S/MIME, and IPSec. All these applications are based on the concept of PKI and perform specific functions. For example, S/MIME is used specifically for securing e-mail messages.

CHAPTER 8: INSTALLING WINDOWS 2000-BASED PKI SOLUTIONS

All the previous chapters gave you a theoretical knowledge of PKI, such as components of PKI, interactions between these components, and applications of PKI. However, this chapter imparts the necessary skills to implement PKI. It demonstrates how to install Certification Authorities (CA), retrieve certificates, and install subordinate CAs. Next, it demonstrates how to revoke a certificate and publish CRLs, and finally how to automatically enroll a certificate by using Group Policy.

CHAPTER 9: INSTALLING AND CONFIGURING WINDOWS 2000 CERTIFICATE SERVER FOR SSL, IPSEC, AND S/MIME

This chapter demonstrates how to install and configure SSL and make a Web site SSL-enabled. Next, it demonstrates how to install and configure IPSec, and finally, how to create and test an IPSec policy.

CHAPTER 10: UNDERSTANDING PGP

This chapter introduces the concept of Pretty Good Privacy (PGP). It discusses different operations performed in PGP, certificates supported by PGP, PGP keys, and key rings. Finally, it discusses the workings of PGP.

CHAPTER 11: PLANNING FOR PKI DEPLOYMENT

This chapter gives you an insight into evaluating PKI solutions. It also explains the operational requirements for PKI. In addition, it provides a brief background to the legal framework that governs PKI.

CHAPTER 12: ALLSOLV, INC. CASE STUDY

This chapter includes a case study that relates to deploying a PKI solution. The case study illustrates using a single Certification Authority (CA) and a hierarchical CA structure for deploying the PKI solution, and demonstrates the deployment of a PGP solution.

APPENDIXES AND GLOSSARY

The four appendixes provide in-depth additional information about the various aspects of cryptography, which we could not include in the chapters because of the scope of the coverage. The glossary defines important terminology.

What Conventions Are Used in the Book

Each icon that is used in this book signifies a special meaning. Here's what each icon means:

Note icons provide supplemental information about the subject at hand, but generally something that isn't quite the main idea. Notes are often used to elaborate on a detailed technical point.

Tips provide special information or advice. They indicate a more efficient way of doing something, or a technique that may not be obvious.

Caution icons warn you of a potential problem or error.

This icon directs you to related information in another section or chapter.

Acknowledgments

We would like to acknowledge the contribution of all those at NIIT and Hungry Minds who were directly or indirectly involved in the creation of this book. My special thanks to the Project Manager at NIIT, Ms. Anita Sastry, and the Graphics Designer at NIIT, Sunil Kumar Pathak. Without their valuable contributions, this book wouldn't be possible. The technical editor for this book was Tim Crothers. He did an excellent job of reviewing the manuscript and offered a lot of constructive suggestions. I also want to thank Ken Brown, the project editor at Hungry Minds.

A very special thanks to Vivek Agarwal, Dimple Walia, Vinay Shrivastava, Nitin Pandey, Meeta Gupta, Mridula Parihar, Ashok Appu, Rashim Mogha, Yesh Singhal Kavita Kochhar, and Sripriya and Angshuman Chakraborty whose timely and indispensable help made this book a reality. Last but surely not the least, I want to thank my parents for being ever so supportive.

Contents at a Glance

Contents

Chapter 1

Cryptography Basics

IN THIS CHAPTER

- ◆ The basics of cryptography
- ◆ Applications of cryptography
- ◆ Digital signatures

FROM THE DAWN OF CIVILIZATION, to the highly networked societies that we live in today – communication has always been an integral part of our existence. What started as simple sign-communication centuries ago has evolved into many forms of communication today – the Internet being just one such example. Methods of communication today include

- ◆ Radio communication
- ◆ Telephonic communication
- ◆ Network communication
- ◆ Mobile communication

All these methods and means of communication have played an important role in our lives, but in the past few years, network communication, especially over the Internet, has emerged as one of the most powerful methods of communication – with an overwhelming impact on our lives.

Such rapid advances in communications technology have also given rise to security threats to individuals and organizations. In the last few years, various measures and services have been developed to counter these threats. All categories of such measures and services, however, have certain fundamental requirements, which include

- ◆ **Confidentiality,** which is the process of keeping information private and secret so that only the intended recipient is able to understand the information. For example, if Alice has to send a message to Bob, then Bob only (and no other person except for Bob) should be able to read or understand the message.

- ◆ **Authentication,** which is the process of providing proof of identity of the sender to the recipient, so that the recipient can be assured that the person sending the information is who and what he or she claims to be. For example, when Bob receives a message from Alice, then he should be able to establish the identity of Alice and know that the message was indeed sent by Alice.

◆ **Integrity,** which is the method to ensure that information is not tampered with during its transit or its storage on the network. Any unauthorized person should not be able to tamper with the information or change the information during transit. For example, when Alice sends a message to Bob, then the contents of the message should not be altered with and should remain the same as what Alice has sent.

◆ **Non-repudiation,** which is the method to ensure that information cannot be disowned. Once the non-repudiation process is in place, the sender cannot deny being the originator of the data. For example, when Alice sends a message to Bob, then she should not be able to deny later that she sent the message.

Before we look at the various mechanisms that provide these security services, let us look at the various types of security attacks that can be faced by an organization:

◆ **Interruption:** In an attack where one or more of the systems of the orga-nization become unusable due to attacks by unauthorized users. This leads to systems being unavailable for use. Figure 1-1 displays the process of interruption.

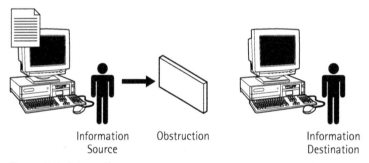

Information   Obstruction   Information
Source   Destination

Figure-1-1: Interruption

◆ **Interception:** An unauthorized individual intercepts the message content and changes it or uses it for malicious purposes. After this type of attack, the message does not remain confidential; for example, if the contents of message that Alice sends to Bob are read or altered during its transmission of message by a hacker or an interceptor. In this situation, Bob cannot consider such a message to be a confidential one. Figure 1-2 displays the process of interception.

◆ **Modification:** The content of the message is modified by a third party. This attack affects the integrity of the message. Figure 1-3 displays the process of modification.

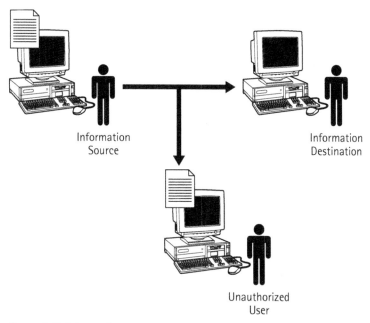

Figure 1-2: Interception

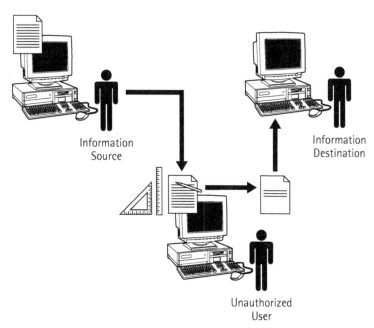

Figure 1-3: Modification

◆ Fabrication: In this attack, a third party inserts spurious messages into the organization network by posing as a valid user. This attack affects the confidentiality, authenticity, and integrity of the message. Figure 1-4 displays fabrication.

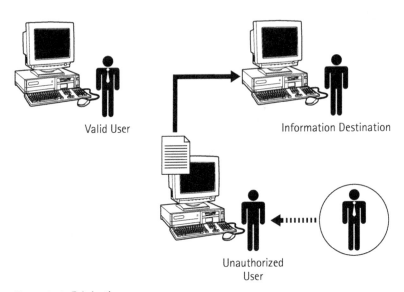

Figure 1-4: Fabrication

From securing sensitive military information to securing personal messages, you often would be confronted with the need of masking information to protect it. One of the most important methods that help provide security to messages in transit is *cryptography*. It helps overcome the security issues as described above, involved in the delivery of messages over any communication channel. This chapter provides an overview of cryptography and popular cryptographic techniques.

 The term *cryptology* has its origin in the Greek kryptós lógos, which means "hidden word." Other examples of cryptography date back to circa 1900 B.C. when Egyptians began using hieroglyphics in inscriptions.

The Basics of Cryptography

Cryptography is the science of protecting data, which provides means and methods of converting data into unreadable form, so that

- ◆ The data cannot be accessed for unauthorized use.

- ◆ The content of the data frames is hidden.

- ◆ The authenticity of the data can be established.

- ◆ The undetected modification of the data is avoided.

- ◆ The data cannot be disowned by the originator of the message.

Cryptography is one of the technological means to provide security to data being transmitted on information and communications systems. Cryptography is especially useful in the cases of financial and personal data, irrespective of the fact that the data is being transmitted over a medium or is stored on a storage device. It provides a powerful means of verifying the authenticity of data and identifying the culprit, if the confidentiality and integrity of the data is violated. Because of the development of electronic commerce, cryptographic techniques are extremely critical to the development and use of defense information systems and communications networks.

History of Cryptography

As already discussed, the messages were first encrypted in ancient Egypt as a result of hieroglyphics. The Egyptians encrypted messages by simply replacing the original picture with another picture. This method of encryption was known as substitution cipher. In this method, each letter of the cleartext message was replaced by some other letter, which results in an encrypted message or ciphertext. For example, the message

```
WELCOME TO THE WORLD OF CRYPTOGRAPHY
```

can be encrypted by using substitution cipher as

```
XFMDPNF UP UIF XPSME PG DSZQUPHSBQIZ
```

In the preceding example, each letter of the plaintext message has been replaced with the next letter in the alphabet. This type of substitution is also known as Caesar cipher.

Caesar cipher is an example of shift cipher because it involves shifting each letter of the plaintext message by some number of spaces to obtain the ciphertext. For example, if you shift the letters by 5, you get the following combination of plaintext and ciphertext letters:

```
Plaintext   A B C D E F G H I J K L M N O P Q R S T U V W X Y Z
Ciphertext  F G H I J K L M N O P Q R S T U V W X Y Z A B C D E
```

However, simple substitution ciphers are not a very reliable type and can easily be broken down. In such a case, an alternative way is to use multiple alphabets instead of one alphabet. This type of a cipher, which involves multiple cipher alphabets, is known as a *polyalphabetic substitution cipher.* An example of the polyalphabetic substitution cipher is the Vigenere cipher.

With the recent advances in mathematical techniques, there has an acceleration in the development of newer methods of encryption. Today, cryptography has emerged so powerful that it is considered rather impossible to break some ciphers.

Cryptography has now become an industry standard for providing information security, trust, controlling access to resources, and electronic transactions. Its use is no longer limited to just securing sensitive military information. In fact, cryptography is now recognized as one of the major components of the security policy of an organization.

Before moving further with cryptography, let us first look at a few terms that are commonly associated with cryptography:

- ◆ Plaintext: Is the message that has to be transmitted to the recipient. It is also commonly referred to as *cleartext.*

- ◆ Encryption: Is the process of changing the content of a message in a manner such that it hides the actual message.

- ◆ Ciphertext: Is the output that is generated after encrypting the plain text.

- ◆ Decryption: Is the reverse of encryption and is the process of retrieving the original message from its encrypted form. This process converts ciphertext to plaintext.

- ◆ Hash algorithm: Is an algorithm that converts text string into a string of fixed length.

- ◆ Key: Is a word, number, or phrase that is used to encrypt the cleartext. In computer–based cryptography, any text, key word, or phrase is converted to a very large number by applying a hash algorithm on it. The large number, referred to as a key, is then used for encryption and decryption.

- ◆ Cipher: Is a hash algorithm that translates plaintext into an intermediate form called *ciphertext*, in which the original message is in an unreadable form.

- ◆ Cryptanalysis: Is the science of breaking codes and ciphers.

Before looking at the details of various cryptographic techniques, let us now look at the steps involved in the conventional encryption model:

1. A sender wants to send a *Hello* message to a recipient.

2. The original message, also called plaintext, is converted to random bits known as ciphertext by using a key and an algorithm. The algorithm

being used can produce a different output each time it is used, based on the value of the key.

3. The ciphertext is transmitted over the transmission medium.

4. At the recipient end, the ciphertext is converted back to the original text using the same algorithm and key that were used to encrypt the message.

This process is also shown in Figure 1-5.

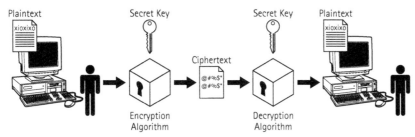

Figure-1-5: Conventional encryption model

Having looked at an overview of cryptography, let us now look at the various cryptography techniques available. For the purpose of classification, the techniques are categorized on the basis of the number of keys that are used. The two main cryptography techniques are

◆ **Single key cryptography:** This cryptography technique is based on a single key. It is also known as symmetric key or private key or secret key encryption.

◆ **Public key cryptography:** This cryptography technique is based on a combination of two keys – secret key and public key. It is also known as asymmetric encryption.

Let us look at each of these methods in detail.

Single Key Cryptography

The process of encryption and decryption of information by using a single key is known as secret key cryptography or *symmetric key cryptography*. In symmetric key cryptography, the same key is used to encrypt as well as decrypt the data. The main problem with symmetric key algorithms is that the sender and the receiver have to agree on a common key. A secure channel is also required between the sender and the receiver to exchange the secret key.

Here's an example that illustrates the process of single key cryptography. Alice wants to send a "For Your Eyes" message to Bob and wants to ensure that only Bob is able to read the message. To secure the transmission, Alice generates a secret key, encrypts the message with this key, and sends the message to Bob.

Figure 1-6 represents the process of secret key cryptography.

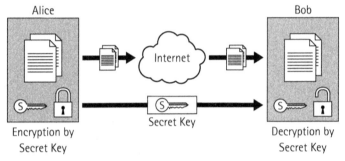

Figure 1-6: Secret key cryptography

Now, to read the encrypted message, Bob would need the secret key that has been generated by Alice. Alice can give the secret key to Bob in person or send the key to Bob by any other means available. If Alice sends the key to Bob in person, it could be time-consuming depending on the physical distance between the two of them or other circumstances such as Bob's availability. After Bob receives the secret key, he can decrypt the message to retrieve the original message.

Many secret key algorithms were developed on the basis of the concept of secret key cryptography. The most widely used secret key algorithms include

◆ Data Encryption Standard (DES)

◆ Triple-DES (3DES)

◆ International Data Encryption Algorithm (IDEA)

◆ RC4

◆ CAST-128

◆ Advanced Encryption Standard (AES)

Let us consider these algorithms in detail in the following sections.

DATA ENCRYPTION STANDARD (DES)

DES, which is an acronym for the Data Encryption Standard, is the common name for the Federal Information Processing Standard (FIPS) 46-3. It describes the *Data Encryption Algorithm* (DEA). DEA is also defined in the ANSI standard X3.92. The DES algorithm is one of the most widely used encryption algorithms in the world. The Data Encryption Standard (DES) algorithm was developed by the IBM team in the 1970s and was adopted by National Institute of Standards and Technology (NIST) for commercial applications.

Refer to RFCs 1827 and 2144 for more information on DES.

DES is still surrounded by controversy. This controversy was originally fueled by the following facts:

♦ The key length used by this algorithm was reduced to 56 bits by the U.S. government, although the original design called for a key length of 128 bits, leading to a compromise on security. Although the algorithm for DES was published, the rationale for the design was never published.

♦ DES became widely available to the U.S. public and to approved users in other countries. However, DES was excluded by the U.S. government from protection of any of its own classified information.

The major weaknesses and attacks that are faced by DES are described below.

BRUTE FORCE ATTACK   The simplest attack to decipher a DES key is the brute force attack. The brute force attack on the DES algorithm is feasible because of the relatively small key length (56 bit) and ever-increasing computational power of the computers. Until the mid-1990s, brute force attacks were beyond the capabilities of hackers because the cost of computers that were capable of hacking was extremely high and unaffordable. With the tremendous advancement in the field of computing, high-performance computers are relatively cheaper and, therefore, affordable. In fact, general purpose PCs today can be successfully used for brute force attacks. Many hackers today are using more powerful techniques, such as Field Programmable Gate Array (FPGA) and Application-Specific Integrated Circuits (ASIC) technology that provide faster and cheaper means of hacking.

You can break through any cipher by trying all keys that possibly exist. However, in brute force attacks, the time taken to break a cipher is directly proportional to the length of the key. In a brute force attack, keys are randomly generated and applied to the ciphertext until the legitimate key is generated. This key decrypts the data into its original form. Therefore, the encryption key length is a major factor that needs to be considered while choosing a key. The longer the encryption keys, the stronger the security. For example, in case of a 32-bit long key, the number of steps required to break the cipher are about 2^{32} or 10^9. Similarly, a 40-bit key requires about 2^{40} steps. This is something which can be achieved in one week by anyone sitting on his personal computer. A 56-bit key is known to have been broken by professionals and governments by using special hardware in a few months time. Today, 128-bit encryption is considered to be the safest and most reliable means of encrypting messages.

On January 19, 1999, a group of computer enthusiasts from all over the world formed a coalition to decipher a DES encrypted ciphertext and as a result recovered the key in a record-breaking time of 22 hours and 15 minutes. This coalition was known as Distributed.Net. Its members worked with DES Cracker and a worldwide network of nearly 100,000 PCs on the Internet to recover the key. The DES Cracker machine was specially designed for this purpose.

For more information on brute force attacks, refer to RFCs 2228 and 2557.

DIFFERENTIAL CRYPTANALYSIS ATTACK   The differential cryptanalysis attack looks specifically at pairs of ciphertexts whose plaintext have some specific differences. It analyzes these differences as the plaintext propagates through the various rounds of DES when they are encrypted with the same key.

This technique chooses pairs of plaintext with a fixed difference. Two plaintexts can be chosen at random, as long as they satisfy specific difference conditions. Then, using the differences in the resulting ciphertexts, different probabilities can be assigned to different keys. As more and more ciphertext pairs are analyzed, one key emerges, as the most probable candidate key.

For more information on differential cryptanalysis attack, refer to RFC 2144.

LINEAR CRYPTANALYSIS ATTACK   Linear Cryptanalysis attack was invented by Mitsuru Matsui in 1993. This method is based on the concept that if you XOR some of the plaintext bits together, XOR some ciphertext bits together, and then XOR the results, you will get a single bit that is the XOR of some of the key bits. A large number of such plaintexts/ciphertexts pairs are then used to guess the values of the key bits. The greater the volume of the base data, the more reliable is the guess.

For more information on linear cryptanalysis attacks, refer to RFC 2144.

TRIPLE DATA ENCRYPTION STANDARD (3DES)

Triple-DES is a minor variation of DES. Although, three times slower than DES, it can be much more secure, if used properly. In today's scenario, Triple-DES is implemented more widely than DES. This is because DES is easy to break with the help of advanced technology that is widely available today. On the other hand, 3DES has proved to be an extremely reliable solution because of the longer key length that it uses. This extended length of key plays an important role in eliminating many of the shortcut attacks that can be used to reduce the amount of time it takes to break DES.

You can increase the effective key length of your cryptographic system by using the Triple Pass DES through the process known as EDE (Encrypt, Decrypt, and Encrypt). When you use triple pass DES, it first encrypts the plaintext data with a 56-bit key. The ciphertext so obtained is then decrypted by using a different key. When you decrypt ciphertext with some different key it gives some garbage. Finally, you encrypt the garbage with the first key. This process of using triple pass DES for encryption, decryption, and again encryption is commonly referred to as EDE.

Figure 1-7 explains the process of 3DES. This is why this encryption method is referred to as "Triple-DES."

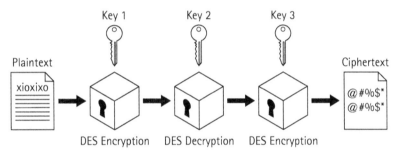

Figure 1-7: Process of 3DES

 Triple-DES has been adopted by ANSI as the standard X9.52 and has been proposed as a revision to FIPS 46, known as draft FIPS 46-3.

 Refer to RFCs 1828 and 2420 for more information on Triple-DES.

INTERNATIONAL DATA ENCRYPTION ALGORITHM (IDEA)

The International Data Encryption Algorithm (IDEA) is a symmetric block cipher developed by Xuejia Lai and James Massey of the Swiss Federal Institute of technology. It uses a 128-bit key to encrypt data in blocks of 64 bits. This is why it is referred to as a block cipher method. IDEA is designed to facilitate both software and hardware implementation.

The major factors that make IDEA a strong algorithm are:

♦ The key length is long enough to prevent comprehensive key searches. IDEA uses a key length of 128 bits, which makes it very secure.

♦ The ciphertext is not easily decipherable from the plaintext and the key. IDEA effectively masks the statistics of how the ciphertext depends on the statistics of the plaintext.

IDEA was developed to provide a high level of security with ease of implementation. Due to its strength and reliability IDEA is now used worldwide in many banking and industry applications.

 You can find more information about the use of the IDEA Encryption Algorithm in a Certificate Management System in RFC 3058.RC2

RC2 or Ron's Code 2 is a 64-bit block cipher that was designed by Ron Rivest. It uses variable-sized keys. This algorithm was designed to replace DES. The code for this algorithm was not made public. However, many companies have licensed RC2 for use in their products. RC2 is being used in a number of software packages, such as Lotus Notes, Microsoft Windows, Internet Explorer, and Netscape Communication's Navigator and Communicator. In addition, RC2 forms an integral component of S/MIME as it provides privacy and interpretability between the export versions and domestic versions of products that use S/MIME.

 You can find more information about RC2 in RFC 2268.

RC4

RC4 is a cipher that was also designed by Ron Rivest, who was the co-inventor of the RSA cipher. It is used in a number of commercial systems like Lotus Notes and Secure Netscape.

For more information on RSA, refer to the RSA section in this chapter.

It is a cipher with a key size of up to 2048 bits (256 bytes). It is listed in the category of relatively fast and strong cipher methods. It is a stream cipher that creates a stream of random bytes and XORs these bytes with the text. Using RC4 with the same key on two different messages makes it very weak. It is thus useful in situations, in which a new key can be chosen for each message.

You can find more information about RC4 in RFC 2246.

RC5

RC5 is yet another block cipher designed by Ron Rivest for RSA Security in 1994. Along with a variable key size, and a variable number of rounds, the size of RC5 data blocks is variable. The block size can range from 32 bits, 64 bits, to 128 bits. Similarly, the number of rounds can range from 0 to 255, while the key can range from 0 bits to 2040 bits in size.

You can find more information about RC4 in RFC 2040.

CAST-128

Carlisle Adams developed CAST-128 in May 1997. This algorithm uses a variable key length and uses block sizes of 64 bits.

The key lengths supported by CAST-128 vary from 40 bits to 128 bits, in increments of 8 bits. For key sizes that range up to 80 bits, the data block undergoes 12 rounds of encryption, while for key sizes of more than 80 bits, the algorithm has 16 rounds. For the keys whose sizes are less than 128 bits, zeroes are added to the rightmost (or the least significant) bits until the total length of the key result is 128 bits. This is done because the algorithm must have an input key of 128 bits in length.

CAST-128 has shown very good encryption/decryption performance. Its implementation has processed up to 3.3 MB/sec on a 150 MHz Pentium processor.

You can find more information about using the CAST-128 Encryption Algorithm in a Certificate Management System in RFC 2984.

ADVANCED ENCRYPTION STANDARD (AES)

With an estimated growth rate of two times every 18 months, computational power is growing in leaps and bounds. This has made Data Encryption Standard (DES) more and more insecure and vulnerable to malicious attacks. As a result, DES, which was the Federal Information Processing Standard (FIPS) until recently, has slowly become redundant. The National Institute of Standards and Technology (NIST) realized this situation and recognized the need for another standard that would be more secure than the DES. However, since DES is a federal standard, it is used widely by many organizations, particularly those in the financial industry.

Advanced Encryption Standard (AES) emerged as a powerful replacement of DES during a competition held by NIST. The competition was organized to develop a substitute of existing DES. The following algorithms reached the final round of the competition to become AES:

- ◆ **MARS:** An algorithm developed by IBM.

- ◆ **RC6:** An algorithm developed by Ron Rivest of RSA Labs, the creator of the widely used RC4 algorithm.

- ◆ **Twofish:** An algorithm from Counterpane Internet Security, Inc. This design was highly suited for large microprocessors and smart card microprocessors.

- ◆ **Serpent:** An algorithm designed by Ross Anderson, Eli Biham, and Lars Knudsen.

- ◆ **Rijndael:** An algorithm designed by Daemen and Rijmen.

Of these algorithms, Rijndael was judged the best and announced to be the new AES. The design of Rijndael was strongly influenced by another cipher called Square, which was also created by Daemen and Rijmen.

Some of the key features of Rijndael are:

- ◆ It is a secret key block cipher.

- ◆ It allows 128-, 192-, and 256-bit key lengths. The block sizes used could be 128-, 192-, or 256-bits long.

- ◆ It gives a vast speed improvement over DES. It is capable of encrypting up to 8.8 MB/sec on a 200 MHz Pentium Pro.

National Institute of Standards and Technology (NIST) chose Rijndael, due to its simplicity and high performance. It is fast, compact, and has a very simple mathematical structure.

PROBLEMS IN SYMMETRIC CRYPTOGRAPHY

The major problem with symmetric cryptography is that the process of transferring keys to the recipient is prone to security risks. Transferring the secret key over the Internet either in an e-mail message or through simple IRC services is insecure. Verbally communicating the key over a phone line runs the risk of eavesdropping. Similarly, snail mail runs the risk of possible interception. The security risks that are involved in secret key cryptography have been overcome to a large extent in another method of cryptography called public key cryptography. Public key cryptography uses a key pair instead of just one secret key. Of this key pair, one key, known as the private key, is always kept secret by the key holder. This private key is not transferred to anyone and is stored securely by the holder of the key and thus public key cryptography eliminates the need for transferring the private key. Let us take an example where Alice wants to send an encrypted message to Bob. If she is using symmetric key encryption, then both Alice and Bob need to first establish a secret key. Only after this secret key has been established, can they both communicate. However, if Alice uses public key encryption, she can send an encrypted message to Bob without first transmitting a secret key. This not only solves the problem of key distribution but also makes the process of key management a lot simpler. In addition to this, public key cryptography also provides data integrity, authentication, and non-repudiation. Public key encryption can also be used for creating digital signatures, which are used for user authentication. Let us now discuss public key cryptography in detail.

Public Key Cryptography

The approach called *asymmetric cryptography* evolved to address the security issues posed by symmetric cryptography. This method solves the problem of secret key cryptography by using two keys instead of a single key. Asymmetric cryptography uses a pair of keys. In this process, one key is used for encryption, and the other key is used for decryption. This process is known as asymmetric cryptography because both the keys are required to complete the process. These two keys are collectively known as the *key pair*. In asymmetric cryptography, one of the keys is freely distributable. This key is called the *public key* and is used for encryption. Hence, this method of encryption is also called public key encryption. The second key is the secret or private key and is used for decryption. The private key is not distributable. This key, like its name suggests, is private for every communicating entity.

In public key cryptography, the data that is encrypted with the public key can only be decrypted with the corresponding private key. Conversely, data encrypted with the private key can only be decrypted with the corresponding public key. Due to this asymmetry, public key cryptography is known as asymmetric cryptography.

HOW DOES PUBLIC KEY CRYPTOGRAPHY WORK?

Let's see how this works out in practice. Consider an example, where Alice wishes to send an encrypted file to Bob. In this situation, Bob would obtain a key pair, retain the private key, and distribute the public key. Alice, therefore, has a copy of Bob's public key. Alice then encrypts the file using Bob's public key and sends the encrypted file to Bob. Since the key pairs are complementary, only Bob's private key can decrypt this file. If someone else intercepts the file, they will be unable to decrypt the file, because only Bob's private key can be used for the decryption. Figure 1-8 explains the process of public key cryptography.

 In today's world, symmetric algorithms are used to handle the data in protocols while asymmetric algorithms are just used for key exchange due to the speed. This helps in striking a balance between speed and security.

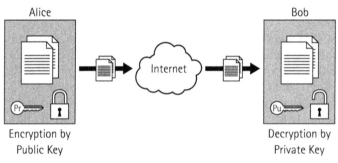

Encryption by
Public Key

Decryption by
Private Key

Figure 1-8: Public key encryption

This method very clearly indicates that the data you send to a user can only be encrypted by the public key. Similarly, the decryption can be done only by the private key, which is supplied by the recipient of the data. So, there is very little possibility of the data in transit being accessed or tampered by any other person. Therefore, messages can be exchanged securely. The sender and receiver do not need to share a key, as required for symmetric encryption. All communications involve only public keys, and no private key is ever transmitted or shared. The above mechanism also brings out the point that every recipient will have a unique key that he will use to decrypt the data that has been encrypted by its counterpart public key. Diffie and Hellman first discussed the process of asymmetric cryptography. One of the most common implementations of this process is the RSA algorithm.

You can find more information about the Diffie-Hellman Key Agreement Method in RFC 2631.

Let us now look at the RSA algorithm in detail.

RSA

RSA refers to a particular implementation of public key cryptography; RSA has become the de facto standard in this field, to the point that RSA and public key encryption are often used as synonyms.

In a cryptographic system with public keys, each object, person or party, must own one public key, which is publicly accessible to all other parties, and one private key, which must be kept secret. Hence, global communication requires only *2n* keys, where *n* is the number of users. The procedure for the sending of a message from User A to User B is performed in the following way:

- ◆ User A obtains the public key of User B from a publicly accessible, authoritative place.

- ◆ User A then encrypts its message using this public key.

- ◆ User B receives the message and decrypts it with his/her private key.

The basic idea of this system was invented by Whitfield Diffie and Martin Hellman and is also used in RSA algorithm.

ADVANTAGES OF RSA   RSA offers a few advantages that have helped in the achievement of manageable and more secure transactions. These advantages include

- ◆ Simplification of the problem of key management: In symmetric encryption the number of keys required to allow *n* entities to communicate is proportional to n^2. Whereas in asymmetric encryption each participant needs two keys; therefore, the total number of keys required is simply *2*n*. The growth in the number of keys with the growth in the number of users is linear and therefore manageable even when there are a large number of users.

- ◆ Enhanced security of the transactions: Not only is the number of keys greatly reduced but the security offered by these keys is highly increased. Every user must have a pair of keys that he/she generates for himself/herself. The secret key must not be shared with anyone and so the problem of transmitting it does not arise, nor do the problems of secure channels and their management; the secret key really is secret, since it is shared with nobody. The public key, however, is shared with everyone, for example in a catalog, which it can be transmitted using the most convenient method, and therefore does not pose any problems regarding its privacy.

RSA has now become an industry standard for encryption. In fact, such is the strength of RSA that the U.S. government has restricted its export to foreign countries.

POSSIBLE ATTACKS ON RSA   The RSA algorithm, although widely prevalent, has some weaknesses. Some of the common attacks that could be faced by RSA are

- ◆ Factoring of the public key: At present RSA seems to be extremely secure. It has survived over 20 years of scrutiny and is in widespread use throughout the world. The attack that is most often considered for RSA is the factoring of the public key. If this can be achieved, all messages written with the public key can be decrypted.

- ◆ Cycle attack: In this attack, the ciphertext is decrypted repeatedly, until the original text appears. A large number of recycles might be able to decrypt any ciphertext. Again, this method is very slow, and for a large key it is not a practical attack.

In spite of all the weaknesses of RSA, it continues to be regarded as a de facto industry standard for encryption, especially data transmitted over the Internet.

Combining Techniques: Symmetric and Asymmetric Encryption

The disadvantage of using public key encryption is that it is a slow process because key lengths are large (1024 bits to 4094 bits). When you compare both processes, secret key encryption is significantly faster as the key length is less (40 bits to 256 bits). On the other hand, there is a problem in transferring the key in secret key encryption. Both these techniques can be used together to provide a better method of encryption. This way you can make use of the combined advantages and over-come the disadvantages.

The steps in data transaction in a combined technique are:

1. Encrypt your file by using a symmetric encryption.

2. Use asymmetric encryption to encrypt only this key using the recipient's public key. Now send the encrypted key to the recipient. The recipient, at his end, can now decrypt the key using his/her private key.

3. Next, send the actual encrypted data. The encrypted data can be decrypted using the key that was encrypted by using the public key from the asymmetric key pair.

Figure 1-9 displays the combined technique of encryption.

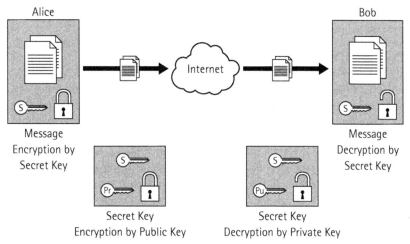

Figure 1-9: Combined technique of encryption

The combined technique of encryption is used widely. It is basically used for Secure Shell (SSH), which is used to secure communications between a client and the server and PGP (Pretty Good Privacy) for sending messages. Above all, it is the heart of Secure Sockets Layer (SSL), which is used widely by Web browsers and Web servers to maintain a secure communication channel with each other.

Applications of Cryptography

By now, you would have understood various cryptography techniques and their advantages and disadvantages. Let us now look at the implementation of cryptography to provide basic security features, which are, confidentiality, integrity, authentication, and non-repudiation.

All these security features can be provided by using any one of the following methods:

◆ Message encryption

◆ Message Authentication Code (MAC)

◆ Hash functions

Let us discuss each of these implementations in detail.

Message Encryption

There are multiple variations of message encryption. Messages can be encrypted either by using secret key encryption or by using public key encryption. Let us look at both the methods in detail.

USING SECRET KEY ENCRYPTION TO PROVIDE CONFIDENTIALITY AND AUTHENTICATION

Conventional encryption methods serve the purpose of authentication, integrity, and confidentiality. Let us look at an example, where Alice wants to send a message to Bob. Only Alice and Bob know the secret key, and no other party knows about the secret key. If Alice sends a message using the secret key to Bob, then Bob knows that the message is coming from Alice, as only Bob and Alice know the secret key. Once the ciphertext reaches Bob, he decrypts the message using the secret key and generates the original plaintext. If Bob recovers the plaintext by using his secret key, this means that the data has not been tampered with during transmission. If Bob is unable to recover the data, this means that someone else might have used the secret key and altered the contents of the message. If the contents of the message are altered then Bob will not be able to decrypt the message.

Figure 1-10 explains this process.

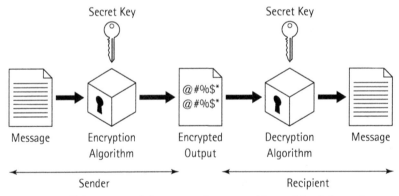

Figure 1-10: Using symmetric key encryption to provide confidentiality and authentication

Hence, the conventional encryption gives both confidentiality and authenticity to messages. However, this method does not provide information about the integrity of data.

USING SECRET KEY ENCRYPTION FOR CONFIDENTIALITY, AUTHENTICATION, AND INTEGRITY

Now let's take an example, where Bob receives a ciphertext from Alice and he decrypts it. Bob can decrypt any ciphertext and produce an output, which will be a plaintext. However, he will get a meaningful output only when Alice has sent the message. Otherwise, the plaintext generated by Bob will be a meaningless sequence of bits. Hence, there must be some automated process at Bob's end to verify that the plaintext he has recovered is a legitimate message and has come from Alice.

If the original plaintext is in a clear message in plain English then determination is easier, because it will generate a meaningless sequence that makes it easier to detect the legitimacy of the message. But if the original message is some binary object file or a digitized image, then it may be difficult to detect the integrity of the message.

To overcome this problem, one solution is to append an error detecting code to the original message, known as *frame check sequence* (FCS). So now if Alice wants to send a message M to Bob, Alice   uses a function FN, which produces an output, FCS. Next, Alice will append this output FCS to the original message M. Then, the entire message along with the FCS will be encrypted using the secret key and will be sent to Bob. Bob will decrypt the entire message with the secret key and will get the message M, and the appended output FCS. Now Bob will put the Message M to the same function, which Alice had used to generate FCS, and produce the FCS. He will compare this FCS with the appended FCS, which has come with the message. If both are the same, then the message is considered legitimate.

This method provides both integrity as well as authenticity. Figure 1-11 explains this process.

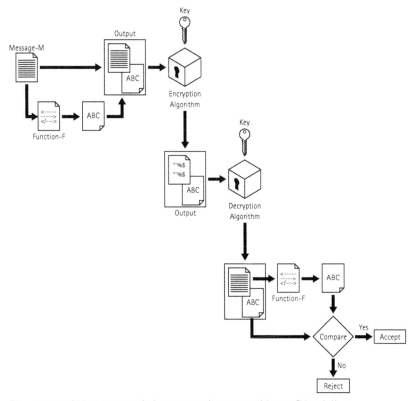

Figure 1-11: Using symmetric key encryption to provide confidentiality, authentication, and integrity

USING PUBLIC KEY ENCRYPTION TO PROVIDE CONFIDENTIALITY

A simple use of public key encryption can provide confidentiality but can't provide authenticity and integrity. Let us take an example where Alice wants to send a message to Bob. She encrypts the message with Bob's public key, and Bob decrypts the message using his private key. This method does not provide any authentication that the message is coming from Alice, because Bob's public key is known to the world. However, it does provide confidentiality to the message, as only Bob can decrypt the message. Figure 1-12 depicts this process.

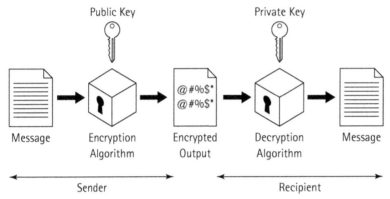

Figure 1-12: Using public key encryption to provide confidentiality

ENSURING CONFIDENTIALITY AND AUTHENTICITY BY USING PUBLIC KEY ENCRYPTION

To provide authentication, Alice must encrypt the message with her private key and Bob will decrypt the message with Alice's public key. This method will provide authenticity, but for integrity there should be a system such as FCS. This system could provide authentication that the message is coming from Alice but it does not provide confidentiality, because Alice's public key is known to all. Hence, anybody possessing Alice's public key can decrypt the message.

To provide both confidentiality and authenticity, Alice will need to encrypt the message first with her private key, which will provide authenticity. Then, she will use Bob's public key to encrypt the message, which will provide confidentiality. Figure 1-13 explains this process.

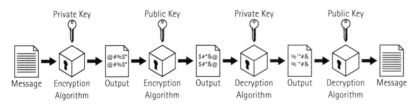

Figure 1-13: Using public key encryption to provide confidentiality and authentication

The disadvantage of the system is that it will be very time consuming and complex as public key encryption and decryption has to be done four times, and the key length of the public key is large (1024 bits to 4094 bits).

Message Authentication Code

To provide authentication and integrity, an alternative method can be used by making use of a secret key to generate a fixed-size block of data. This fixed-size block of data is called *Message Authentication Code* (MAC).

Let's take an example where Alice wants to communicate with Bob. Both Alice and Bob will share a secret key. When Alice wants to send a message to Bob, she will calculate the MAC of the message using the secret key and will append it to the message. When Bob receives the message he will use the shared secret key to generate the MAC of the message, and if both the appended MAC and the generated MAC match, both will be sure of the integrity of the message, as well as the authenticity of the message, as only Bob and Alice know the key. Figure 1-14 explains this process.

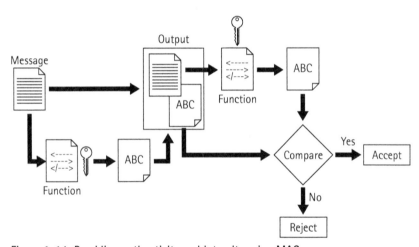

Figure 1-14: Providing authenticity and integrity using MAC

The only difference between MAC and message encryption is that MAC can only be a one-way function, which is not reversible. Once MAC has been generated, the original message can't be regenerated back from the MAC.

The process mentioned above does provide authenticity and integrity but does not provide confidentiality. To provide confidentiality, Alice needs to encrypt the message. The MAC can be appended to the message before encryption. Figure 1-15 displays this process.

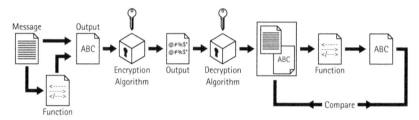

Figure 1-15: Providing authentication, integrity, and confidentiality using MAC

The MAC can also be appended to the message after encryption. In this case, the MAC will be generated by using the ciphertext and not with the original message. Figure 1-16 explains this process.

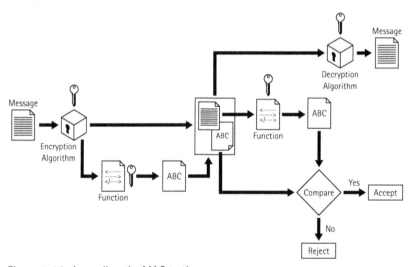

Figure 1-16: Appending the MAC to the message

Hash Functions

A hash function is a variation of the message authentication code. A *hash function,* H, is a conversion method that takes an input *m,* which is the message, and returns a fixed-size string, which is called the *hash value h* (that is, $h = H(m)$) or message digest. This output is fixed in size and is irreversible, which means that the original content can never be recovered. The hash function output could be *weakly collision free,* which means that there is a very rare chance that a similar output could be produced by another message. The output could also be *strongly collision free,* which means that a similar output can never be produced by another message.

If any two hash functions produce the same set of hash values at any time, it is termed as a *collision*. A hash function is considered to be up to the standard, only if the risk of collision is minimal.

Hash functions are normally used to provide the digital fingerprints of files to ensure that the content of the file has not been altered in transit.

There are various ways how hash functions can be used in communication between two individuals. Let us take an example to explain this communication process.

Alice wants to send a message to Bob; Alice will append the hash value of the message with the message and encrypt the message with the secret key. This will provide authenticity, because only Alice and Bob know about the secret key, and encryption is used to provide confidentiality to the message. Figure 1-17 displays this process.

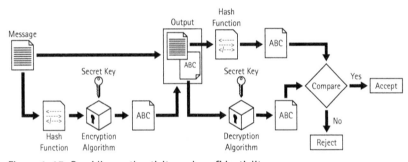

Figure 1-17: Providing authenticity and confidentiality

Alice will encrypt the message digest or the hash value by using her private key. This will generate Alice's digital signature, because only Alice can provide the encrypted hash value. Figure 1-18 explains this process.

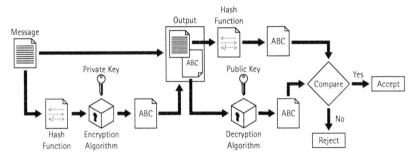

Figure 1-18: Encrypting a message by using the private key

Let's take an example, when Alice wants to send a message to Bob. Bob should know that the message is coming from Alice. Thus, Alice will append her digital signature to the message and encrypt the entire message by using the conventional secret key. Bob will use the corresponding key to decrypt the message. Figure 1-19 explains this process.

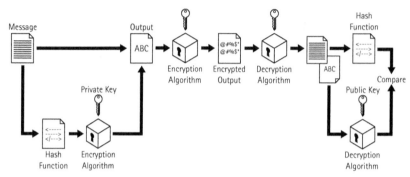

Figure 1-19: Providing integrity, authentication, and confidentiality

There are several hash functions available. The description of some of the most commonly used hash functions is given below:

♦ **Secure Hash Algorithm (SHA-1):** Also known as *Secure Hash Standard (SHS)*, this hash algorithm was published by the United States government. This algorithm can produce an output of a 160-bit hash value. This algorithm has been well taken and appreciated by experts.

♦ **MD2, MD4:** These algorithms were released by RSA Data Security Inc. Several security leakages have been discovered in these algorithms, and they are no longer used to implement encryption. Newer algorithms like MD5 have been developed.

♦ **MD5:** This algorithm was also released by RSA Laboratories. This algorithm can produce an output of a 128-bit hash value. As in the case of MD4, some security loopholes have been found in MD5 too.

♦ **RIPEMD-160:** This hash algorithm was designed to replace MD4 and MD5 and provide better and safer hashing methodology. It can produce a 20 bytes or 160 bits message digest.

When using algorithms to create encrypted hash values, you need to ensure that you keep track of the input string and enter an appropriate input string. This is because a small change in the input characters can cause a major bit-shift on the entire output string. A shift of 1 bit in the input string will cause a shift of about half of the total bits in the resulting string. This is called the *avalanche effect*.

Digital Signatures

Any process of authentication protects two parties against a third party. However, this process does not protect the parties against each other. This means that in situations where there isn't complete trust between the sender and the recipient, something more than authentication is required. This problem can be solved using a digital signature. A digital signature is analogous to a handwritten signature and verifies the author, date, and time of signature. The signature should also be able to authenticate the content at the time of the signature. The main requirements of a digital signature are:

◆ It is unique to the sender.

◆ It should be recognizable and verifiable.

There are a variety of approaches for digital signatures, which fall broadly into two categories—*direct* and *arbitrated*.

Direct Digital Signatures

A direct digital signature can be formed by encrypting the entire message with the sender's private key or by encrypting a hash value of the message with the sender's private key. Figure 1-20 explains the process of creating digital signatures.

The output is called a digital signature and is attached to the message. To verify the signature, the recipient does a computation involving the message, the signature, and the sender's public key. If the result conforms, the signature is considered to be authentic. Otherwise, the signature is considered either to be a fake or the message has been tampered with. This is because the computed value is based on the signature and the contents of the message. Any change in the values of the digital signature or the contents of the message results in a mismatch between the computed value and the value that is received. This indicates that either the signatures have been faked or the message contents have been modified.

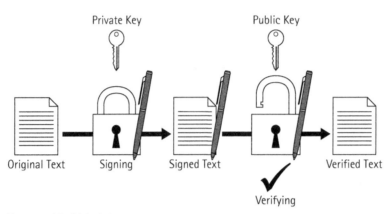

Figure 1-20: Digital signatures

Further encrypting the entire message plus the digital signature can provide confidentiality. It is important to add the digital signature to the message and then to encrypt the entire message. Rather than encrypting the message first, the digital signature must be calculated and added to the signature. If the latter approach is taken, then a third party needs to access the decryption method to read the message. Otherwise, only plaintext and the digital signature can be kept for future dispute resolutions.

This direct digital signature scheme has a single drawback – the entire scheme depends on the validity of the sender's private key. If the sender disowns the responsibility that he has sent the message and claims that private key is lost or compromised then somebody must have forged the signature.

Arbitrated Digital Signature

Arbitrated digital signature scheme is used to overcome the problem of non-repudiation encountered in a direct digital signature. In this scheme, every signed message from the sender, which has been sent to the recipient, first goes to an arbitrator who checks the signature about its origin and content. The message is then dated and sent to the recipient. The presence of the arbitrator solves the problem of sender disowning the signature. For example, when Alice sends a digitally signed message to Bob, an arbitrator first validates Alice's signature. After the signature has been validated, the message is then sent to Bob along with the date of validation and notice that the signature does belong to Alice.

How Does a Digital Signature Work?

The manner in which a digital signature works is quite simple.

Let's suppose that you want to send important documents to your business partner, who is out-of-town. After you send the documents, you need to assure your partner that the documents have not been modified and are not different from the ones that you sent, and that you actually own them. To ensure the authenticity of the documents that you are sending in an e-mail message, you need to get a hash for your document and then encrypt the hash by using the private key from the key pair that you have obtained from an authority. So where's your digital signature? The hash that you encrypted by using the key is your digital signature. In this way, the hash function is converted to a digital signature and an e-mail that you can send to the receiver. Each time that you create a digital signature for a message, your digital signature will be different because a different hash has been created each time.

Now let's look at the recipient's side.

The message reaches your business partner. How does he verify that it is a valid and authentic document? Your business partner will first create a hash for the message. Then he will decrypt the message hash that you sent. How will he do it? He will use the public key to decrypt it. Finally, he needs to match the hash you sent with the hash that was created at his end. If the two match, it is proof that your message is a valid one.

There are several standard algorithms that have been developed for creating digital signatures. One of them is Digital Signature Standard (DSS) developed by the U.S. National Security Agency (NSA) in 1994. It has been used to generate digital signatures for electronic documents.

Summary

In this chapter, you learned about the various techniques that are used to encrypt data to prevent it from being violated during transit. You learned how cryptography provides the means and methods of hiding data, establishing its authenticity, and preventing its undetected modification or unauthorized use. You learned that there are two types of cryptography:

♦ Symmetric cryptography, which uses one single key to encrypt as well as decrypt data. DES, 3DES, IDEA, RC2, RC4, RC5, CAST-128, and AES are various algorithms that are used in symmetric cryptography.

♦ Asymmetric cryptography, which uses a pair of keys – public and private keys – for data encryption and decryption. Asymmetric cryptography is based on the RSA algorithm. RSA is one of the most powerful encryption/decryption algorithms available today.

Next, you learned about the various applications of cryptography, which include

♦ Message encryption

♦ Message Authentication Code

♦ Hash functions

Message encryption allows the encryption of data using symmetric as well as asymmetric encryption mechanisms. Message Authentication Code, on the other hand, is an irreversible encryption method that uses a secret key to generate fixed-sized data blocks. Hash functions are a variation of MAC and allow strong collision-free output.

Finally, you learned about the role and use of digital signatures in modern encryption/decryption mechanisms. You learned that digital signatures work exceptionally well between entities that do not trust each other. Therefore, digital signatures have emerged as the most common method of data authentication over that most untrustworthy of mediums – the Internet.

Chapter 2

Public Key Infrastructure Basics

IN THIS CHAPTER

◆ What is PKI?

◆ Components of PKI

◆ Working with PKI

◆ Processes in PKI

IN THE PREVIOUS CHAPTER, we looked at public key cryptography. However, public key cryptography on its own is not sufficient to ensure the security of e-business transactions. E-business organizations need a framework that provides policies to generate keys and procedures to distribute these keys. Public Key Infrastructure (PKI) provides one such framework.

PKI is a framework that consists of security policies, encryption mechanisms, and applications that generate, store, and manage keys. PKI also provides procedures to generate, distribute, and utilize keys and certificates. PKI provides a mechanism to publish the public keys that are part of public key cryptography. It describes the policies, standards, and software that are used to regulate certificates, public keys, and private keys. In this chapter, we examine the basics of PKI. We discuss the roles of different authorities in PKI. Next, we examine the components of PKI, and finally, we review the processes that are typically carried out in PKI.

What Is PKI?

Trust forms the basis of all communication, be it physical or electronic. In physical communication, building trust is relatively easy as you can identify the entity or person by either face-to-face interaction or certain identification marks such as signatures, notary stamp, or even the letterhead. However, in case of electronic communication, building this trust is quite difficult as the identity of the other entity remains concealed, and also most of the identification or security methods that you take for granted in a non-electronic or physical communication are not present. This trust cannot be established until and unless both entities are sure about each others' identities and that the information they are exchanging over a network is completely secure from any kind tampering.

For example, when you walk into a store you are quite sure about the legitimacy of the company. You can see and touch the product, you might even know the salesperson, and when you hand over your credit card to the billing clerk you might not feel the risk of your credit card being misused in any way. However, when you conduct similar a transaction over the Internet, you are not quite sure about the legitimacy of the company or the product. You are not even sure about the identity of the person to whom you are sending your credit card number.

It is to address these underlying problems of trust, authentication, and security over the network that PKI is used. PKI brings the security and trust of the physical world to the electronic world by enabling trusted electronic communications and transactions.

As discussed in the previous chapter, the core security functions provided by cryptography are confidentiality, non-repudiation, authentication, and integrity. In addition to these core security functions, it is necessary to have the following for secure and trustworthy electronic interactions:

- ◆ Policies that specify rules for operating cryptographic systems.

- ◆ Mechanisms for managing, storing, and creating keys.

- ◆ Guidelines for managing, storing, distributing, and creating keys and certificates.

In other words, what is needed is PKI. To reiterate, PKI is a framework that consists of hardware, software, policies, and procedures that are required to manage, create, store, and distribute keys and digital certificates. To integrate all entities of this framework, there are various components of PKI. The next section discusses these components in detail.

Components of PKI

As discussed in the previous sections, PKI is a framework that consists of hardware, software, policies, and procedures for managing keys and certificates. For this framework to be functional, you need various components of PKI. These components are

- ◆ Certification Authority (CA)

- ◆ Registration Authority (RA)

- ◆ PKI clients

- ◆ Digital certificates

- ◆ Certificate Distribution System or repository

In a PKI deployment, each of these components has a specific role to perform. Let us now discuss each of these components in detail.

Certification Authority

The CA is a trusted third party that authenticates entities taking part in an electronic transaction. To authenticate an entity, the CA issues a digital certificate. This certificate is a digital document that establishes the credentials of the entities participating in a transaction. The digital certificates issued by CAs contain information, such as the name of the subscriber, the public and the private key of the subscriber, and the issuing CA's public key. This information depends upon the policy of the company that issues the certificates.

Before issuing a digital certificate, the CA verifies the request for a certificate with a Registration Authority (RA). For validating certificate requests, a CA uses its own procedures. These procedures depend on an organization policy and the infrastructure available to validate the request. If the request is validated, the CA issues the certificate.

Registration Authority

An RA is responsible for the interaction between clients and CAs. Often, because of the bulk of certificate requests, it is not possible for the CA to accept certificate requests, validate the requests, and issue the certificates. In such cases, the RA acts as an intermediary between the CA and the client. The tasks performed by the RA are given below:

◆ Receive entity requests and validate them

◆ Send the requests to the CA

◆ Receive the processed certificate from the CA

◆ Send the certificate to the correct entity

RAs are especially useful for scaling PKI applications across different geographical locations. For example, a CA can delegate its responsibilities to different RAs and assign an area of operation to each RA, such as an RA for northern region, southern region, and eastern and western regions.

PKI Clients

The entities which request CAs or RAs to issue certificates are commonly referred to as PKI Clients. To obtain a digital certificate from a CA, a PKI client needs to perform the following steps:

1. Send a request to generate a public-private key pair. A CA or the client can do this task. The key pair contains the details of the client.

2. After the key pair is generated, a request is sent to the CA for the CA certificate. This request can be routed through an RA.

3. After the client receives the certificate from the CA, it can use the certificate to identify itself as being an authenticated certificate holder.

All communication between a client and the CA is kept secure. Additionally, the client is responsible for ensuring the safety of its private key. This is because if the private key is lost, then the encrypted message cannot be decrypted. In addition, if the private key is compromised, any unauthorized person can use this private key to decrypt the messages. In such situations, the need for securing the private key becomes all the more apparent. You can ensure the safety of your private key by using several hardware components that are available, such as tokens and smart cards. A token is a physical device, which you can carry with you and can use to authenticate a user to a network. Similarly, a smart card is also a physical device, very much like your credit card, which contains a microprocessor for storing security information. This microprocessor does not work until you specify your Personal Identification Number (PIN). In this way, you can secure your private keys.

As can be seen, an important component of PKI deployment is digital certificates. These certificates form the basis of implementing a PKI solution.

Digital Certificates

It is important to ensure the security of a public key to avoid security breaches related to impersonation and key modification. Therefore, a data integrity mechanism is required to ensure that a public key that is modified does not go undetected. However data integrity mechanisms alone are not sufficient to guarantee that the public key belongs to the claimed owner. A mechanism is required which binds the public key with some globally trusted party that can ensure the identity and authenticity of the public key. The desired mechanism should accomplish the following two goals:

◆ Establish the integrity of the public key

◆ Bind the public key and its associated information to the owner in a trusted manner

In the PKI environment, digital certificates accomplish these goals. Certificates ensure that only the public key for a certificate that has been authenticated by a certifying authority works with the private key possessed by an entity. This eliminates the chance of impersonation.

A certificate includes the following elements:

◆ Serial number of the certificate

◆ Digital signature of the CA

◆ Public key of the user to whom the certificate is issued

◆ Date of expiration

◆ Name of the CA that has issued the certificate

After a digital certificate is obtained, the entity can use it to communicate with recipients of information in the following manner:

1. The subscriber digitally signs the message with his or her private key to ensure message integrity and its own authenticity and sends the message to the recipient.

2. The recipient, after receiving the message, verifies the digital signature with the subscriber's public key and queries the global directory database to check the validity of the subscriber's digital certificate.

3. The Global directory database returns the status of the subscriber's digital certificate to the recipient. The transaction is completed only if the certificate is valid.

The CA signs the digital certificates. To verify a signature, the CA's public key is needed. The public key is part of the CA's digital certificate. These certificates are typically pre-installed in Web browsers.

After a certificate has been issued, it needs to be distributed to users and organizations. This is done by a Certificate Distribution System (CDS) or a repository.

Certificate Distribution System (CDS) or Repository

The Certificate Distribution System (CDS) distributes certificates to users and organizations. These certificates can be distributed in two ways depending on implementation of PKI in the organization. Either the certificates can be distributed by users themselves or they can be distributed by a directory server that uses LDAP to query the user information that is stored in an X.500 compliant database. CDS distributes certificates in cooperation with the directory service server. The distribution system is used to do the following tasks:

◆ Generate and issue key pairs

◆ Certify the validity of public keys by signing the public key

◆ Revoke expired or lost keys

◆ Publish the public keys in the directory service server

After knowing the various components of PKI, let us now look at how PKI works.

Working with PKI

Before we discuss about working with PKI, let us first look at various functions that a PKI needs to perform in order to provide trust and security to electronic communication. These functions are

- ◆ Generating public key and private pairs for creating and authenticating digital signatures

- ◆ Providing authentication to control access to the private key

- ◆ Creating and issuing certificates to authenticate users

- ◆ Registering new users to authenticate them

- ◆ Maintaining history of keys for future references

- ◆ Revoking certificates that are not valid

- ◆ Updating and recovering keys in case of key compromise

- ◆ Providing a means for key validation

All these functions are very imperative for PKI to achieve its basic purpose of providing trust. Just like public key cryptography, PKI also uses a pair of keys to provide information security. The following steps are involved in working with PKI:

1. Generating the key pair

2. Applying digital signatures to identify the sender

3. Encrypting the message

4. Transmitting the symmetric key

5. Verifying sender's identity by using a CA

6. Decrypting the message and verifying its contents

Let us now look at each of these steps in detail.

Generating the Key Pair

This is the first step that is involved in working with PKI. Here, the user who wants to encrypt and send the message first generates a key pair. Generating a key pair refers to the creation of two keys by the user, one private key and the other public key. This key pair is unique to each user of PKI. First the private key is created and then by applying a one-way hash on that private key, the corresponding public key is created. The private key is used for signing the data, and the corresponding public key is used for verifying the signature. When a user wants to encrypt any message he/she uses the public key. A message encrypted with a public key can only be decrypted by its corresponding private key.

Applying Digital Signatures to Identify the Sender

A digital signature attached with an encrypted message identifies the sender of the message. It is interced to have the same legal binding as a normal signature. The digital signature is a mathematical function that is derived from the sender's private key and the original message. To derive a digital signature and attach it to the message, the following steps need to be performed:

1. Convert the original message into a string of fixed length by applying a hash function on the message. This process is also known as *hashing,* and the fixed-length string so obtained is known as *message digest.*

2. Encrypt the message digest with the sender's private key. The resultant encrypted message digest is referred to as a digital signature.

3. Attach this digital signature with the original message.

Encrypting the Message

After applying the digital signature to the original message, you can secure it by encrypting it. To encrypt the message and the attached digital signature, you use a symmetric key. This symmetric key is common to both the sender and the receiver of the message and is used once each for encryption and decryption.

Transmitting the Symmetric Key

After encrypting the message and the digital signature, the symmetric key that was used to encrypt the message needs to be transmitted to the receiver. This is because the same key is used to decrypt the message. This can pose as a major security threat because, if this key is compromised, anyone can decrypt the encrypted message by using this key. As a result the symmetric key also needs to be protected. This is done by encrypting the symmetric key with the receiver's public key. This way only the receiver can decrypt the encrypted symmetric key by using his/her corresponding private key. After being encrypted, the session key and the message are transmitted to the receiver.

Verifying Sender's Identity by Using a CA

As discussed, the CAs act as trusted third parties to verify the identity of the entities taking part in the transaction process. When a receiver receives an encrypted message, the receiver can request the CA to verify the digital signature attached with the message. Upon receiving the request, the CA verifies the digital signatures, and a successful verification ensures that the sender is who he/she claims to be.

Decrypting the Message and Verifying Its Contents

After the encrypted message is received it needs to be decrypted. This message can only be decrypted by using the encrypted symmetric key that was sent along with the message. Hence, before decrypting the message, the encrypted symmetric key should be decrypted by using the receiver's private key. After being decrypted, the symmetric key then decrypts the message. The digital signature attached with the message is decrypted by using the sender's public key, and the message digest is extracted from it. This decrypted message is hashed again to obtain a second message digest. Both these message digests are then compared, to check for any possible tampering of the message in transit. If both the digests match it indicates that the message has not been tampered with.

In addition to providing the core security features this framework also provides trust and legal status for electronic communications. For any transaction, electronic or physical, to be legal and enforceable, the transaction should meet the following basic criteria of

◆ **Non-repudiation:** All the entities involved in the transaction should not be able to deny being a part of the transaction.

◆ **Transmission security:** There should be a proper mechanism to ensure security of the message in transit. Any tampering or modification done to the message should be easily visible.

◆ **Privacy:** Any unauthorized access to the message should be denied.

◆ **Authentication:** The identity of entities taking part in the transaction process should be known to both the parties.

◆ **Enforceable:** The transaction should be verifiable and signed by all entities involved.

PKI ensures that all transactions meet these legal requirements by providing the necessary infrastructure and environment.

After having understood the basic working of PKI, let us now discuss the different processes that are involved in PKI.

Processes in PKI

Applications can achieve four principal security functions by using PKI. These functions are confidentiality, integrity, authentication, and non-repudiation.

Each process in a PKI solution accomplishes the above-mentioned security requirements. Let us examine the different processes in a PKI solution and look at how they are used to ensure the authenticity of data.

Certificate Requests

To obtain a digital certificate from the CA, the user needs to send a certificate request. There are many standards for sending certificate requests, the most common being PKCS#10. The certificate request consists of the following fields:

- Distinguished name (DN) of the CA

- Public key of the user

- Algorithm identifier

- Digital signature of the user

The digital signature is created by the user's private key. It also acts as a proof of possession of a private key. The user sends the PKCS certificate request to a CA through a secure channel. If the channel is not secure, the user downloads the CA's public key and encrypts the certificate with the CA's public key to make the certificate secure.

SENDING REQUESTS
The certificate request is sent to the CA as an e-mail that uses the PEM (Privacy Enhanced Mail) format. The certificate request needs to be sent in PEM format because the request is originally generated in a binary format. The binary format cannot be transmitted using e-mail. Therefore, binary message is converted to the PEM format, which is ASCII based. This eliminates the problem of sending certificate requests through e-mail.

With digital signatures in certificate requests, the CA can be sure that the sender has a private key related to the public key. Therefore, the sender has a proof of possession.

A client can also submit key requests through a Web browser. In this case, PKCS #10 is used with SSL. The client makes an SSL connection with the certificate server and then transfers the certificate request through a secure channel.

POLICIES
The security policy defines an organization's direction in terms of information security, processes, and principles for cryptography usage. It defines how the organization manages public and private keys and other information such as the level of control required to manage security risk factors.

Some PKI systems are operated by trusted third parties called *Commercial Certificate Authorities* and therefore require a Certification Practice Statement (CPS), which outlines the details of operational procedures. The CPS defines how these policies would be implemented and supported; how certificates would be issued, accepted, and revoked; and how the keys would be generated, registered, and certified. The CPS also defines the location of these keys and how they would be made available on a user's request.

Certificate Revocation

As you already know, certificates are used to authenticate the identity of users. All certificates have a validity period. A certificate is usually valid through its validity period. Validity of a certificate means that from the time the certificate is issued and until the time it expires, the certificate can be used to authenticate users. However, at times, a certificate might lose its validity before the lapse of its validity period. In such a situation, the certificate can no longer be used for authentication purposes. These situations generally arise when either the certificate security has been compromised or when the person holding the certificate is no longer authorized to perform the tasks that he or she performs by using the certificate. Such a situation, when a certificate loses its validity before its expiry date, is known as certificate revocation. A certificate that has undergone revocation, or to put it simply, a revoked certificate, can be used to validate information that was encrypted at the time when the certificate was valid.

Communicating Certificate Revocation

When a certificate is revoked, the information about the revoked certificate needs to be published because the certificate's public key has been compromised. Information about revoked certificates can be posted on a certificate server so that the users are warned from using those certificates. Another method, which is commonly used, is the use of Certificate Revocation Lists (CRL). CRLs contain a list of certificates that have been revoked. To ensure that the list does not become too long, when a revoked certificate encounters its expiration date, the entry for the certificate is removed from the CRL. This does not lead to an unintentional use of the revoked certificate because the certificate would have expired in any case.

A CA maintains the CRL, who distributes the list at regular intervals. These intervals need to be short enough to prevent use of the certificate after it is revoked and before it is published in the CRL.

Client-to-Client Communication Through PKI

Whenever two or more PKI clients want to communicate securely, they need to validate each other and negotiate the various encryption, authentication, and data integration algorithms. The protocols that are used to negotiate are

- ◆ ISAKMP (Internet Security Association and Key Management Protocol)
- ◆ IKE (Internet Key Exchange)
- ◆ Oakley
- ◆ Skeme

The ISAKMP and IKE protocols need Security Associations (SA) to identify their connection parameters. SAs describe the utilization of security services for communicating securely. IKE is a hybrid protocol that implements the Oakley key exchange, and Skeme key exchange in the ISAKMP protocol. The Oakley and Skeme protocols are used to derive authenticated keys. Let us examine the IKAMP and IKE protocols in detail.

Internet Security Association and Key Management Protocol (ISAKMP)

The ISAKMP protocol defines the various procedures and packet formats required to establish, modify, negotiate, and delete Security Associations. A Security Association (SA) contains all the information that is required to carry out all network security-related activities in the organization. It defines payloads for exchanging key generation and for authenticating data. This framework is independent of the key management protocol being used, the encryption algorithm being used, and the authentication mechanism in use. This protocol is independent of IPSec and is compatible with both IPv4 and IPv6.

Internet Key Exchange Protocol

The IKE protocol is used in conjunction with the IPSec standard. The IKE protocol automatically negotiates IPSec SAs and enables IPSec communications. It also specifies the validity of the IPSec SA. When the IPSec communication is enabled, it permits CA support for building manageable and scalable IPSec implementations. IPSec is used for the authentication and encryption of IP packets. IKE works in two phases, main mode and quick mode. Let us examine these phases in detail.

PHASES OF IKE PROTOCOL

The two phases in which IPSec operates are the main mode and the quick mode. The main mode is also referred to as aggressive mode. A description of the two phases is given below:

- ◆ Main mode: In main mode, the clients present their digital certificates to each other. Digital certificates contain the CA signature to facilitate the authenticity of the client. Therefore, if one client does not trust the CA of the other client, the authentication fails and no further communication takes place. If the two clients trust each other's CA, the authentication is completed and the two clients form a secure channel for phase 2 negotiation. This channel is known as a phase 1 SA. The encryption channel is based on encrypting the information with the receiver's public key. The phase 1 SA is used to protect the network traffic from eavesdroppers.

- ◆ Quick mode: In quick mode, the two clients negotiate the IPSec SA. Once both entities trust each other, they start the second phase of negotiation. In this phase, various parameters are negotiated, such as key type, key length, symmetric key algorithm, encryption algorithm, hash functions, and so on.

The quick mode is faster than the main mode. Also, in this mode the information exchange takes place without setting up of a secure channel and hence can result in a threat of hackers discovering the source of SA. When you use IKE, you do not need to manually specify the IPSec SA parameters for the peer devices. Also, when no policy is specified, the default policy is applied, and it contains the default value for each parameter.

Summary

In this chapter, you learned about the basics of PKI. You learned that PKI is a framework that consists of security policies, encryption mechanisms, and applications that generate, store, and manage keys. Then, you learned about the different components of PKI. These components are

- Certification Authority (CA)
- Registration Authority (RA)
- PKI clients
- Digital certificates
- Certificate Distribution System or repository

Next, you learned about the workings of PKI. You learned that the steps involved in the working of PKI are

- Generating the key pair
- Applying digital signatures to identify the sender
- Encrypting the message
- Transmitting the symmetric key
- Verifying sender's identity by using a CA
- Decrypting the message and verifying its contents

Finally, you learned that processes typically implemented in a PKI solution are certificate issue, certificate revocation, and client-to-client communication.

- A CA issues certificates, after a client sends the request. The request can be sent through an RA.
- Certificates are revoked when their integrity is compromised or when the user is no longer authorized to use the certificate. Information about certificate revocation is published in CRLs.
- Client to client communication in PKI happens with the help of the ISAKMP and IKE protocols. These protocols need security associations to identify their connection parameters.

Chapter 3

PKI Architecture

PKI is being implemented today by many organizations as a tool to secure sensitive corporate resources. However, with varied needs, processes, and ambiguities associated with every business, a standardized model for PKI is not quite feasible. For this purpose, there are various PKI architectures, which an organization can deploy to best suit their needs. However, irrespective of the PKI architecture that can be implemented, one thing that remains at the core of each architecture is trust.

This chapter details the various PKI architectures available and advantages and disadvantages of each architecture. It introduces the three primary trust models in use today, which can be used according to the needs of the organization.

Introduction to PKI Architecture

You learned in Chapter 2 that PKI brings trust of the physical world to the electronic world by enabling trusted electronic communications and transactions.

Let us take an example to understand how trust is established in a PKI environment. Suppose Alice has received a document that has been digitally signed by Bob. To verify the validity of Bob's signature on this document Alice needs to use Bob's public key. Here arises the question of trust. How does Alice ensure that the public key which she is using is in fact Bob's public key and not of any other person impersonating Bob. The answer to this problem is a digital certificate. As you already know, a digital Certificate is a document that binds the information of the certificate holder to a public key. This certificate is digitally signed by a third party, also referred to as a *Trusted Third Party* (TTP) or a *Certification Authority* (CA). Hence, to verify Bob's certificate, Alice needs to first obtain the CA's public key. Here once again the question of trust arises, as to how can Alice now trust the CA's public key. Alice can obtain the CA's public key out-of-band. This way Alice can trust the CA's public key as she is now assured of the validity of the public key. By using this trusted public key Alice can now verify Bob's certificate and hence Bob's digital signatures.

Out-of-band refers to a dedicated transmission channel, other than the usual transmission channels that are used to transmit data.

In addition to certifying users, CAs can certify other CAs, by distributing keys in the same trusted manner. These CAs can further certify other CAs and so on. In this way, every entity can trust the other entity, provided it is able to establish the chain from its trusted CA to the other entity's trusted CA. This chain is referred to as the certificate path. The number of CAs in a certificate path and the arrangement of these CAs determine the different PKI architectures. The following section discusses the different PKI architectures in detail.

A CA in an organization can either be an external party or be internal to the organization. The decision of having an external party act as a CA or establishing a CA within an organization depends on the business model of the organization. For example, an organization can make it mandatory that every employee of the organization has to present a proof of identity to the other employees of this organization while transacting or communicating. In this situation, the organization can establish a CA within the organization to issue and verify the identity of employees in the form of digital certificates. The most widely used certificate specification is found in the International Telecommunications Union's X.509 standard.

Types of PKI Architecture

PKI architectures can be implemented in the following ways:

- ◆ Single CA architecture
- ◆ Enterprise PKI architecture
- ◆ Hybrid PKI architecture

These different types of architecture are based on the number of CAs, their arrangement, and the relationship between them. Let us now discuss these architectures in detail.

Single CA Architecture

The Single CA architecture is the most basic type of PKI architecture. In this type of architecture, there is just one CA who issues and distributes certificates and Certificate Revocation Lists (CRLs) to the entities. All these entities trust this CA. In addition, these entities use only those certificates that are issued by this CA. There are no CA trust relationships in a single CA architecture because there exists only one CA. The single CA architecture does not allow for any new CAs to be added to the PKI.

All the entities in this architecture communicate with each other in a trusted environment, as there is a common point of trust, which is the CA, for all the entities. For example, Alice and Bob are two entities who trust a CA, CA-1. Therefore, both of them can validate and verify each other's certificates and then communicate. Figure 3-1 displays the single CA architecture.

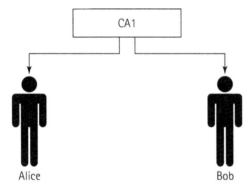

Single CA Architecture

Figure 3-1: PKI with a single CA

Deploying a single CA architecture is also quite easy because it involves establishing only one CA. A single CA architecture presents a single point of failure. This is because there is only one CA that holds the key information for all the entities. If the private key of this CA is compromised then all certificates issued by this CA will become invalid, and this might result in a complete breakdown of the PKI system. In case the CA's private key is compromised, every entity should immediately be informed about it.

Also, if the private key of the CA has been compromised, the CA needs to be re-established. To re-establish a CA, all the certificates issued by the CA should be deemed invalid and should be reissued. The information about the new CA should then be passed on to the entities. Thus, the CA should have procedures in place for maintaining its private key and should also have a secure mechanism for online verification of the certificates issued to different entities.

The single CA architecture suffers from scalability issues. Although it is quite suitable for a small organization with a limited number of users, as the size of the organization increases the single CA architecture becomes limited in scope. For example, Alice and Bob are employees of the AllSolv, Inc. company. AllSolv CA is the single CA that issues certificates to the employees of AllSolv, Inc., and thus both Alice and Bob trust AllSolv CA. Due to an increase in the business of AllSolv, Inc., its employees are now required to communicate with the employees of other companies. However, the scope of AllSolv CA is limited to the employees of AllSolv, Inc. only. Hence, when Alice and Bob have to communicate with Charlie of IntelliSol, Inc., they need to have additional CAs that can communicate with Charlie in a trusted manner. This is where the scope of single CA architecture gets limited, as it does not allow addition of CAs to the architecture.

An enhancement to the single CA architecture is the Basic Trust List model.

Basic Trust List Model

In the Trust List model, PKI services are provided by a number of CAs. However, these CAs do not establish a trust relationship between them. As a result, there are no certification paths in this architecture, but only single certificates. Entities have to maintain a list of CAs that they trust. These entities use only those certificates and CRLs that have been issued by the CAs in their list of trusted CAs. Hence, the entities can work with only a single certificate or with CRLs that have been issued to them by any of the CAs listed in the trust list.

According to the single CA architecture, for one entity to communicate securely with the other entity, both of them should be members of the same CA. But if that is not the case, then the entities need to be members of each other's CAs. For example, consider a case where Alice needs to communicate with Bob but both of them trust two different CAs. Alice trusts CA-1, and Bob trusts CA-2. According to the single CA architecture, there is just one CA and there exists no trust relationship. As a result, CA-1 would not trust CA-2. In this situation, both Alice and Bob will not be able to communicate with each other in a trusted manner as their CAs do not trust each other. For Alice to trust Bob, she needs to get her certificate from Bob's CA. Figure 3-2 displays this process.

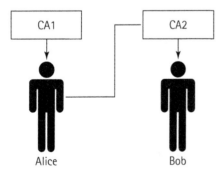

Figure 3-2: Trusting two CAs

If Alice gets her certificate from Bob's CA, then she would also be required to maintain some vital information about Bob's CA. For this purpose Alice needs to create a list of all the CAs she trusts. This type of an architecture where an entity maintains a list of trusted CAs is known as *Basic Trust List architecture.*

As against the single CA architecture where new CAs cannot be added to the PKI, in this architecture you can add new CAs by making changes in the Trust List. Although the Trust List model has a distinct advantage of being very simple in design it can become quite complicated at times. With an increase in the number of CAs trusted by an entity, there is also an increase in the number of entries in the Trust List. Also, vital information about the trusted CAs needs to be maintained by every entity. Updating this information can prove to be an uphill task for the entities as the number of CAs increases. Also, there might be situations where an entity adds a CA in her Trust List without informing that CA. Let us look at an example to explain the situation. In case the key of a CA is compromised, then the CA can immediately inform about this key compromise to those entities which the CA trusts. But the same information cannot be passed on immediately to those entities that have included the CA in their Trust List without the CA's knowledge. Furthermore, these entities might carry on trusting the certificates issued by this CA until they are informed about it.

To use the public key inside a certificate, any PKI application needs to first validate the certificate. To validate this key, the application needs to first verify the existence of a valid certificate path. A certificate path is a series of certificates, in which the entity that has issued the first certificate is a trust point. The subject of the last certificate is known as the end entity. There can be a number of trust points in a certificate path, depending on the number of CAs.

Before using a certificate, a certificate path needs to be constructed between the trust points and the certificates. This process of certificate path construction involves gathering all the certificates (from the issuer's certificate to a root certificate) that are required to form a trust path.

CERTIFICATE PATH CONSTRUCTION IN A SINGLE CA AND BASIC TRUST LIST ARCHITECTURE

Certificate path construction is the simplest in a single CA architecture. This architecture consists of only one CA or trust point, and as a result only one certificate can connect any subject to the trust point. In other words, it can be said that there is no path construction in a single CA architecture, and a single certificate represents the entire path. Figure 3-3 shows a single CA certification path. Here, Alice and Bob trust CA-1. As mentioned, a single CA represents the certification path.

The certification paths for Alice and Bob can be depicted as follows:

- ◆ [CA-1 → Alice]
- ◆ [CA-1 → Bob]

The notation CA → User indicates that the CA, in this case CA-1, is issuing the certificate to the user, in this case Alice. In addition, the certificate issued by the CA-1 to Alice is the complete certification path and comprises just one certificate.

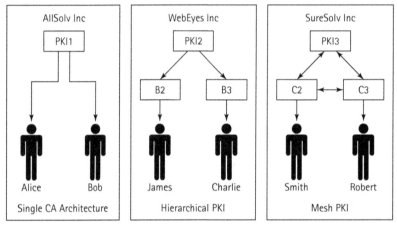

Figure 3-3: Certificate path construction in single CA architecture

The certification path shows that in a single CA architecture the complete certification path is composed of just one certificate that has been issued to the entity. In case of a Trust List also, the certificate path comprises a single certificate. Therefore, a single certificate is needed to connect the entity to the trust point.

Figure 3-4 depicts a certification path in Trust List architecture.

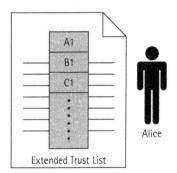

Figure 3-4: Certificate path construction in Trust List architecture

Alice has CA-1 and CA-2 listed in her Trust List, and Bob has CA-2, CA-3, and CA-4 in his Trust List. The certification path for Alice can either be:

◆ [CA-1 → Alice]

◆ [CA-2 → Alice]

Similarly, the certification path for Bob can be one of the following:

◆ [CA-2 → Bob]

◆ [CA-3 → Bob]

◆ [CA-4 → Bob]

The certification path in the Trust List architecture is the same as that of a single CA architecture and contains only a single certificate. The more complex is the PKI architecture, the more difficult it becomes to construct the certificate path. Let us first discuss some more complex PKI architectures.

Enterprise PKI Architecture

As organizations grow, the delegation and distribution of management becomes a key factor for the effective and efficient management of systems. With the increase in business operations, the transaction scope also increases beyond the physical boundaries of an organization. PKI is no exception to this rule. Although the single CA model can serve the requirements of a small organization, however, as the needs of the organization grow or interoperability between different organizations increases, there arises a need for delegating the task of a single CA.

This requires the distribution of operations of a single CA between multiple CAs that are arranged either in a hierarchy or mesh. The mechanisms used for enterprise PKI architecture are either Superior-subordinate (hierarchical PKI) or Peer-to-peer (mesh PKI).

Hierarchical PKI Architecture

This is the most common PKI architecture deployed by organizations. In this architecture, PKI services are provided by multiple CAs. Unlike the Trust List architecture, all CAs in a hierarchical PKI architecture share a trust relationship among them. The CAs in this type of architecture are connected through superior-subordinate relationships.

The CA hierarchy is an inverted tree-like structure having root at the top, referred to as root CA, which in turn contains branches or nodes. These nodes are referred to as the subordinate of the root CA. These subordinate CAs are like any other CA and perform all the functions of a CA; they can also delegate the responsibility of certificate issuance to other subordinate CAs beneath them. Whenever the root CA assigns a subordinate, the root CA will issue a certificate to the subordinate, indicating what type of work the subordinate can perform.

The root CA usually issues certificates to subordinate CAs and not to the users. However, the subordinate CAs can issue certificates to both users and subordinate CAs at lower levels. In a hierarchical PKI, subordinate CAs do not issue certificates to their superior CA or root CA. Except for the root CA, all other CAs have a single superior CA. The issuer is the superior CA, and the subject is the subordinate CA. To add a new CA to the architecture, the root CA or any current CA issues a certificate to the new CA.

The following example illustrates the hierarchical PKI architecture.

When a root CA issues the certificate to its subordinate CAs, say CA-1 and CA-2, the purpose of the certificate is mentioned clearly in the certificate. Suppose the purpose of the certificate is that the root CA trusts CA-1 and CA-2 for issuing certificates to subordinates only; this forms the first level of nodes in the hierarchy. CA-1 issues a certificate to another subordinate CA-3 for the purpose of issuing the certificates only to end users or entities. Figure 3-5 illustrates this trust in the hierarchy.

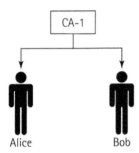

Figure 3-5: Hierarchical PKI architecture

Similarly, CA-1 trusts CA-4 to issue certificates to subordinates only like CA-7 and CA-8 and CA-7 and CA-8 to issue certificates to end user or entities.

Similarly, the root CA issues certificates to CA-2. This CA-2 is subordinate to root CA, and it also issues certificates to CA-5 and CA-6 down the hierarchy. A superior CA can impose certain restrictions on the subordinate CAs according to their requirements.

Some important properties that have contributed to the success of hierarchical PKI architecture are:

◆ Scalability: Hierarchical PKIs are quite scalable. They can easily meet the demands of a growing organization. To include a new entity in the PKI system, the root CA simply establishes a trust relationship with that entity's CA (subordinate CA). As shown in Figures 3-6 and 3-7, a new CA can either be added directly under the root CA or under a superior CA as a subordinate CA.

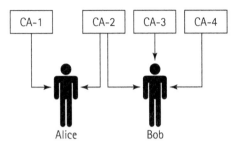

Figure 3-6: Adding a new CA to the root CA

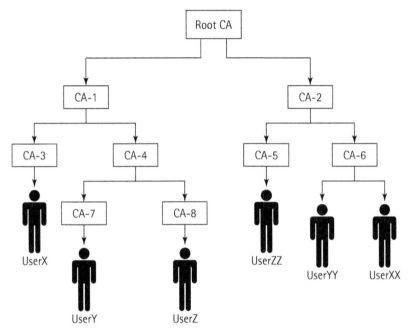

Figure 3-7: Adding a new CA to the superior CA

◆ **Ease of Deployment:** Being uni-directional, the hierarchical PKI architecture is quite easy to deploy. The path for the entity to the root or the issuer CA can be determined quickly and easily.

◆ **Short Certification Path:** The certification paths in a hierarchical PKI architecture are quite short. The biggest path in the PKI is equivalent to the CA certificate for each subordinate CA plus the end entity's certificate.

However, the hierarchical PKI architecture suffers from a major drawback that there is a single point of trust, the root CA, which controls the complete hierarchical PKI architecture. In case of a compromise of the root CA, the complete PKI architecture will break down. The compromise of subordinate CAs can still be handled, as the superior CAs can revoke their certificates and establish them again. However, the root CA is at the top of the hierarchy, and any loss of trust on the root CA leads to a complete loss of trust across the entire PKI architecture. Also, transition from a set of isolated CAs to a hierarchical PKI may be logistically impractical because all entities must adjust their trust points. To overcome this limitation of a single trust point, the mesh PKI architecture is used. Before discussing about Mesh PKI architecture let us first discuss certificate path construction in Hierarchical PKI architecture.

CERTIFICATE PATH CONSTRUCTION IN A HIERARCHICAL PKI ARCHITECTURE

Certificate path construction in a hierarchical PKI architecture starts with the end entity certificate, although certificate paths begin at the root and end at the end entity.

This end entity certificate consists of two optional identifier extensions that help in finding the right CA certificate.

◆ Issuer identifier: This extension is used to locate CA certificates in the repository by matching this issuer identifier with the subject identifier in CA certificates. This is an optional extension and is used in case of a reuse of the X.500 name for different entities.

◆ Authority key identifier: This extension identifies the key that is used to sign the certificate. This field is also optional, and just like the issuer identifier field this too is used in case of a reuse of the X.500 name for different entities.

Figure 3-8 depicts the certification path in a hierarchical PKI architecture.

As can be seen in the figure, for every entity there exists only one certification path.

For example, the certification path for Alice can be depicted as follows:

◆ [Root → CA-3]: [CA-3 → CA-2]: [CA-2 → CA-1]: [CA-1 → Alice]

Bob's certification path can be depicted as follows:

◆ [Root → CA-3]: [CA-3 → CA-2]: [CA-2 → CA-1]: [CA-1 → Bob]

James's certification path can be depicted as follows:

◆ [Root → CA-4]: [CA-4 → James]

The certification path for Alice and Bob shows that four CAs, namely the root CA, CA-1, CA-2, and CA-3 and thus the certification path comprises four certificates. But, the certification path for James has two CAs, namely the root CA and CA-4. As a result James's certification path comprises two certificates.

Let us now discuss the mesh PKI architecture in detail.

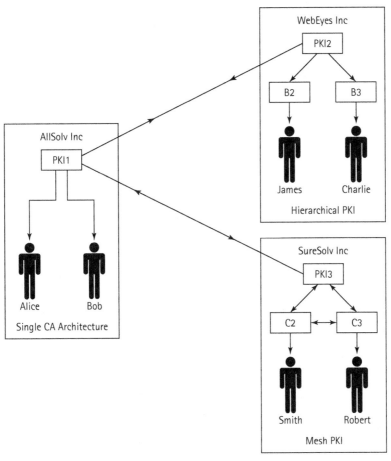

Figure 3-8: Certificate path construction in hierarchical PKI architecture

Mesh PKI

In the mesh PKI architecture, the CAs have a peer-to-peer relationship, rather than a superior-subordinate relationship. All CAs in a mesh PKI can be trust points, and there is no single CA around which the complete PKI architecture revolves. Since CAs issue certificates to each other, they share a bi-directional trust relationship.

In a mesh PKI architecture, all CAs need to cross-certify each other. Cross-certification is the process of connecting two CAs. In this process, a mutual trust relationship is established between both the CAs. Two CAs will cross-certify whenever their respective entities need to communicate securely.

There are multiple trust points in a mesh PKI architecture, and hence the compromise of a single CA cannot result in a breakdown of the complete PKI. Even if a CA is compromised, then the entities with other CAs as their trust points continue to communicate with other entities. The certificate of the compromised CA can be revoked by the CAs who have issued the certificates to that CA. Also, the compromise of the CA affects only the entities associated with that CA and not the entire PKI.

New CAs can easily be added to the mesh PKI architecture. All that is required to add a new CA is that the existing CAs issue a certificate to at least one other CA in the mesh. Figure 3-9 illustrates a mesh PKI architecture.

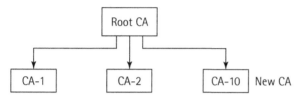

Figure 3-9: Mesh PKI architecture

In this figure, all CAs have a peer-to-peer relationship.

All the CAs have a bi-directional peer-to-peer relationship. In this example, Alice and Bob trust CA-1. James trusts CA-2, and Charlie trusts CA-3. If Alice wants to establish a secure session with Charlie then she has to build a path to get to Charlie. Since CA-1 has a direct peer-to-peer trust relationship, then Alice will have two certificates. If CA-1 connects to CA-2 through CA-3, then Alice will have three certificates.

Certification path construction in a mesh PKI architecture is more complex than in a hierarchical PKI architecture. Unlike a hierarchy, building a certification path from a user's certificate to a trust point is non-deterministic.

CERTIFICATE PATH CONSTRUCTION IN A MESH PKI ARCHITECTURE
In a mesh PKI architecture, the certification path construction is initiated at the trust point, and it moves toward the issuer of the end entity certificate. The end entity certificates are issued directly by their trust point. But this CA can be different from the trust point for the entity that is constructing the path. In addition, this CA will have many certificates, each issued by a different CA and each leading to a different location in the mesh.

This makes path construction more complex since there are multiple choices. Some of these choices lead to a valid path while others result in useless dead-ends. It is possible in a mesh PKI to construct an endless loop of certificates. The maximum length of a certification path in a mesh PKI is the number of CAs in the PKI.

In addition, mesh architecture involves construction of different certification paths by different users. Since a trust point is usually a CA that has issued a certificate to the entity, therefore when Alice constructs a certification path for Bob, the initiation point is the CA that has issued Alice's certificate and the end point is Bob's certificate. Similarly, when James constructs a certification path for Bob, it begins with James's issuer CA and ends with Bob's certificate. In both situations, the certification paths will not be the same until both Alice and James have the same issuer CAs or trust point.

Since mesh contains many bidirectional relationships between the CAs, there is usually more than one certification path between any entity and a trust point. In a hierarchy, building a certification path from the user's certificate to the highest trust point is deterministic while in mesh it is nondeterministic. The path discovery is more difficult in case of peer-to-peer architecture. The path length may be longer than hierarchical PKI.

Figure 3-10 depicts a certification path in a mesh PKI architecture.

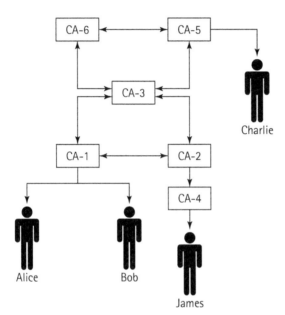

Figure 3-10: Certificate path construction in mesh PKI architecture

As can be seen in the figure different certification paths can be constructed for each user. For example, Alice can construct the following certification path for Bob:

◆ [CA-1 → Bob]

But for James, she can construct the following certification paths:

◆ [CA-1 → CA-2]: [CA-2 → CA-3]: [CA-3 → Bob]

◆ [CA-1 → CA-2]: [CA-2 → James]

The single CA, hierarchal PKI, and the mesh PKI architectures are combined to create a hybrid PKI.

Hybrid PKI Architecture

PKI architectures that you have learned so far cater to the needs of an enterprise or a user group. However, in quite a few instances organizations need to interact with other organizations to conduct their business. The architecture of these organizations might not always be the same. For example, one organization might have a hierarchical PKI architecture, while the other might have a mesh PKI architecture. In such situations, PKI needs to provide an optimum solution that enables organizations to interact with each other in a trusted environment. PKI provides such an environment through a hybrid architecture. A hybrid architecture allows organizations with multiple PKI architectures to interoperate between themselves.

Let us look at a generic hybrid PKI architecture that involves a single, hierarchical, and mesh PKI architecture. Consider three organizations having three different types of architecture. AllSolv, Inc. has a single CA architecture named PKI1, WebEyes, Inc. has a hierarchical PKI architecture named PKI2, and SureSolv, Inc. has a mesh PKI that is named PKI3. Each of these organizations has subordinate CAs according to their needs and end-entities. Such a situation is depicted in Figure 3-11.

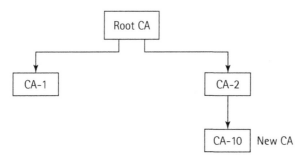

Figure 3-11: Hybrid PKI architecture

Alice and Bob are members of PKI1, James and Charlie are members of PKI2, and Smith and Robert are members of PKI3. All these users have received their certificates from their respective CAs.

The three types of Hybrid PKI architectures are:

◆ **Extended Trust List architecture:** This extends the Trust List architectures to support certification paths of lengths greater than one.

◆ **Cross-certified PKI architecture:** Enterprise PKI establishes a peer-to-peer relationship to enable secure communication.

◆ **Bridge CA architecture:** Provides support to multiple PKI architectures.

Let us now discuss each of these hybrid architectures in detail.

Extended Trust List Architecture

In the extended trust list architecture, end entities maintain a list of multiple trust points. Each trust point refers to a PKI, which the entity trusts. This can be a single CA, hierarchical, or mesh PKI.

As shown in Figure 3-7, Alice receives a certificate from CA-1. According to the extended trust list architecture, Alice must trust PKI2 and PKI3 to communicate with James, Charlie, Smith, and Robert. Alice can trust any one CA in PKI2 or PKI3, or she can add the entire organization to her trust list.

The extended Trust List of Alice is shown in Figure 3-12.

As shown in Figure 3-12, Alice trusts CAs A1, B1, and C1, and therefore she includes them in her ETL.

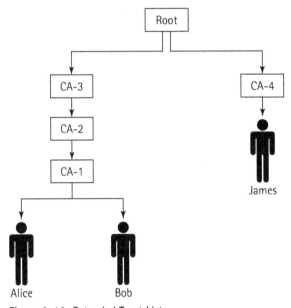

Figure 3-12: Extended Trust List

CERTIFICATE PATH CONSTRUCTION IN A EXTENDED TRUST LIST PKI ARCHITECTURE

The extended Trust List might contain both hierarchical and mesh PKI architecture. One entry in the trust might correspond to the root CA of a hierarchy, and another entry could correspond to a CA within a mesh. When a hierarchical PKI architecture is encountered, then the straightforward certification path construction method is used, but in case of mesh architecture a more complex method is used.

However, just by looking into an end entity certificate one cannot determine whether it belongs to a hierarchical PKI architecture or a mesh PKI architecture. The initialization of the certification path construction is also difficult because unless the certificate was issued by one of the trust points, it is not clear from which trust point should the certification path begin.

To encounter all such issues, the extended Trust List generates a *certificate cache*. This cache consists of all the possible certification paths. Therefore, instead of constructing a certification path, you can refer to the cache and search for the appropriate path with the help of the certification path value. This value is based on the complexity of the certification path. Simple certification paths are assigned a higher value than complex paths.

 Cygnacom Solutions has developed a Certificate Path Development Library (CPL) that is freely available. The CPL can discover all possible paths from an entity certificate to a trusted root and return them in a prioritized order. The CPL does not provide code to obtain and/or cache the needed certificates, but instead provides callouts for this activity.

Cross-Certified Enterprise PKIs

In a cross-certified architecture, either the root CA or the subordinate CA of a particular PKI establishes a peer-to-peer trust relationship with the root CAs or subordinate CAs of another PKI. For example, in Figure 3-9, the root CA of AllSolv Inc. makes a peer-to-peer trust relationship with the other two PKIs, PKI2 and PKI3. Similarly, the Root CA of PKI2 establishes a trust relationship with the Root CAs of PKI1 and PKI3.

Each user will have a single trust point. The cross-enterprise relationship is peer-to-peer. Once the CAs have cross-certified each other, their entities can validate entities in the other PKI. Therefore, a single action enables secure communications among all the users across the PKIs. While in an extended trust list architecture, both Alice and Robert need to update their own Trust Lists. This architecture is good for a small number of enterprise PKIs that need to establish the trust relationship.

Figure 3-13 illustrates a cross-certified PKI architecture.

According to Figure 3-13, three peer-to-peer relationships need to be established, and for establishing these relationships six certificates are needed.

 Cross-certifying in enterprise PKIs requires *(n*n-n)/2* peer-to-peer relationships and *(n*n-n)* certificates.

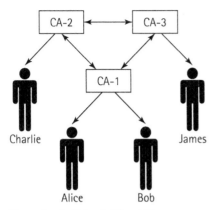

Figure 3-13: Extended Trust List

CERTIFICATE PATH CONSTRUCTION IN A CROSS-CERTIFIED PKI ARCHITECTURE

Just like the mesh and the extended trust list PKI architecture, in cross-certified PKI architecture, different users construct different certification paths for the same end entity certificate. The certification path begins at the trust point that is associated with the native PKI. For example, if Alice is a part of the hierarchical PKI then the certification path will begin at the root CA, but if she is a part of the simple or mesh PKI, then her certification path will begin at the CA that issued her the certificate. One cross certificate can connect to the root CA of a hierarchy, and another cross certificate can connect to a CA within a mesh.

In cross-certified PKI architecture also, the straightforward certification path construction method is used within a hierarchy, but this ends when an outside root is reached. Then, a more complex certification path construction associated with a mesh PKI architecture must be used to identify one or more cross certificates to reach the trust point.

Figure 3-14 depicts the certification path construction in cross-certification PKI architecture.

The following certification paths would be constructed by Alice for Bob:

◆ [CA-1 → Bob]

The following certification paths would be constructed by Alice for James:

◆ [CA-1 → CA-2]: [CA-2 → CA-4]: [CA-4 → James]

◆ [CA-1 → CA-3]: [CA-3 → CA-2]: [CA-2 → CA-4]: [CA-4 → James]

The following certification paths would be constructed by Alice for Charlie:

◆ [CA-1 → CA-3]: [CA-3 → CA-5]: [CA-5 → Charlie]

◆ [CA-1 → CA-2]: [CA-2 → CA-3]: [CA-3 → CA-5]: [CA-5 → Charlie]

◆ [CA-1 → CA-2]: [CA-2 → CA-3]: [CA-3 → CA-6]: [CA-6 → CA-5]: [CA-5 → Charlie]

As we just discussed, cross-certified PKI architecture is suitable for establishing a relationship between only a few organizations. The bridge CA architecture is designed to overcome the limitations of the two basic PKI architectures, the hierarchical PKI and the mesh PKI.

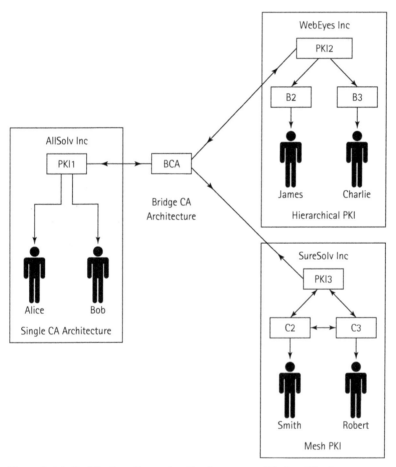

Figure 3-14: Certificate path construction in cross-certified architecture

Bridge CA Architecture

The bridge CA architecture is the most suitable architecture to link PKIs that implement different architectures. Unlike a mesh PKI CA, the bridge CA does not issue certificates directly to users. The bridge CA establishes peer-to-peer trust relationships with the CAs of different entities. These relationships are combined to form a "bridge of trust" enabling entities to interact with each other through the bridge CA.

The establishment of a trust relationship in a bridge CA architecture depends on the type of PKI architecture with which the trust is being established. For example, in case of a hierarchical PKI architecture, the trust is established with the root CA, while in case of a mesh PKI architecture, a trust relationship can be established with any CA in the PKI. The CA that establishes a relationship with the bridge CA is referred to as the *Principal CA*. The trust relationships between a principal CA and a bridge CA are all peer-to-peer.

It is easy to add new CAs or entire enterprise PKIs to a bridge-connected PKI. The change is transparent to users as no change in trust points happens.

Figure 3-15 shows a bridge CA that has established trust relationships with a mesh PKI and a hierarchical PKI. In the example, Alice has received her certificate from a CA in the hierarchical PKI and uses the root CA of the hierarchy as her trust point. James received his certificate from a CA of the mesh PKI and uses that CA as his trust point. Alice and James can use the "bridge of trust" to establish a relationship that enables them to interact with each other in a trusted manner.

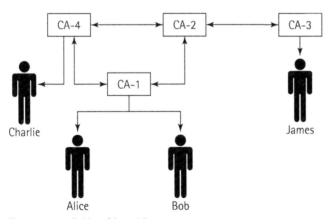

Figure 3-15: Bridge CA architecture

The bridge CA architecture is sometimes also known as a "hub and spoke" PKI. This is because the bridge PKI connects multiple PKIs at a common point or a hub. In a bridge CA architecture, if a principal CA is compromised then the bridge CA revokes its certificate. In this way, other relationships are not affected. In case of a compromise of the bridge CA, the principal CAs revoke the certificates issued to the bridge CA.

CERTIFICATE PATH CONSTRUCTION IN A BRIDGE CA ARCHITECTURE

Bridge CA architecture is an improvement over the cross-certified PKI architecture. Here, different users construct different certification paths for the same end entity certificate, and the path begins at the trust point associated with the native PKI. But, in a bridge CA architecture certificate path construction, there is only one cross certificate that links the native PKI to all the outside or foreign PKIs.

In comparison to a mesh PKI, certification path discovery becomes easier in bridge CA architecture. The users typically know their path to the bridge CA; they need to determine only the path from the bridge CA to the entity's certificate. In addition, a BCA-architected PKI will typically have shorter trust paths than a random mesh PKI with the same number of CAs. The Certification path discovery is still more difficult than in a hierarchy, and the typical path length is approximately doubled.

Figure 3-16 depicts certification path construction in bridge CA architecture.

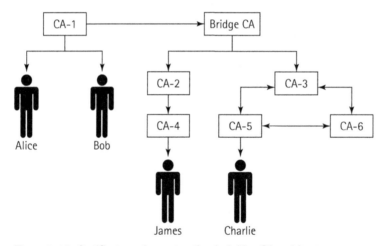

Figure 3-16: Certificate path construction in bridge CA architecture

Alice will construct the following certification path for Bob:

◆ [CA-1 → Bob]

Alice will construct the following certification path for James:

◆ [CA-1 → Bridge CA]: [Bridge CA → CA-2]: [CA-2 → CA-4]: [CA-4 → James]
◆ [CA-1 → Bridge CA]: [Bridge CA → CA-3]: [CA-3 → CA-2]: [CA-2 → CA-4]: [CA-4 → James]

The following certification paths would be constructed by Alice for Charlie:

♦ [CA-1 → Bridge CA]: [Bridge CA → CA-3]: [CA-3 → CA-5]: [CA-5 → Charlie]

♦ [CA-1 → Bridge CA]: [Bridge CA → CA-3]: [CA-3 → CA-6]: [CA-6 → CA-5]: [CA-5 → Charlie]

After the certificate path has been created, you need to validate it.

Certificate Path Validation

Certificate path validation is the process that involves validating each certificate in the certification path to determine whether or not the key in the certificate is trustworthy. Certificate path validation verifies that the binding between the signer's identity and their public key is valid and the integrity of the public key is assured. The process of key validation does not depend on the type of PKI architecture. For each certificate, one needs to perform the following steps:

♦ Verify the digital signature of the certificate.

♦ Ensure that the certificate had not expired at the time of transaction.

♦ Check the revocation status to ensure that it was valid at the time the transaction/document was signed.

♦ Check any applicable policies, key usage restrictions, name constraints, and so on.

After the certificate path has been validated the certificate can be trusted by the entities.

Which PKI Architecture Should You Implement?

Choosing the most appropriate PKI architecture for your organization is indeed quite a tedious job. There are no hard and fast rules for choosing a particular PKI architecture as no architecture provides a complete solution to all situations. Understanding of the organization's requirements and working is one of the basic criteria for implementing a particular architecture.

If your organization is a small and uniform unit, then implementing a single CA type of architecture seems to be the most appropriate choice. However, when your organization has a well-defined and formalized organizational structure, then you can implement a hierarchical PKI architecture. Hierarchical PKI architecture is closely associated with the organization structure. You can create a hierarchical PKI structure on the basis of your organizational structure. For example, if your organization structure is more of a vertical structure, that is, with many layers, then you can first implement a root CA. This root CA is the most trusted CA and has the greatest authority. After the root CA has been established you can then implement subordinate CAs thus forming a hierarchy. Mesh PKI architecture is suitable for organizations that do not support a defined organizational structure. As already discussed, mesh PKI architecture supports a peer-to-peer relationship between the CAs rather than a superior-subordinate relationship. Thus, in organizations where there exists no well-defined organization structure, it is easier to implement mesh architecture, as in these organizations there are more peer-to-peer relationships rather than superior-subordinate relationships. Cross-certified PKI architectures are implemented when there exist only a few PKI, for example between PKIs of two partner organizations. Bridge PKI architecture, as discussed in the previous section, is best suited to link PKIs that implement different architectures.

Summary

In this chapter, you learned that PKI architecture reflects the arrangement of CAs in an organization and the relationships between each of them. You learned that there are three basic types of architecture, namely:

- Single CA architecture
- Enterprise PKI architecture
- Hybrid PKI architecture

Single CA architecture is the most basic type of PKI architecture, and there is just one CA who issues and distributes certificates and CRLs to the entities. An enhancement over the single CA architecture is the Trust List architecture in which an entity can trust more than one CA. Each of these CAs is maintained in the Trust List of that entity.

Then you learned about the enterprise PKI architecture. An enterprise PKI architecture can be implemented in two ways, either superior-subordinate (hierarchical PKI) or peer-to-peer (mesh PKI).

Next, you learned about hybrid PKI architecture. There are three types of hybrid PKI architectures, namely:

- Extended Trust List architecture
- Cross-certified enterprise PKI
- Bridge CA architecture

You learned about certification path construction and certificate path validation. A certification path is a series of certificates, in which the entity that has issued the first certificate is a trust point. Certificate path validation is the process that involves validating each certificate in the certification path to determine whether or not the key in the certificate is trustworthy.

Chapter 4

CA Functions

IN THIS CHAPTER

- ◆ Issuing certificates
- ◆ Revoking certificates
- ◆ Formulating a certificate policy
- ◆ Implementing the Certification Practice Statement (CPS)

THE PREVIOUS CHAPTERS gave you an overview of cryptography and PKI. You learned that PKI is a framework that is comprised of hardware, software, policies, and procedures that are required to create, manage, store, and distribute keys and digital certificates.

You also learned that the various roles that are involved in a PKI organization are

- ◆ Certification Authorities (CA) that manage and sign certificates for an institution
- ◆ Registration Authorities (RA) that operate under the auspices of the CA and validate users as having been issued certificates
- ◆ PKI management tools, including software to manage revocations, validations and renewals
- ◆ Directories to store certificates, public keys, and certificate management information
- ◆ Databases and key management software to store escrowed and archived keys
- ◆ Applications that can make use of certificates and can seek validation of others' certificates
- ◆ Trust models that extend the realm of secure communications beyond the original CA
- ◆ Policies that identify how an institution manages certificates, including legal liabilities and limitations, standards on contents of certificates, and actual campus practices

A Certification Authority (CA) plays a pivotal role for an effective PKI deployment, which forms the foundation of an increased use of digital certificates and e-commerce. This chapter introduces you to the various functions that are performed by a CA. You'll learn about the process of issuing certificates, revoking certificates, formulating certification policies, and the Certificate Practice Statement (CPS). For a better understanding and practical implementation of CPS, we have included a sample CPS at the end of the chapter.

Functions of a CA

You already know that a CA is trusted third party that issues digital certificates to authenticate entities taking part in an electronic transaction. Although authenticating users is one of the most fundamental functions of a CA, the role of a CA is not limited to just issuing certificates for authenticating entities. In addition to issuing digital certificates, other functions of a CA include revoking certificates and formulating certificate policies and Certification Practice Statement (CPS). All these functions form the basis for implementing PKI. To ensure that PKI is implemented successfully, a CA has two principal roles to perform:

- ◆ Ensure that the public key that is associated with a private key belongs to the person specified in the public key. If the public key belongs to a person other than the one specified, the entire purpose of PKI is defeated. Therefore, the CA performs the important task of issuing certificates and revoking them if they are compromised.

- ◆ Establish its credibility, so that all parties can trust the CA. A CA uses its private key to sign certificates. The public key corresponding to this private key is stored in a certificate. Further, this certificate enables a user to establish a trust relationship with a CA.

Let us now discuss in detail each of the functions that are performed by a CA. We'll start with the most fundamental function performed by a CA, which is issuing certificates.

Issuing Certificates

As discussed, a CA authenticates users by issuing digital certificates. You would recall from the previous chapters that a digital certificate is an electronic document that is issued by a CA to authenticate entities taking part in an electronic transaction. These digital certificates can be issued to users, other CAs, or to both. However, before issuing a certificate, the CA needs to verify the credentials of the certificate applicant. When a CA issues a certificate, it asserts that the certificate owner has the private key corresponding to the public key that is contained in the certificate.

While issuing a certificate, the CA digitally signs the certificates with its private key. This digital signature of the issuing CA in the certificate helps users to identify whether the CA who has issued the certificate is their trusted CA or not. To ensure the authenticity of the certificate, users can verify the signature of the CA by using the public key of the CA. It is this signature of the CA that forms the very basis of trust for certificates issued by that CA.

CAs can only issue certificates if they are requested to do so. To obtain a certificate from a CA the user needs to perform the following steps:

1. Generate his or her key pair.

2. Once a key pair has been generated, the user needs to register his or her public key with a CA.

3. Send the request for certificate issue to the RA in a predefined format.

4. The RA checks the user identification and assures itself of the identity of the user. Once done, the RA forwards the request to the CA.

5. The CA signs a certificate by using its private key and sends the certificate to the RA. The signing of the certificate binds the subscriber to his or her public key.

6. The RA forwards the certificate that it receives from the CA to the concerned user.

7. The user presents this certificate whenever desired in order to demonstrate the legitimacy of his or her key.

The certificates that are issued have to be in a specified format so that they are recognized globally. One such format that is globally recognized is the X.509 standard. Let's now look at the structure of a digital certificate based on the X.509 standard.

STRUCTURE OF AN X.509 DIGITAL CERTIFICATE

In 1988, the International Telecommunications Union recommended the X.509 standard for digital certificates. Since then the X.509 has become a de facto industry standard for authenticating users on open systems, such as the Internet. The latest version of X.509 certificate is X.509 v3. Figure 4-1 illustrates the structure of an X.509 certificate.

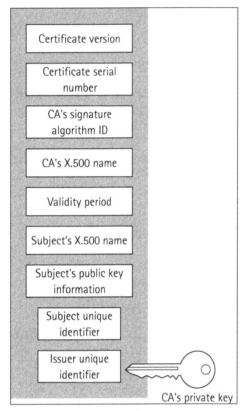

Figure 4-1: X.509 v3 certificate

As can be seen from the figure, a X.509 v3 digital certificate consists of the following fields:

◆ **Certificate Version:** This describes the version of the certificate.

◆ **Certificate Serial number:** This is a unique integer that a CA associates with each certificate.

◆ **CA's Signature algorithm:** Identifies the CA's signature algorithm.

◆ **CA's X.500 name:** Identifies the CA that has signed and issued the certificate.

◆ **Validity period:** Contains two dates, the date from which the certificate validity period begins and the date when the certificate validity period ends.

◆ **Subject's X.500 name:** Identifies the entity to which the private key is issued. This private key is associated with the subject's public key.

◆ **Subject public key information:** Contains the public key along with the identifier of the algorithm with which the key is used.

◆ **Subject unique identifier:** Similar to the Issuer unique identifier, this field ensures the uniqueness of the subject of the certificate.

◆ **Issuer unique identifier:** This field contains a unique ID of the certificate issuer. Although the CA's X.500 name field also exists, this field ensures that the identifier is unique to the issuing CA and doesn't identify some other CA.

These fields provide the required information about a certificate and the entity to which the certificate has been issued.

All issued certificates are published in the repository database of the CA to make the identification of the subscriber available online for verification. The repository is an online database of certificates and other information used in the digital signature verification process.

Once a certificate has been issued it is valid for a particular lifetime. However, there might be certain situations that can lead to a certificate becoming invalid prematurely. Such a certificate then needs to be revoked. Revoking a certificate is another important function of a CA. The following section discusses the reasons of revoking a certificate and how a CA revokes a certificate.

Revoking Certificates

As we just discussed, every certificate has a validity period. However, some of the reasons that can result in a certificate becoming prematurely invalid are:

◆ Compromise of an entity's private key

◆ A certificate holder leaves the company

◆ Change in the attribute information of the entity, such as entity name, or relationship with the organization

◆ Compromise of the Certification Authority (CA) key

Some of the methods that a CA can use to revoke certificates are:

◆ Periodic Publication Mechanisms: This mechanism includes the use of Certificate Revocation Lists (CRL) and Certificate Revocation Tress (CRT). A Certificate Revocation List (CRL) is a signed list of certificates that have been revoked or suspended. CRT is a revocation technology, which is based on Merkle hash trees, where the tree represents all known certificate revocation information relevant to some known set of PKI communities.

◆ Online Query Mechanisms: Online Query Mechanisms comprise Online Certificate Status Protocol (OCSP) and Online Transaction Validation Protocols. OCSP is used to obtain online revocation information about certificates, and Online Transaction Validation Protocols are used for online validation, such as business transactions through credit cards.

There is an indirect relationship between the information contained in the certificate and its useful lifetime. Generally speaking, the more the information in a certificate, the shorter is its usefulness. This is because the information in the certificate might change. This may result in an old certificate being revoked and a new certificate being issued before the first expires.

You will learn more about certificate revocation and methods for certification revocation in Chapter 5.

One of the most important aspects of certificate revocation is the timeliness with which the revocation information is updated and published. This is because if users are not informed about a revoked certificate they might end up trusting an invalid certificate. The difference between the time when a CA receives the information that a certificate needs to be revoked and when the CA actually publicly publishes the revocation information is known as revocation delay. This revocation delay should be as minimal as possible and should be specified in the certificate policy.

A certificate policy is a document that specifies a security policy for managing certificates. Formulating a certificate policy is yet another function of a CA.

Formulating a Certificate Policy

A certificate policy, though not comparable with a concept such as company policy, can be regarded parallel to it. A certificate policy is a documented set of rules and commitments made by a CA to indicate the applicability of a certificate to a particular group of users or set of applications.

Though the primary purpose of certificate policies is to determine the security policy that is followed by a certification organization, it can also be used as a reference for other organizations that need to establish a domain-trust relation with your organization. This is required to ensure that their data will be secure after establishing the relationship. A certificate policy does not give insights into how the policy is implemented. It is merely a reiteration of the organization's commitment toward ensuring security of certificates. Because software policies are application independent, they can be applied across a wide range of certificates for different applications. Furthermore, they can remain in effect for a long time, even when the application that has implemented the policy has changed.

A certificate policy effectively is a statement of authenticity for a certificate user, signifying that the public key of the CA is bound to the certificate that is referred to by the certificate policy. Different certificates that are issued follow different practices and procedures and may be suitable for different applications and/or purposes. However, all these certificates, though differing in their application, can be covered under the purview of one certificate policy.

A certificate policy can apply to one organization or to a number of organizations. A certificate policy can also belong to an industry. In this case, the organization might implement that certificate policy to associate itself with the industry. For example, an IT company might implement SEI-CMM standards to associate itself with those standards and benefit from them.

Writing Certificate Policies

When a certificate policy is drafted, security analysts and application owners should evaluate it. This ensures that the policy covers all security aspects of a certificate and can be implemented with the given application. For writing certificate policies, you can use the RFC 2527 format. You can obtain this format from the URL http://www.ietf.org/rfc/rfc2527.txt. This format ensures that all the critical aspects of the certificate policy are included in a policy.

A certificate policy can apply to a single CA or to multiple CAs that issue certificates by using this policy.

Certificate Policies and CAs

A certificate policy is usually associated with a single CA when the CA serves as the trust point and is responsible for issuing all certificates. A certificate policy is associated with multiple CAs when a single CA is not the trust point. A CA should ensure that all subordinate CAs working on its behalf or the registration authority comply with the certificate policies.

Certificate policies are also useful in the approval of CAs. Each CA is approved against one or more certificate policies that the CA implements. Let us examine how CAs create trust policies between themselves by examining their certificate policies. When one CA issues a CA certificate for another CA, the CA assesses the certificate policies of the other CA. The CA, having evaluated the certification policy of the other CA, communicates the policies that are acceptable to the other CA. Once the set of policies that the CA has accepted has been conveyed to the other CA, the trust relationship between the two CAs is established.

The information about a certificate policy is distributed to the users in the form of object identifiers (OID). In a certificate each policy OID corresponds to a single CA. The following section discusses policy OID in detail.

Policy Object Identifiers

Users need to have a source of obtaining certificate information. If a user uses multiple certificates, associating certificate policies and CPS with the correct certificates might pose a problem. This is accomplished by the use of policy object identifiers, referred to as OID. An OID is a simple data type defined by ANS.1 and is a sequence of integers that are separated by dots or periods, for example 3.4.2 or 5.2.1.

Each OID maps to a certificate policy, which is, in turn, related to one or more CPS. Once an OID is associated with a certificate policy, you cannot make major modifications to the policy. If you make major modifications, the certificate policy needs to be associated with a new OID. As a result you can use OIDs to easily distinguish one certificate policy from another.

An OID is indirectly related to a CPS. To explain this concept, let us take an example. AllSolv Inc. has three departments: Sales, Manufacturing, and Legal. The Legal department performs functions that are not even remotely related to the functions of the Sales and Manufacturing departments. Therefore, a separate certificate policy exists for the Legal department. However, the Sales and Manufacturing departments have some procedures in common, and a single, exhaustive certificate policy has been defined for both the departments. Since the organization has two certificate policies, it will have two OIDs associated with it.

However, the organization needs to develop a separate CPS for each of these departments. This is because each department performs a specialized job. Moreover, the employees of each department are concerned with work that is related to their job profile. In such a scenario, the company can implement three separate CPSs for each of its departments. However, the CPS for the Sales and the Manufacturing departments will be derived from the common certificate policy.

Certificate policies are documented and practiced by using a Certification Practice Statement (CPS). You will learn more about CPS in the following section. CA operations are based on its CPS, which in turn define the security policy.

Certification Practice Statement (CPS)

A Certification Practice Statement (CPS), as the name suggests, specifies how certification is practiced. That is, the statement describes how the practices that are identified in the certificate policies are implemented and enforced. A CPS specifies the policies and procedures that a company follows for issuing and managing certificates. Though it appears similar to certificate policies, a CPS is essentially a detailed description of the procedures implemented by an organization. The description includes any application-specific details that an organization might deem relevant to the document.

To clarify the relationship between certificate policies and CPS, consider an example. Consider a company that states its certificate policy as "Each document that is exchanged electronically will be tracked." A CPS corresponding to this certificate policy can be: "The company uses Microsoft BizTalk Server 2000 to exchange documents with its trading partners. Details of all documents interchanged by BizTalk Server 2000 are, by default, maintained in the Tracking database. A system administrator, from time to time, retrieves the details of such documents and archives them." In the example mentioned here, the CPS describes the procedure by which the object listed in the certificate policy is implemented.

A CPS provides a good insight into the working of a CA. It can be used by organizations to evaluate the maturity of an organization's processes before partnering with the organization. In this way, the organization that owns the CPS can demonstrate its competence to manage certificates.

Role of CAs in CPS

A CA is responsible for issuing a CPS. The tasks that a CA should perform for formulating a CPS are given below:

◆ Issue a CPS.

◆ Ensure that the RA and the subscribers are aware of the policies and CPS.

◆ Ensure that any CA with whom it cross-certifies complies with certificate policies and CPS that are mutually agreed. Cross-certified CAs are those CAs whose certificate policies have been evaluated and have been accepted.

Starting right from establishing the identity of an applicant through the applicant's initial certificate registration request to renewing a certificate, the role of a CA in CPS is well defined and documented. It has to abide by the obligations and liabilities as per the CPS.

Writing a CPS

A CPS should conform to the certificate policies supported by the CA. Often the same template that is used for creating certificate policies is used for creating a CPS. However, a CPS is generally more specific than a certificate policy. Therefore, even when you use the RFC 2527 format for creating a CPS, you can be more specific by getting into the insights of a process or by naming the personnel who will be involved in performing a given set of operations. A CPS typically includes the following type of information:

◆ The CA with which the CPS is associated

◆ The certificate policies implemented by the CA. A CA can implement one or more certificate policies

◆ The CA policy for issuing and renewing certificates

◆ The validity period of the CA certificate

◆ The conditions in which the CA might revoke the user certificate

◆ The CRL policies that mention the publishing interval and distribution point

◆ The cryptographic algorithm used for a CA certificate

RFC 2527 format for a CPS contains a number of components for a CPS. These components are

◆ Introduction

◆ General Provisions

◆ Identification and Authentication

◆ Operational Requirements

◆ Physical, Procedural, and Personnel Security Controls

◆ Technical Security Controls

◆ Certificate and CRL Profile

◆ Specification Administration

Although all these components need to be part of the CPS, the two most important components are

◆ Identification and Authentication

◆ Operational Requirements

Let's discuss each of these in detail.

IDENTIFICATION AND AUTHENTICATION

Before a CA issues a certificate, the CA should first authenticate the certificate applicant. An applicant can be identified by the credentials presented by the applicant in the certificate application during certificate registration process. The various ways in which an applicant can be identified are

◆ E-mail ID of the user as given in the certificate application

◆ Face-to-face appearance before a CA or an RA

◆ Applicant's unique name

◆ Presenting credentials to collect registered/certified mail

OPERATIONAL REQUIREMENTS

The operational requirements component of the CPS ensures that a certificate is issued or revoked by a CA only when appropriate. According to RFC 2527, operational requirements components consist of the following sections:

- Certificate Application

- Certificate Issuance

- Certificate Acceptance

- Certificate Suspension and Revocation

- Security Audit Procedures

- Records Archival

- Key Changeover

- Compromise and Disaster Recovery

- CA Termination

For a better understanding of these components and CPS, let us now look at the following sample CPS for a fictitious company called AllSolv. The CPS clearly defines the policies and procedures that are followed by the AllSolv CA in order to perform CA functions and to provide certification services.

Sample CPS for AllSolv, Inc. Company

In this section, we will discuss the CPS of AllSolv, Inc. This is a sample CPS and can be used as an example to see what an actual CPS looks like. As discussed earlier, a CPS consists of several sections as described in RFC 2527. However, these sections can differ from organization to organization based on the requirements and policies of the organization. For example, according to the RFC 2527 format, a CPS should also contain a section on fees. This section contains provisions regarding fees charged by CAs, repositories, or RAs. This fee can be charged for certificate issuance or revocation, certificate access, or revocation or status information access. Since the AllSolv CA is an internal CA, therefore there exists no provision for fees in the CPS of AllSolv.

Let us now look at the sample CPS for AllSolv, Inc. and discuss the various sections that are a part of this CPS.

AllSolv CA

CERTIFICATION PRACTICE STATEMENT
© AllSolv, Inc.
Version: 1.2
Date: 5 November 2001
Prepared by: AllSolv CA Certification Services

1.   Introduction

1.1   OVERVIEW
This AllSolv CA Certification Practice Statement (CPS) defines the policies, practices, and standards that are used by AllSolv CA to provide CA Services and to exhibit trust by substantiating the methods that are used to manage and complete tasks associated with generating and issuing certificates.

1.2   EXTENT OF ALLSOLV CA CERTIFICATION SERVICES
AllSolv CA Certification Services are designed to support secure electronic transactions and other security services to meet the needs of AllSolv users for digital signatures and other network security services. To do this, AllSolv CA serves as a trusted third party, issuing, managing, renewing, and revoking certificates in accordance with published policies.

AllSolv CA provides the following services:

- ◆ Application of Certificate

- ◆ Issuance of Certificate

- ◆ Publication of Certificate

- ◆ Revocation of Certificate

- ◆ Expiration of Certificate

- ◆ Management of CRL

1.3   IDENTITY OF ALLSOLV CA
AllSolv CA manages certificates of the following organization:

Organization Name: AllSolv, Inc.

Registered Office: AllSolv, Inc

                          15 Marina Village Parkway

                          Alameda, CA – 94501

Telephone:	**510-464-5441**
Fax:	**510-464-9643**
Electronic mail:	`http://allsolvca@acs.us`

2.   AllSolv CA Infrastructure

2.1   OVERVIEW

AllSolv CA acts as a trusted third party that authenticates the identity of AllSolv users by issuing a certificate. A certificate, i.e., a digitally signed document that is issued by AllSolv CA, confirms the authenticity of the AllSolv users. Managing the certificates of AllSolv includes registration, naming, authenticating, issuance, revocation, and audit-trail generation.

2.2   CERTIFICATION AUTHORITY (CA)

AllSolv Certification Authority operates according to this CPS and issues, manages, and revokes certificates. Its functions include the following:

- ◆ Application of Certificate
- ◆ Issuance of Certificate
- ◆ Publication of Certificate
- ◆ Revocation of Certificate
- ◆ Expiration of Certificate
- ◆ Management of CRL

To ensure security, Certification Authority will accept Certificate Requests approved by the Registration Authority Officer on the Registration Authority Console only. AllSolv CA neither generates nor holds the private keys of certificate users.

The private key of AllSolv is protected against compromise by hardware products.

Registration Authority (RA)

AllSolv Registration Authority examines and approves or rejects certificate applications, exclusively on behalf of the AllSolv CA that actually issues the certificates.

To manage and validate certificate applications' identity and confirm the information they provide while applying, a Registration Authority Officer is assigned.

To approve certificate applications after the Registration Authority Officer has validated them, a Registration Authority Manager is assigned. This Registration Authority Manager is different from the Registration Authority Officer and also ensures that the whole certification application process is performed according to the CPS.

After the Registration Authority Manager has approved the certificate request the Registration Authority Officer submits the certificate to the Certificate Authority through the Registration Authority Console. This Registration Authority Console is the only machine which communicates with the CA server to manage digital certificates.

Certificate Repository

Certificate Repository is an internal database that stores all issued or revoked certificates, private Certificate Revocation List (CRL), pending certificate requests, etc. The CA or the RA can only update this database. Users can access this database by using the Web user interface and query their certificate request status.

A directory server, based on the LDAP standard, acts as a public repository of CRl, and user and CA certificates. To retrieve certificates for applications such as S/MIME or SSL client authentication a standard LDAP interface is provided to the native clients.

3.   Application of Certificate

3.1   OVERVIEW

This section describes the Application process for a certificate. It comprises the key pair generation requirements and the security information required for each certificate.

3.2   CERTIFICATE APPLICATION

To obtain a certificate the applicants need to complete the following procedures:

◆ Generate a key pair and demonstrate its functioning to the AllSolv CA.

◆ Secure their private key from any type of compromise.

◆ Submit a certificate application to AllSolv CA and agree to the AllSolv CA certificate owner agreement.

◆ Authenticate users with a valid Network Account and Password.

AllSolv CA follows an online enrollment process. After completing this online enrollment process, the certificate applicant confirms that:

◆ Certificate applicant accepts the certificates issued by AllSolv CA.

◆ Certificate applicant has read and abides by the terms of the certificate owner agreement.

◆ Certificate applicant information is authentic.

After completing the validation process, the AllSolv CA sends an e-mail message to the e-mail address specified by the applicant in the certificate application. This e-mail contains a URL that authorizes the certificate applicant to acquire the certificate from AllSolv CA.

4.   Certificate Application Validation

4.1   OVERVIEW
This section includes requirements for validating the certificate applications. It also lays down the procedures for applications that fail validation.

4.2   REQUIREMENTS FOR CERTIFICATE APPLICATION VALIDATION
When the AllSolv CA receives a certificate application, it shall validate all the information of the application by validating all information prior to certificate issuance.

Once a certificate is issued, AllSolv CA shall not monitor and investigate the information in a certificate, unless AllSolv CA is notified about the compromise of that certificate. This notification should be in accordance with the CPS.

4.3   CERTIFICATE APPLICATION APPROVAL
After successful validations of certificate application, AllSolv CA shall approve the certificate application and issue a certificate according to this CPS.

4.4   CERTIFICATE APPLICATION REJECTION
If the validation fails, AllSolv CA shall reject the certificate application, notify the certificate applicant of the validation failure, and provide the reason for failure. AllSolv CA shall communicate to the applicant by using the same method as was used to communicate the certificate application to AllSolv CA. A person whose certificate application has been rejected may thereafter reapply.

5.   Issuance of a Certificate

5.1   OVERVIEW
This section provides information about issuance of a certificate.

5.2   ISSUANCE
After a certificate application is approved the AllSolv CA issues a certificate. The issuance of a certificate indicates that the certificate application has been approved by AllSolv CA.

5.3   PUBLICATION
AllSolv CA shall publish the issued certificate and the public key in the AllSolv Certificate Repository and the AllSolv LDAP directory server, which is a public repository.

5.4   VALIDITY PERIOD

All certificates shall be considered valid if they meet all of the following criteria:

◆ Issued by AllSolv CA

◆ Published on the AllSolv Directory Server

◆ Can be verified by a valid AllSolv Certification Authority certificate

◆ Have not expired

◆ Are not included in the AllSolv CA CRL

5.5   FORMAT OF CERTIFICATE

The format of all certificates issued by AllSolv CA should be in ISO/IEC 9594 X.509 Version 3 format.

6.   Revocation of Certificate

6.1   OVERVIEW

This section explains the conditions under which a certificate may or must be revoked. It also defines the procedures for revoking certificates.

6.2   REVOCATION REASONS

A certificate shall be revoked if:

◆ The private key of the subject of the certificate has been compromised.

◆ The certificate of the subject of the certificate has been modified.

◆ The person is not able to meet his/her obligations under this CPS due to a natural disaster, communications failure, or other cause beyond the control of the person, and as a result another person's information is materially threatened or compromised.

◆ The subject of the certificate breaches a material obligation under this CPS.

6.3   ALLSOLV CA CERTIFICATE REVOCATION

AllSolv CA shall revoke a certificate under the following conditions:

◆ A material fact represented in the certificate is known or reasonably believed to be false by AllSolv CA.

◆ A prerequisite to certificate issuance was not fulfilled.

◆ The private key was compromised, affecting the authenticity of the certificate.

◆ The subject of the certificate breaches a material obligation under this CPS.

6.4   REQUEST FOR REVOCATION

To get a certificate revoked, the owner of the certificate must make a formal request to AllSolv CA. The request needs to be made in one of the following ways:

◆ Sending a paper Certificate Revocation Request form to AllSolv CA. This form must be duly signed with the same signature as on the original application for the certificate and should be accompanied with a valid proof of identity.

◆ Online Submission of a digitally signed Certificate Revocation Request Form. A valid AllSolv CA certificate must digitally sign the online submission of the Certificate Revocation Request Form.

7.   Expiration of Certificate

7.1   OVERVIEW

This section provides information about the expiration and renewal of certificates.

7.2   EXPIRY OF CERTIFICATE

AllSolv CA will notify certificate owners twenty (20) days before the expiration date, via e-mail, about expiration of their certificates.

7.3   RENEWAL OF CERTIFICATE

For renewal of a certificate, the certificate owner shall submit a signed, written request to AllSolv CA before the expiration. Requests that are received after the expiration of the certificate will not be accepted.

Requirements for renewal are subject to change at AllSolv CA's discretion.

8.   Rights, Responsibilities, and Liability

8.1   CERTIFICATE OWNERS' RIGHTS AND RESPONSIBILITIES

AllSolv users acknowledge that AllSolv CA has provided him/her with complete information to become familiar with digital certificates before applying for, using, and relying upon a certificate.

By using a certificate issued by AllSolv CA, the applicant certifies to and agrees with AllSolv CA, and to all who rely on the information contained in the certificate that, until notified otherwise by the certificate owner, of the following points:

◆ All information made by the certificate owner to AllSolv CA regarding the information contained in the certificate is true.

- ◆ Each digital certificate created using the private key corresponding to the public key listed in the certificate is the digital certificate of the certificate owner and the certificate has been accepted and is operational at the time of generation of the digital certificate.

- ◆ Private key of the owner of the certificate has not been compromised.

- ◆ The certificate owner is an end-user certificate owner and not an Issuing Authority. He/She will not use the private key corresponding to any public key listed in the certificate for purposes of signing any certificate or CRL, as an Issuing Authority or otherwise, unless expressly agreed in writing between certificate owner and AllSolv CA.

By accepting a certificate, the owner of the certificate assumes a duty to retain control of the private key of the owner of the certificate and to take precautions to prevent its loss, disclosure, modification, or unauthorized use. The user must revoke his certificate when there has been a loss, theft, modification, unauthorized disclosure, or other compromise of the private key of the certificate with AllSolv CA.

By accepting a certificate, the certificate owner guarantees AllSolv CA of causing no harm to AllSolv CA from any acts resulting in liability, any loss or damage, and any expenses that AllSolv CA may incur, due to:

- ◆ Misrepresentation of fact by the owner of the certificate.

- ◆ Inability of the owner of the certificate to present some material fact in case misrepresentation was made negligently.

- ◆ Inability of the owner of the certificate to protect his/her private key, to prevent its compromise, loss, disclosure, modification, or unauthorized use.

8.2   CERTIFICATE OWNER'S LIABILITY

Owner of the certificate is liable for any misrepresentation he/she makes in certificates to third parties that rely on the representations contained therein.

8.3   ALLSOLV CA'S RIGHTS AND RESPONSIBILITIES

AllSolv CA doesn't generate or store the private keys of the owners of the certificates. Neither does AllSolv CA enforce any particular private key protection requirements of the owner of the certificate.

Upon receipt of a certificate application, AllSolv CA shall make the necessary validations before issuing a certificate, as follows:

- ◆ The certificate applicant is the person identified in the request.

- ◆ All the information provided in the certificate is authentic.

Once a certificate is issued, AllSolv CA shall not monitor and investigate the information in a certificate, unless AllSolv CA is notified about the compromise of that certificate. This notification should be in accordance with the CPS.

Unless otherwise provided in this CPS or mutually agreed upon by both AllSolv CA and the certificate owner, AllSolv CA underwrites to the certificate owner

- ◆ To promptly revoke certificates upon request of the certificate owner

- ◆ To notify certificate owners of any facts known to it that materially affect the validity and reliability of the certificate it issued to such certificate owner

Upon certificate owner's acceptance of the certificate, and verification by AllSolv CA, AllSolv CA shall publish a copy of the certificate in the AllSolv CA repository. Certificate owners may publish their AllSolv CA certificates in other repositories.

8.4   ALLSOLV CA'S LIABILITY
AllSolv CA

- ◆ Does not warrant the accuracy, authenticity, completeness, or fitness of any unverified information contained in certificates or otherwise compiled, published, or disseminated by or on behalf of AllSolv CA.

- ◆ Shall not incur liability for representations of information contained in a certificate, provided the certificate content substantially complies with the CPS.

- ◆ Does not warrant "non-repudiation" of any certificate or message.

Summary

In this chapter, you learned about the process of issuing certificates and the basics of certification revocation. You also learned about the certificate policy, which defines the use of certificates in specific applications and situations. You learned how certificate policies and CPS are accessed by certificate users through Policy Object Identifiers. Next, you learned about the Certification Practice Statement (CPS) that implements these policies. Finally, you looked at a sample CPS of AllSolv CA.

Chapter 5

Certificate Management

IN THIS CHAPTER

♦ Certificate enrollment and Registration Authority (RA)

♦ Maintaining keys and certificates

♦ Issuing multiple certificates to users

♦ Certificate retrieval and validation

♦ Methods of certificate revocation

CERTIFICATES ARE THE BUILDING BLOCKS of the PKI system. The certificate management process starts with the user requesting the registration of a certificate. A Registration Authority (RA), on behalf of a Certification Authority (CA), can carry out this registration process. Once it is issued, a certificate remains valid for a certain period of time. This is known as the certificate lifetime, which is determined by the CA policy. Certificates can become invalid before their expiration date. For example, if a private key is compromised, or even if the compromise is suspected, it can cause a certificate to become invalid before expiry.

Before processing data that is received from the network, a user checks for the validity of the certificate by viewing its expiration. When a certificate has been compromised, the expiration date might not indicate if the certificate is valid. In such a scenario, how will you ascertain if the certificate is valid?

This is where the Certificate Revocation List (CRL) comes into the picture. A CRL is a list of all revoked certificates. In addition to the list of revoked certificates, the CRL also contains information on why the certificate was revoked.

In this chapter, you will learn about the certificate enrollment process. You will also learn about the RA that registers the certificate requests of the users. Then, you will learn about the process of key backups and certificate expiry and archiving. You will also learn about the certificate retrieval and validation process. Next, you will learn about the basics of CRLs and their different versions. You will learn about the different CRL extensions. Finally, you will learn about the process of distribution of CRLs.

Certificate Enrollment and Registration Authority

Certificate enrollment is the process by which a user sends a request for a certificate to a CA. The process involved in *certificate registration* might involve another authority that is different from the CA. This authority is the RA and assists a CA in performing the registration tasks. The RA can be designated by a CA or can be specific to an organization.

The industry associations decided to standardize the entire process of certificate enrollment for the following three reasons:

◆ To make the PKI clients and RA or CA from different vendors compatible.

◆ To enable the issue of certificates uniquely and smoothly. This would ensure that the revocation process is equally smooth.

◆ To use X.509 standards for certificates.

 PKIX or Public Key Infrastructure X.509 is the recommendation to address specific certificate and CRL profiles associated with the Internet. The PKIX group of the Internet Engineering Task Force (IETF) was founded in 1995 and has produced a number of RFCs and Internet Drafts that define the format and transportation of information between different PKI entities. The RFCs produced by PKIX include RFC2459, RFC2511, RFC2560, and RFC2587. This working group had been substantial in bringing PKI to the Internet.

The RA acts as an interface between the user and the CA. The RA typically receives requests from a user to issue certificates. These requests are made through a registration form, which is provided by the RA. The main functions of the RA include

◆ Verifying the identity of a user on receiving a request

◆ Handling certificate enrollment

◆ Passing on the information to the CA to complete the registration process

 The complete registration process is described in the next section, "Certificate Registration."

Typically, the RA consists of three components – Registration authority console, Registration authority officer, and Registration authority manager. Let us consider each component individually.

- ◆ **Registration authority console:** This is a server on which the registration requests are received from the users. The server, in turn, communicates with the CA servers.

- ◆ **Registration authority officer:** This is an individual who processes, verifies, and approves certificate requests. When the CA issues the corresponding certificates, the RA officer distributes them to the users.

- ◆ **Registration authority manager:** This is an individual who manages the RA officers and ensures that all of the dealings are fair. Before the RA officer passes the certificate requests to the CA, all of the verified requests need to be approved by the RA manager.

Certificate Registration

Certificate registration is the process of receiving the registration requests from users. These requests are then processed and validated by the RA. The following steps describe the process of certificate registration:

1. The user sends a request for a registration form to a RA. The RA predefines the format of the registration form. This request for the registration form can be made online depending on the policy under which the RA functions.

2. On receiving the request, the RA sends the registration form to the user.

3. The user submits the completed registration form to the RA.

4. Based on the information in the registration form, the RA verifies the identity of the user and sends the registration request to the corresponding CA.

 The verification that is performed by the RA in Step 4 is as per the policy under which the RA is operating and contingent on how the certificate is used in future. For example, if the user intends to use the certificate for a financial transaction, the verification process might be strict. However, if the certificate is to be used for normal code signing, the verification process might not be as strict.

5. After verifying the request, the CA sends back its response to the RA. The response can be negative if the user does not fulfill a mandatory condition.

6. If the response from the CA is positive, the RA registers the user and passes the registration information to the user.

Figure 5-1 illustrates the certificate registration process.

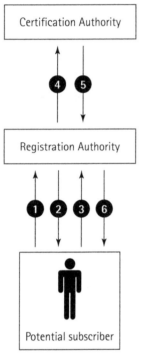

Figure 5-1: Registration process

After the registration process is complete, a key pair is generated. The key pair is important for aspects such as non-repudiation, authentication, etc. The public key of this key pair is bound with the certificate, which is then issued to the user.

Key Generation

A key pair can be generated at the client-end or the CA-end. Deciding where to generate the key pair, to a large extent, depends on the availability of resources to generate the key pair and also on the intended use of the certificate. For example, if a user needs to use the key pair for authentication purposes, either the CA or the user can generate the key pair. However, if the user does not have the required resources for generating the key pair, the CA carries out this task.

TIP In case of non-repudiation, it is advisable that the user generates the key pair. If the CA generates the key pair, it would also have the private key of the generated key pair. This private key has to be transferred to the user, which might lead to certain security threats. For example, if this private key is compromised during its transition, some other user can use it to carry out transactions without the knowledge of the original user. In such a situation, the original user would not have any idea of the transactions that have been carried out and subsequently deny being a part of the complete transaction process. If the key pair is generated at the user-end, the private key doesn't need to be transferred because the owner generates the key; the owner cannot deny being a part of the transaction.

In CA Key Pair Generation, the CA signs the key pair by using a predefined cryptographic algorithm. It also involves the transfer of the generated private key to the user. To accomplish this, the CA needs to have procedures for transferring the private key safely to the owner. In addition to transferring the private key, the CA also needs to publish the certificate along with the corresponding public key in the global directory database.

The CA and the users should not only have adequate resources for generating the keys, but also have resources for performing the key backup. A backup needs to be made once the key is generated. This backup copy can be used to decrypt the messages in case the user loses the original key. The private key of the key pair should always be kept in the safe custody of the owner. This would minimize any intrusion threats to the key. The owner of the private key should also have a proper key backup facility.

After the key pair has been generated and the private key has been secured, a certificate is generated. The public key of the corresponding key pair is then associated with this certificate.

Maintaining Keys and Certificates

A certificate binds the identification information of the subscriber with its public key. A CA always creates a certificate irrespective of where the key pair is generated. If the key pair is generated at the user's end, the public key is sent to the CA along with a request for certificate generation. However, if a trusted third party or CA generates the key pair, the private key that corresponds to the key pair also needs to be distributed to the owner through a secure mechanism.

Some PKI implementations include a provision for a dual key pair model. In this model, one pair is used for signing and signature verification while the other pair is used for encryption and decryption purposes. Therefore, in a dual key pair model, two certificates are distributed to the user.

Key Backup

Another activity that is involved with key management, which needs to be closely looked at at this point, is key backup. A CA performs a key backup to ensure that if a user loses his or her private key, the data that was encrypted by using the corresponding public key can be decrypted. A key is usually backed up when the certificate is generated. Either a CA or a user can back up keys. In case the private key is used for signing the documents, the CA need not back it up. As such, there are no well-defined rules for backing up keys. These policies essentially depend upon the use of the keys.

 If two key pairs are used, one for data encryption and another for digitally signing the documents, the key that is used for the digital signature doesn't need to be backed up at all. Even if the key is lost, there would be no encrypted data that needs to be decrypted by this key.

Certificate Expiry and Archiving

Certificates associated with the public key of the user are valid for a limited period. When this period is over, the certificate becomes invalid. Sometimes a certificate can become invalid even before the expiration date.

A CA can revoke an invalid certificate. The issuing CA, upon the receipt of the revocation request from the owner, invalidates the original certificate and enters the certificate information in a new Certificate Revocation List (CRL).

A CA must be able to establish the validity of certificates after they have expired. This is because even after the certificate has expired, all transactions that were done by using the certificate when it was valid should be permissible. Therefore, CAs should be able to maintain sufficient archival information to validate the actual identity of the person or system named in a certificate, and verify that the certificate was valid at the time the document was signed. This can be accomplished by cryptographic timestamps.

An archive is a long-term secure storage of information. An archive reiterates that the information was correct at the time it was obtained and has not been modified while in the archive. Archives play a minor role in the daily operations of a PKI, but demand strict technical and procedural controls.

Certificate Updates

Certificates are valid for a fixed period, starting from the day they were issued. When a certificate is due for expiration, a new public/private key is generated and the public key is associated certificate. This is referred to as *key update*. Key updates should occur automatically once 70 to 80 percent of the key lifetime is exhausted, and the new keys should be used for future cryptographic operations. This would give a reasonable transition period for end entities to acquire the new certificates. When the new certificate is acquired in reasonable time, entities can conduct business without downtime that is related to possession of the expired certificate.

To issue a new certificate, a CA issues a pair of key rollover certificates simultaneously. A description of the two keys in the key rollover certificates is given below:

- ◆ The first certificate contains the old public key and is signed with the new private key. This rollover certificate allows subscribers that have certificates signed with the new private key to construct a valid certification path to the certificates previously signed with the old private key.

- ◆ The second certificate contains the new public key and is signed with the old private key. This rollover certificate allows the subscribers with certificates signed by the old private key to construct a valid certification path to the certificates signed with the new private key.

In this way, subscribers with certificates signed by the old private key and subscribers with certificates signed with the new private key can validate each other's certificates.

Issuing Multiple Certificates to Users

Smith, the owner of AllSolv Inc., requests a certificate of authentication from a CA for signing an e-mail. He also requests another certificate from the CA to sign e-commerce transactions. Therefore, as users deploy more and more applications that use secure communication, the number of key pairs deployed would increase.

Different certificates that are issued to the same user or organization may be associated with different applications for different uses. A key pair in that case could be identified for a specific use by the cryptographic algorithm that is used or by the choice of implementation that is imposed. For example, a Digital Signature Algorithm (DSA) key pair cannot be used for encryption and decryption. Similarly, a Diffie-Hellman (DH) key pair cannot be used for signing data and verifying the signature. Furthermore, a key pair might be usable for Internet Protocol Security (IPSec) user authentication and not Secure Sockets Layer (SSL) user verification.

If a user has multiple key pairs through multiple certificates, the user is likely to have multiple certificates because the format of the certificate usually does not allow the user to have more than a single public key. Furthermore, in the case of rollover certificates, a valid public key would appear simultaneously in several valid certificates. However, if a single public key is present in multiple certificates, such a situation may allow a hacker to substitute one certificate for another. Therefore, if a single user has multiple certificates issued by a Certification Authority, the user must be ensured that each one of the certificates contains a separate public key to avoid substitution attacks.

Another issue is the use of valid private keys for a given transaction. Key selection usually occurs automatically and transparently. If an SSL session is being established, the client software may search the user's certificates for the one with the appropriate extension for SSL and then use the corresponding private key for user authentication.

Therefore, putting a single public key in several certificates may lead to security risks. It may be necessary to distinguish between key types and uses, such as key usage extension and policy OIDs that use key extensions.

Certificate Retrieval and Validation

After a certificate is issued, it undergoes various phases, such as revocation, expiration, etc. Therefore, it is important to establish the credibility of a certificate before the certificate is used to trust the certificate owner.

Establishing the identity of a user involves two tasks, retrieving the certificate and validating the retrieved certificate. For example, James, a user in AllSolv Inc., has been issued a certificate by a CA. Charlie, a user in Solutions Inc., wants to communicate with James. To accomplish this, Charlie has to ensure that the person he communicates with is James. Thus, to establish James's identity, Charlie first retrieves James's certificate, which contains the information that is related to James's identity and is duly signed by a trusted CA. Charlie then verifies the digital signature on James's certificate using the CA's certificate. In this manner, Charlie authenticates James's identity. Now let us look at the certificate retrieval and validation processes in detail.

Certificate Retrieval

In order to validate the identity of an entity, you need to retrieve the certificate issued to that identity and also the certificate of the issuing CA.

Certificate retrieval depends upon the location of a certificate. A certificate can be distributed by the means of a secure e-mail using Secure Multipurpose Internet Mail Extensions (S-MIME) or can be published in an X.500 directory. If the certificate is published in the X.500 directory, a user can then retrieve it by using

Lightweight Directory Access Protocol (LDAP). LDAP enables applications running on multiple platforms to obtain directory information, such as e-mail addresses and public keys. A CA can populate an LDAP directory with a new employee's details. The CA can use employee information in the LDAP directory to issue multiple certificates simultaneously for users that match a criterion. LDAP directory can also be integrated with the Certificate Manager to automatically retrieve certificate information from the Certificate Manager and update it in the directory.

You can learn about the X.500 protocol in Chapter 6.

Certificates might need to be published based upon the PKI implementation. Let us consider a scenario to explain this concept.

James and John are employees of AllSolv Inc. The organization is planning to implement PKI for a secure communication on an intranet. To facilitate certificate retrieval, either the owner of the certificate can transfer the certificate to other users as per the established requirements or all certificates can be published in the local directory database. Whenever James wants to send some secure information to John, James retrieves John's certificate from the local directory database and encrypts the message by using the public key in the certificate. Then he sends this encrypted message to John, who can decrypt it by using his private key.

Due to its expansion, AllSolv has decided to acquire the CA certificate from a root CA in order to generate and distribute certificates to its employees. The certificates that are distributed to employees can be used to make financial transactions with other organizations or external entities over the Internet. In this situation, the public key certificates of the employees, if they are stored in the local directory database, will not serve the purpose. The reason is because the certificate users are now spread outside the organization limits and cannot retrieve certificates that are stored inside the local directory database of AllSolv, Inc. Therefore, the public key certificates of the employees need to be published on an online X.500 compliant global directory database so that certificates are made available globally for verifying and validating all of the intended users.

Certificate Validation

After retrieving certificates, you need to validate them. Certificate validation involves the following processes:

- Verifying that the signature is valid
- Verifying that a trusted CA has issued the certificate

◆ Ensuring that the certificate can be used for intended purposes

◆ Determining if the certificate has been revoked

The process of certificate validation is explained in the following scenario.
James needs to validate John's certificate. In the first level of validation, James performs the following tasks:

◆ Checks the validity date of the certificate to ensure that the certificate has not expired.

◆ Checks the policy object in the certificate to ensure that the certificate issued to John is not being misused.

Next, James checks the authenticity of the certificate by performing the following tasks:

◆ Examines his list of trusted CAs, to find whether John's CA is on the list. If the CA is not on the list, James tries to find the trusted CA in the certificate path in the CA hierarchy.

◆ After finding the trusted CA, James verifies the digital signature on John's certificate. To verify the signature, James creates a hash for the message. Next, he decrypts the message hash that John sent by using his public key. Finally, he matches the decrypted hash with the hash that was created at his end. James retrieves the public key certificate of the CA that has issued the certificate to John. He computes the hash value by using hash algorithm on the message and matches it with the retrieved message hash after decrypting it. If both the values match, it proves that the certificate has not been altered since its issuance and is authentic.

After James is satisfied that John's certificate is authentic, he retrieves the latest Certificate Revocation Lists (CRL) to verify that the certificate has not been revoked for any reason.

Methods of Certificate Revocation

Certificate revocation is the process of removing the validity of a certificate prematurely. There could be multiple reasons for revoking a certificate; some of the reasons are stated below:

◆ The certificate holder leaves the organization.

◆ The name and/or details of the certificate holder change.

♦ The issuing authority ceases to exist or the relationship between the issuing authority and the organization ceases to exist.

♦ There is a suspicion of private key compromise.

Certificate Revocation can be implemented in a number of ways. A revocation method is selected by an organization based on the cost, infrastructure, and volumes of transactions that are expected. One mechanism is to use a periodic publication mechanism. Another method is to use an online query mechanism. A description of these mechanisms is given below:

♦ **Periodic Publication Mechanisms:** This mechanism includes the use of Certificate Revocation Lists (CRL) and Certificate Revocation Tress (CRT).

- **CRL:** A CRL is a list of all certificates that have been revoked before their expiration date. CRLs are issued, maintained, and updated on a regular basis by the issuing authority or a CA.

- **CRT:** Is another certification method that was introduced by Valicert, a U.S.-based company. This revocation technology is based on Merkle hash trees, where the tree represents all known certificate revocation information relevant to some known set of PKI communities. The major drawback of this method is that the CRTs have to be recomputed with every update. This leads to an increase in the load on the processor, and it also reduces the timeliness of the CRT.

♦ **Online Query Mechanisms:** Online Query Mechanisms comprise Online Certificate Status Protocol (OCSP) and Online Transaction Validation Protocols.

- **OCSP:** OCSP is used to obtain online revocation information about certificates.

- **Online Transaction Validation Protocols:** Online Transaction Validation Protocol is used for online validation, such as business transactions through credit cards.

In this section, we examine the CRL and OCSP methods of certificate revocation in detail.

CRL

Once a certificate is revoked, the revocation information is published in a CRL.

Usually, the CA who has issued the certificate issues the CRL for the corresponding certificates. The CRL is digitally signed by the CA to prove its authenticity.

There may be a time difference between when the certificate is revoked and when the revocation information is posted in the CRL. This time difference is known as *revocation delay*. The revocation delay is based on the CA policy and should be kept at a minimum amount of time. A CA generally issues CRLs on an hourly or daily basis depending on the CA policy.

Let's now look at how CRLs are used to validate a certificate. To validate a certificate, the user performs the following steps:

1. Checks the validation date field of the certificate.

2. If the certificate has not expired, the user issues a request to the trusted CA for the latest CRL.

3. On receipt of the CRL, the user validates the digital signature of the issuing CA on the CRL.

4. Finally, the user looks into the CRL to check if the certificate's serial number is present on the CRL. If the certificate serial number is present on the CRL, it signifies that the certificate has been revoked.

The user needs to follow the above-mentioned process each time to verify the validity of a certificate. However, this process might not be feasible at times. For example, the user might not be connected to the Internet. As a result, the latest CRL cannot be accessed for the verification of a given certificate. To verify a certificate in such circumstances, *cached CRLs* are used. The cached CRLs are stored locally by users on their machines. This considerably speeds up the certificate verification process because the user does not have to query the CA for the CRLs each time to verify a certificate.

TIP Cached CRLs might result in obsolete information. Therefore, the user needs to update the cached CRL regularly by downloading the latest copy of the CRL.

CRLs that contain revocation information about CA certificates are also called *Authority Revocation List* (ARL). ARLs, as the name suggests, contain certificate revocation information of the CA certificates but do not contain the revocation information of the user certificates.

EVOLUTION OF CRL

CRLs came into existence with the advent of the X.509 specification. It defined the information that must be a part of a certificate and the format in which this information should be included in the certificate. The X.509 specification led to the development of the various versions of CRL.

VERSION 1 CRL   Popularly known as CRL V1, this standard defines the basic structure of a CRL. It also specifies the information that needs to be stored in the CRL and the information of the certificate that needs to be revoked. In addition to the signature, this CRL contains the following information:

♦ **Serial Number:** This field contains the serial number of the certificate that is assigned by the issuing authority.

♦ **Signature Algorithm Identifier:** This field contains the algorithm that is used by the CA to issue the certificate.

♦ **Issuer Name:** This field contains the name of the issuing authority. Generally, this is the CA.

In the case of top level CA certificates, such as root, the issuing authority signs its own certificates.

♦ **Validity Period:** This field contains the start date and time and end date and time through which the certificate is valid.

♦ **Subject Name:** This field contains the name of the entity whose public key is identified by the certificate.

♦ **Subject Public Key Information:** This field contains the public key of the entity that issued the certificate. This public key, along with the algorithm that is specified in the Signature Algorithm Identifier field, specifies the crypto-system to which the public key belongs.

Since it was first developed and used, the Version 1 CRL has undergone a number of changes due to the following reasons:

♦ **Security:** Information in the Version 1 CRL could be replaced without the CA's or user's knowledge. Therefore, incorrect information about a CRL could be passed on to the user.

♦ **Size:** Version 1 CRL does not have a mechanism to control or limit its size.

♦ **Flexibility:** Version 1 CRL does not allow any additional information provided by extensions to be associated with the CRL.

All of these issues are addressed by Version 2 CRL (CRL V2). CRL V2 introduced the concept of extensions, similar to introduction of extensions with X.509 version 3 public key certificates. These extensions are based on certificates that are a part of the CRL and some extensions that are based on the CRL itself.

VERSION 2 CRL   A major change in CRL V2 is the inclusion of *extensions* to make the CRL more flexible and scalable than version 1. An extension allows additional attributes, such as attributes for managing the certification hierarchy and CRL distribution, to be associated with the user or public keys. The fields that are included in a CRL are shown in Figure 5-2.

Figure 5-2: Version 2 CRL

A description of these fields is given below:

- ◆ Version: This field indicates the version of the CRL. The value of this field, if present, is always 2 because this field was first introduced in CRL Version 2.

- ◆ Signature: This field contains the algorithm identifier by which the issuing CA signs each CRL digitally.

- ◆ Issuer: This field contains the X.500 distinguished name (DN) of the CA issuing the CRL.

- ◆ This update: This field contains the date on which this CRL was issued.

- ◆ Next update: This field contains the date on which the next CRL will be issued or this CRL expires.

- ◆ List of revoked certificates: This field contains entries for revoked certificates. The information that is associated with a revoked certificate is shown in Figure 5-3. As shown in the figure, there is one entry per revoked certificate along with the certificate information, such as the certificate serial number, the date of revocation, certificate-based extensions, etc.

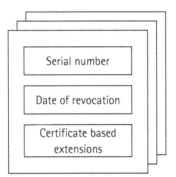

| Serial number |
| Date of revocation |
| Certificate based extensions |

Figure 5-3: Revoked certificate information

 In some reference material, this field might be referred to as a structure rather than a field.

◆ CRL Extensions: This field was introduced in CRL Version 2 and contains additional information, such as reason for revocation of certificate, name of certificate issuer, code for certificate suspension, and certificate invalidity date, related to the CRL and the certificate.

 CRL V2 allows users to define their own extensions and include them in the certificates.

CRL EXTENSIONS

CRL extensions, as defined in X.509 v3 and CRL V2, provide a mechanism for adding additional attributes for users of public keys. CRL extensions were defined to facilitate the additional information to be enclosed within the CRLs, thus making CRLs extensible. Some of the most commonly used extensions today are AuthorityKeyIdentifier, KeyUsage, and AlternativeNames.

On the basis of the CA policy, an extension can be defined as *critical* or *non-critical*. A critical extension is one that has to be processed by an application involved in the verification process of the CRL. On the other hand, a non-critical extension might not be processed. A CRL validation fails if a critical but unrecognized extension is encountered. However, if during the CRL validation an unrecognized non-critical extension is encountered, it is merely ignored.

 Industry associations encourage non-critical extensions. This is because CRLs with non-critical extensions don't need to be processed. Therefore, validation does not take long.

Organizations can define their own private extensions for domain-specific use. These extensions are specific to the organization. Based on their functions, extensions are categorized into

◆ Certificate-based extensions

◆ CRL-based extensions

Let us examine these extensions separately.

CERTIFICATE-BASED EXTENSIONS   Certificate-based extensions help you to identify the revoked certificates easily. A certificate-based extension, apart from containing the identification information of the certificate, such as certificate serial number, CA name, and entity name, also contains the following information:

◆ Reason code: This is a non-critical extension. It identifies the reason for certificate revocation. Reason code includes any of the following values:

■ Key compromise

■ Affiliation changed

■ Superceded

■ CA compromise

■ Cessation of operation

■ Certificate hold

■ Unspecified

■ Remove from CRL

◆ Invalidity date: Invalidity date is the date on which a certificate becomes invalid.

◆ Certificate issuer: This extension facilitates a CRL to include the revocation information of certificates that are issued by different CAs. This extension also identifies the CA that has issued the certificate to be revoked. CRLs containing such information are known as *indirect CRLs*.

◆ **Hold instruction code:** Apart from containing a list of revoked certificates, the CRL also contains a list of *suspended certificates.* Suspended certificates are those certificates that are not yet revoked but cannot be used unless they are activated again. The reasons for the temporary suspension of a certificate are based on the CA policy. The hold instruction code extension comprises an object identifier, or OID, which identifies this extension. Based on the OID value, an application or a user decides the action that is to be performed on the suspended certificate. You can perform the following actions on a suspended certificate:

  ▪ Interacting with the CA for re-enabling the certificate

  ▪ Rejecting the certificate

  The hold instruction code extension supports the following instruction codes:

  ▪ id-holdinstruction-callissuer: This instruction code forces the applications to call the certificate issuer. If this cannot be done, the certificate is rejected.

  ▪ id-holdinstruction-reject: This instruction code forces the applications to reject the certificate.

  ▪ id-holdinstruction-none: This instruction code, if encountered, results in the rejection of the certificate.

Generally, applications are not configured to take advantage of the hold instruction code extensions because calling a CA might not be feasible sometimes. As a result, this extension is not often used.

CRL-BASED EXTENSIONS   CRL-based extensions make CRLs more flexible. By using these extensions CAs can control the size of CRLs. A number of CRL-based extensions exist. The detailed information of CRL-based extensions is given below:

◆ **Authority key identifier:** A CA digitally signs each CRL. These CRLs are verified by the issuing CA's public key certificate. The CA can use more than one key for a digital signature. For example, the CA can use one key for signing a CRL and another for signing a certificate. An authority key identifier extension identifies the key that is used for signing the CRL. The fields contained within the authority key identifier extension include:

  ▪ **keyIdentifier:** This is an optional field that contains the key identifier extension from the CRL issuer's certificate.

- authorityCertIssuer: This is also an optional field that contains the name of the issuing authority. This field can contain more than one name. If this field is used, a value for the authorityCertSerialNumber must also be specified.

- authorityCertSerialNumber: This is also an optional field that contains the serial number of the certificate of the CRL's issuing authority.

♦ Issuer alternate name: This extension is used to provide additional information to identify the CA apart from the CA distinguished name. The Issuer alternate name extension can also contain a user-friendly name to identify the issuer, such as the host name or an e-mail address, etc.

A CRL-based extension can be critical or non-critical, based on the CA policy.

♦ Issuing distribution point: This is a critical extension that identifies the location of a CRL and the types of certificates that are contained in the CRL. If this extension is not recognized in the certificate validation process, the CRL is rejected. This extension indicates whether the CRL contains the list of revocations for user certificates, CA certificates, or reason codes.

One CRL issuing authority may support multiple distribution points. In such cases, each distribution point that is supported by the same CRL issuing authority would have the same signing key.

♦ CRL number: This is a non-critical extension that contains a unique number that identifies the CRL. This field also represents the sequence of the CRL, which is issued by the issuing authority.

♦ Delta CRL indicator: This field always contains a base CRL number for which the updates have been distributed. To keep the size of a CRL under control, and simplify the distribution process, the CRL is distributed partially. When distributing a CRL for the first time, the complete CRL is distributed, which is known as the base CRL. However, for the subsequent distributions, only the updates are distributed instead of the complete CRLs. These updates or partial CRLs are referred to as *Delta CRLs*. Since Delta CRLs contain only updates to the base CRL, they help in keeping the size of distributed CRLs small and also decrease the network traffic and processing load. This is a critical extension.

A CRL is used to store the complete certificate revocation information that is related to one CA. Complete CRL postings simplify the process of verification of certificates as the revocation information about a CA can be found in a single CRL. It works fine in a small subscriber base but is not practical in situations where the numbers of subscribers is large because as the numbers of subscriber increases, the revocation list also grows. Since there is only one revocation list that pertains to a CA, such a list can lead to scalability problems on the CA side. Downloading the entire list from the client side can result in the possibility of network congestion.

◆ **Indirect CRL:** Typically, a CA that has issued a certificate also issues the CRL. However, this may not be the case every time. The indirect CRL method proposes the consolidation of CRLs. Let's say, for example that a group of CAs has entrusted one single authority with the responsibility of issuing CRLs. This trusted authority would contain the revocation information from multiple CAs and therefore share the load of other CAs. An indirect CRL also simplifies the verification process that is performed by users, who do not need to retrieve multiple CRLs from multiple authorities.

 The authority that is entrusted by a group of CAs to issue CRLs is generally referred to as Indirect CRL Authority (ICRLA).

DISTRIBUTION OF CRLS

In the preceding sections, you learned about CRLs and their extensions. The most important factor in managing CRLs is their distribution. To make the distribution process simple and to access the CRLs with ease, a CA can define multiple CRL distribution points. For example, one distribution point can be for the user CRLs and another for the CA CRLs. This reduces the size of CRLs as well as saves the network from possible congestion. It also considerably reduces the time required by a user to process the CRLs.

CAs can distribute CRLs on the basis of changing business requirements. An organization's CA can divide the CRL on the basis of various departments and issue the CRLs to users of the corresponding departments. Let's say for example, James, a user in the research department, needs to view the certificate of Charlie who is from the Sales department. Instead of viewing the CRLs of the entire organization, James can verify the certificate of Charlie directly from the CRLs of the Sales department.

The process of partitioning a CRL has certain limitations. When a certificate is issued to a user, the CRL distribution point for the user is decided then. This distribution point cannot change once the user has been assigned the certificate. Therefore, portioning is not a flexible solution, because the distribution points might need to be changed if the CRL increases in size. Therefore, some flexibility is required while deciding upon the distribution points. This flexibility is offered by *redirect CRLs*.

REDIRECT CRLS

Redirect CRLs are the CRLs that point to multiple CRL distribution points where the CRLs are located. When an organization uses redirect CRLs, the CRL information can be changed without affecting the status of the certificate. This approach is quite flexible as compared to the fixed distribution point approach where the CRL location cannot be changed.

The following example explains the process of redirect CRLs. James, a user in AllSolv Inc., is issued a certificate from a CA. To verify this certificate, Charlie, another user in AllSolv Inc., needs to look into the CRL distribution point extension that is pointing to a redirect CRL. Charlie, upon retrieving the redirect CRL information, can retrieve the concerned CRL. Figure 5-4 illustrates this process.

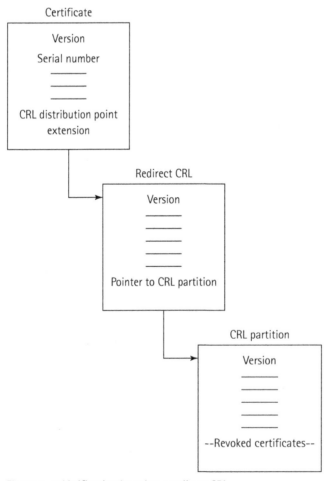

Figure 5-4: Verification by using a redirect CRL

Online Certificate Status Protocol (OCSP)

Redirect CRLs work fine even when the certificates are verified offline or by using a cached CRL. But this might involve some risks when the CRLs are updated. Keeping this concern in mind, another method has been defined for checking the status of certificates online. This method is known as *Online Certificate Status Protocol* (OCSP).

An *OCSP responder* is used to process the information relating to all OCSP verification requests. The OCSP responder is a trusted entity, which, on receiving the requests for the revocation information, replies to the sender of the request with status information about the online certificates.

The process for obtaining online revocation information involves the following sequence of steps, which is illustrated in Figure 5-5:

1. A user sends an OCSP request to the OCSP responder. This request consists of information such as the name of the CA, the certificate serial number, and the protocol version number.

2. Upon receiving the request, the OCSP responder processes the request and replies with the status information of the certificate. This status information also has the validity period of the information and the certificate identifier. A certificate's status can have three valid values: good, revoked, or unknown. A description of these values is given below:

   ■ A good certificate: This status indicates that the certificate is valid and has not been revoked.

   ■ A revoked certificate: This status indicates that the certificate has been revoked.

   ■ An unknown certificate: This status indicates that the information regarding the status of the certificate could not be retrieved.

3. Based on the certificate status information, a user can take appropriate action.

The OCSP responder digitally signs the response before sending it to the user. This ensures the authenticity of the response. OCSP is gaining popularity, but it doesn't offer a foolproof verification method. Some of the limitations with OCSP are listed below:

◆ Although OCSP is an online protocol, it cannot be assumed that there is no revocation delay while using OCSP.

◆ OCSP does not define how the information is retrieved from the CRL repository at the OCSP responder's end.

◆ The responder's response is digitally signed. Therefore, it can lead to possible performance degradations.

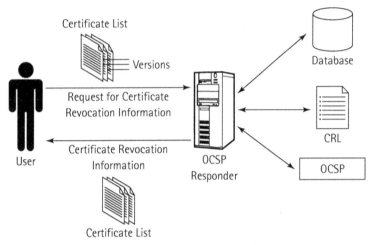

Figure 5-5: Online Certificate Status Protocol (OCSP)

In spite of all these limitations, OCSP enables organizations to validate certificates in an efficient and cost-effective manner. In addition, by using OSCP, organizations can enhance the security of their business transactions. OCSP allows organizations to link to multiple responders for carrying out their business transactions. In this way, if one responder does not have the required information, it can connect to other responders to obtain the information. Such a network of responders enables a flexible validation of foreign certificates and helps to facilitate business over the Internet.

Other Certification Revocation Mechanisms

Although CRLs and OCSP are the two most popular Certificate Revocation mechanisms that are in use, there are certain other revocation mechanisms that are also available. These mechanisms are listed below:

◆ OCSP-X, also called OCSP extensions, provides additional features as compared with OCSP. With these extensions, an entity can delegate the task of deciding if a certificate can be relied on.

◆ Data Certification Server is a trusted third party that is used to verify the correctness of the data that has been submitted to it. This method can be used to verify a digital signature and can also be used to verify the revocation status of a certificate.

◆ Certificate Revocation Status Directory is a repository that stores a list of authenticated, issued certificates that have not yet expired. For the certificates that have not yet expired, it contains detailed information about the contents of the certificate.

Summary

In this chapter, you learned about the process of certificate registration and key pair generation. You learned that the key pair generation could take place at both the user-end as well as the CA-end, depending upon two factors, which are:

- Availability of adequate resources
- Intended use of the key

Then, you learned about key backup and certificate expiration. You also learned that the key backups are performed to ensure that if the original key is lost then the data is decrypted and retrieved by using the backed-up key.

Next, you learned about certificate retrieval and validation process. You learned that in order to establish the identity of a user, the certificate issued to the user should first be retrieved and then validated.

You learned about the Certificate Revocation Lists (CRLs) and their need. Then, you learned about the evolution of CRLs and the two versions of CRLs, namely:

- Version 1 CRL (also known as CRL V1)
- Version 2 CRL (also known as CRL V2)

You also learned about the enhancements that have been incorporated in CRLs in the form of CRL extensions. You learned that the CRL extensions are categorized into two categories based on their functionality:

- Certificate-based extensions
- CRL-based extensions

Next, you learned about the CRL distribution point and redirect CRL, and online verification of certificates using Online Certificate Status Protocol (OCSP).

Chapter 6

PKI Management Protocols and Standards

IN THIS CHAPTER

- ◆ PKI management protocols
- ◆ Public-Key Cryptography Standard (PKCS)#10
- ◆ Public-Key Cryptography Standard (PKCS)#7
- ◆ Certificate Management Protocol (CMP)
- ◆ Simple Certificate Enrollment Protocol (SCEP)
- ◆ X series standards

AS DISCUSSED IN THE PREVIOUS CHAPTERS, a user requests a certificate from a Certification Authority (CA) or a Registration Authority (RA). To issue a certificate, the CA must verify the authenticity of the user and the information provided by the user in the certificate. Moreover, the CA must maintain a list of certificates that are no longer valid. At the same time, the private key of the CA should be secure from any intrusion or unauthorized access. To ensure the secrecy of private key, the CA uses the PKI management protocols, which interact with other components of PKI on behalf of the CA.

These PKI management protocols obtain the information needed by CAs to issue or revoke certificates. The most commonly used PKI management protocols are PKCS#10, PKCS#7, Certificate Management Protocol (CMP), Certificate Management using CMS (CMC), and Simple Certificate Enrollment Protocol (SCEP).

In this chapter, you'll learn about the working of these protocols and their evaluation criteria.

PKI Management Protocols

As discussed, PKI management protocols enable CAs to collect information needed for issuing and revoking certificates. The most commonly used PKI management protocols are:

- ◆ PKCS#10

- ◆ PKCS#7

- ◆ Certificate Management Protocol (CMP)

- ◆ Certificate Management using CMS (CMC)

- ◆ Simple Certificate Enrollment Protocol (SCEP)

PKCS#10 and PKC#7 protocols are a part of the Public Key Cryptographic Standards (PKCS) that define various standards for PKI cryptography. Table 6-1 illustrates the standards that are part of PKCS:

TABLE 6-1 PKCS STANDARDS

Standard Number	Standard Name
PKCS#1	RSA Cryptography Standard
PKCS#2	This standard has now been incorporated into PKCS#1
PKCS#3	Diffie-Hellman Key Agreement Standard
PKCS#4	This standard has now been incorporated into PKCS#1
PKCS#5	Password-Based Cryptography Standard
PKCS#6	Extended-Certificate Syntax Standard
PKCS#7	Cryptographic Message Syntax Standard
PKCS#8	Private Key Information Syntax Standard
PKCS#9	Selected Attribute Types
PKCS#10	Certification Request Syntax Standard
PKCS#11	Cryptographic Token Interface Standard
PKCS#12	Personal Information Exchange Syntax Standard
PKCS#13	Elliptic Curve Cryptography Standard
PKCS#14	Pseudorandom Number Generation Standard
PKCS#15	Cryptographic Token Information Format Standard

For more information on all these PKCS standards, visit the Web site at

http://www.rsa.com/rsalabs/pkcs/

Before discussing each of the PKI management protocols in detail, let us first look at a basic criterion for evaluating these protocols. These evaluation criteria should be kept in mind while implementing these protocols and can also be used to compare different protocols.

Evaluation Criteria for PKI Management Protocols

The evaluation criteria for PKI Management protocols are listed below:

- These protocols must support the creation and publication of certificates and CRLs. In other words, they should allow entities to make certificate and revocation requests.

- These protocols should be extensible, so that they can be used over disparate systems. They should also be able to address the needs of the organization's local network.

- They should support both two-party and three-party transactions. The design of the protocol should facilitate the use of a single protocol by the entities irrespective of whether they are interacting with a CA or an RA.

- These protocols should be algorithm-independent. Since organizations might need to use different algorithms for their key pairs, these protocols should have the ability to recognize the type of algorithm that is used. Some of the common algorithms that are used in cryptography are MD5, RSA, and DSA.

- PKI management protocols must support different transport mechanisms, such as HTTP, FTP, and TCP/IP.

Having looked at the evaluation criteria, let us now look at each of the PKI management protocols in detail.

PKCS#10

PKCS#10, or Certificate Request Syntax Standard, defines the syntax for certificate requests. According to the PKCS#10 standard, a certificate request comprises the following three elements:

- Certificate request information

- A signature algorithm identifier

- A digital signature on the certification request information

The certificate request information is composed of the Distinguished Name (DN) of the entity, the public key of the entity, and some other attributes that are optional. These attributes contain additional information about the entity, such as the postal address to which the signed certificate should be returned if electronic mail is not available. These attributes may also contain a "challenge password" which the entity can use when requesting for the revocation of the certificate at a later stage. Figure 6-1 depicts the format for a certificate request as per PKCS#10.

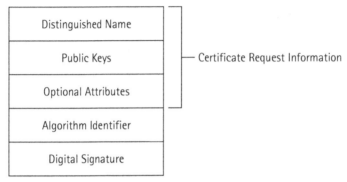

Figure 6-1: Certificate request format as per PKCS#10

Lets now look at an example of how PKCS#10 is used during a certification request process. Suppose Bob requests the AllSolv CA for a certificate. Now to request for a certificate according to PKCS#10, Bob needs to perform the following steps:

1. Generate a CertificateRequestInfo value as per the PKCS#10 specification from his public key and user name. As already discussed, this CertificateRequestInfo value consists of the distinguished name of the entity, in this case Bob, and the public key of the entity.

2. After generating the CertificateRequestInfo value, Bob needs to sign this value with his private key.

3. Finally, Bob needs to generate a CertifcateRequest value as per PKCS#10 from the CertificateRequestInfo value and his signature.

Lets now discuss each of these steps in detail.

Generate a CertificateRequestInfo Value

Bob generates a CertificateRequestInfo value by using his distinguished name and public key. Let us assume that Bob's common name is "Bob" and he works for the organization "AllSolv, Inc." situated in "US". This CertificateRequestInfo value is DER encoded, resulting in an octet string. This resultant value can be represented as:

```
20 83 b4
05 08 00                                                         version = 0
20 43                                                            subject
21 0a
20 08
02 09 44 01 08        attributeType = countryName
19 01 20 45                           attributeValue = "US"
26 2b
20 2c
02 09 44 01 0b              attributeType = organizationName
17 18                           attributeValue = "AllSolv Inc"
54 87 56 5c 80 5b 32 30 3d 64 54 53 5a 62 3b 72
57 98 4f 5a
71 14
20 14
03 04 55 02 02                     attributeType = commonName
17 0a                              attributeValue = "Bob"
45 56 78 38 30 44 78 56 37 31 42
20 4c
subjectPublicKeyInfo
20 0a                                                   algorithm
05 03                                algorithm= rsaEncryption
5b 68 67 23 g4 0c 02 02 02
03 00                                                   parameters
= NULL
04 5b                           subjectPublicKey = RSAPublicKey
encoding
00 20 74 03 60 ... 02 02 00 02
```

CertificateRequestInfo comprises the following components:

♦ **Version:** Represents the version number so that it is compatible with any future modifications. As can be seen from the preceding example, the version number is 0.

♦ **Subject:** Represents the distinguished name of the subject of the certificate.

♦ **SubjectPublicKeyInfo:** Represents the public key information of the subject of the certificate, which is to be certified.

♦ **Attributes:** Represents additional information about the subject of the certificate such as the subject's common name and the organization name.

After generating the CertificateRequestInfo value, Bob then needs to sign this value.

Sign the CertificateRequestInfo Value

After the CertificateRequestInfo value has been generated, Bob needs to sign it by using his private key. He can use any specified signature algorithm such as PKCS#1's MD5RSAEncryption for this purpose. This process of signing the CertificateRequestInfo value consists of three steps:

1. An MD5 message digest is added to the encoded CertificateInfo.

2. A DigestInfo value is encoded from the message digest and the CertificateInfo value.

```
20 30
20 0b                                              digestAlgorithm
07 09 4b 67 54 67 e6 0a 01 03     algorithm = md5
06 01                               parameters = NULL
05 20                                             digest
ed b4 ad e2 ... 87 86 74 ad
```

3. Finally, this encoded DigestInfo value is encrypted by using Bob's private key. This encryption of the DigestInfo value results in an octet string or a signature. This signature can be represented as:

```
05 ac 63 bc 21 e2 56 4a 5b 11 ca 4a 76 90 32 04
03 54 aa cb aa 3b 6a 44 6e a3 19 36 42 a6 32 65
4g 9b 7e 3b gg ab 68 b4 d2 6b 17 a8 7c 17 8b 34
6a 48 a2 a3 03 9a c4 b0 59 47 34 a2 3b 3c 9d ac
```

After signing the CertificateRequestInfo value, Bob needs to generate the CertificateRequest value.

Generate a CertificateRequest Value

CertificateRequestInfo value and the signature are together used to generate the CertificateRequest value as per PKCS#10. It is this value that is sent to the CA as a certificate request. The CertificateRequest value so generated can be represented as follows:

```
20 83 c4
20 83 c3 02 ... 02 02 00 02                  certificationRequestInfo
20 0a                                         signatureAlgorithm
05 03                             algorithm = md5WithRSAEncryption
5b 68 67 23 g4 0c 02 02 01
03 00                                         parameters = NULL
03 41                                         signature
00 02 ca 48 ab ... 6b 3c 9e ac
```

CertificateRequest comprises the following components:

- ◆ **CertificationRequestInfo:** Represents the Certification Request Information value, which is being signed.

- ◆ **SignatureAlgorithm:** Represents the signature algorithm that is used to sign the Certificate Request Information.

- ◆ **Signature:** Represents the resultant of encoding the CertificateRequestInfo with the subject's private key.

After generating the CertificateRequest value, Bob sends this value as a certificate request to the CA. After authenticating Bob's credentials by verifying his signatures and the information contained in the CertificateRequest value, the CA can issue a certificate to Bob.

PKCS#10 is the most common standard for certificate requests. Since most of the PKI applications have become Web-enabled, certificate requests can be made online. However, PKCS#10 does not support HTTP protocols. When a certificate request is made over the Web by using HTTP, the CA is unable to authenticate the entity. Therefore, PKCS#10 is used most commonly with the Secure Sockets Layer (SSL) for making certificate requests.

Generally, PKCS#10 and SSL are used in a three-party transaction; in which an RA authenticates the request after an entity has submitted it to the CA.

The following process takes place in a third-party transaction when PKCS#10 is used with SSL:

1. An SSL connection is established between the client and the CA.

2. The client submits a PKCS#10 request to the CA.

3. The CA sends the request to the RA for verification.

4. An SSL session is established between the RA and the CA.

5. Based on the verification of the information, the RA processes the request. The RA can approve or deny the request.

6. If the RA approves the request, the CA issues a certificate.

 The request for comments for this protocol are in RFC 2314.

Although PKCS#10 is the most widely used certificate format, it suffers from some inherent limitations.

Limitations of PKCS#10

A few limitations of PKCS#10 are:

- ◆ PKCS#10 is not algorithm-independent. Just like an RSA algorithm, it also assumes that the private key might be used for creating the digital signature.

- ◆ The digital signature on a PKCS#10 request does not provide all the information that a CA needs to authenticate the users. In addition, there is no well-defined mechanism to ensure that a certificate request has not been altered during its transit.

- ◆ PKCS#10 defines the syntax for only one message type, which is a certificate request, and not for the complete protocol. It does not specify the syntax and protocol for any other types of messages such as certificate revocation requests. Hence, messages other than certificate requests have to be implemented by using other protocols, such as HTTP

Consequently, PKCS#10 is considered the industry standard for certificate requests.

PKCS#7

PKCS#7 or Cryptographic Message Syntax Standard defines the syntax for cryptographic data, such as digital signatures. PKCS allows for authentication of attribute information in addition to authenticating the content of the messages.

Some of the important uses of PKCS#7 are:

- ◆ The CAs use the PKCS#7 standard as a response to the entity requesting a certificate.

- ◆ It is used to authenticate the certificate messages sent to an entity.

- ◆ It provides complete information to the CA for processing certificate requests.

- ◆ It is used by many protocols such as S/MIME for providing security.

PKCS#7 stipulates that the format of a message must consist of two fields:

- ◆ Content type
- ◆ Content

Let us look at each of these fields in detail.

CONTENT TYPE

The content type field outlines the specifications for the format of the content and is referred to as an object identifier. The six content types defined by PKCS#7 are:

◆ Data

◆ Signed data

◆ Enveloped data

◆ Signed and enveloped data

◆ Digested data

◆ Encrypted data

Content types can also be classified into two classes:

◆ **Base:** In the base class, the content type is composed of non-cryptographic data. The data content type is included in this class.

◆ **Enhanced:** The content types other than the data content type fall in this class.

We'll discuss only the signed data content type because it is used most commonly for PKI cryptography.

SIGNED DATA

The fields that are included in the signed data content type are:

◆ **Version:** It is the version number of the content.

◆ **Digest algorithms:** These are the encrypted message digest algorithms of the content.

◆ **Content Info:** It is the digitally signed content.

◆ **Certificates:** These are the set of X.509 certificates and/or PKCS#6 certificates. This is an optional field.

◆ **CRLs:** This is also an optional field and contains a set of CRLs.

◆ **Signer Info:** The signer info field contains the following information:

  ■ The version of the certificate

  ■ The issuer and serial number

  ■ Authenticated attributes

  ■ Digital signature algorithm

  ■ Digital signature

  ■ Unauthenticated attributes

The following steps take place for creating a signed data content type:

1. A message digest for each user is calculated based on a signer-specific message digest algorithm.

2. The user's private key encrypts this message digest and the associated information. The encrypted message digest and other signer-specific information together form the signer info value.

3. After the signer info value has been generated, certificates and CRLs are collected.

4. Finally, for all of the users, the signer info values, certificates, CRLs, and message digest algorithms are collated to form the signed data content type.

In the previous section where we discussed PKCS#10, we looked at how Bob obtained a certificate by using PKCS#10. Let us now look at how Bob can use PKCS#7 to create a digitally signed message by using PKCS#7. Bob needs to perform the following steps to create a digitally signed message by using PKCS#7:

1. Encode a value of type ContentInfo as per PKCS#7 for the data that he wants to sign.

2. Digest the data to be signed as per PKCS#7.

3. Encode a value of type DigestInfo as per PKCS#7 from the message digest.

4. Encrypt the encoded DigestInfo with his private key.

5. Encode a SignedData type value as per PKCS#7 from the first ContentInfo value, the encrypted message digest, and other information such as his certificate and the message digest algorithm identifier.

6. Encode another ContentInfo type value from the SignedData value as per PKCS#7.

Let's now discuss each of these steps in detail.

Encode a ContentInfo Value

To create a digitally signed message Bob needs to first encode a ContentInfo value as per PKCS#7. This value contains Bob's message in the form of an OCTET STRING.

Suppose Bob wants to encode the message "Alice is the new system administrator." The content type of Bob's message is a PKCS#7 data and has an object identifier value of

{3   2   520   126731 3   6   2}

When Bob's encodes the ContentInfo value it can be represented as:

```
20 36
03 06                                                    contentType
= data
1b 76 84 78 d6 0c 03 06 02
b0 2a                                                           [0]
EXPLICIT
03 21        content = OCTET STRING value: "Alice is the new system
administrator"
34 84 45 65 80 3d 3s 70 30 32 31 12 24 45 53 30
41 52 26 89 30 5d 77 88 2f
```

After encoding the ContentInfo, the next step is to digest the data.

Digest the Data

Bob can use any specified algorithm such as MD2 to digest the message content as per PKCS#7. This results in a message digest. It can be seen from the previous step that the original content in the ContentInfo value is represented as:

```
34 84 45 65 80 3d 3s 70 30 32 31 12 24 45 53 30 41 52 26 89 30 5d 77
88 2f
```

When Bob digests this value with MD2, it results in a message digest that is represented as:

```
2c 23 ac 11 7e 3a 63 dc 67 48 c2 2b cd ea dc b2
```

Bob then uses this message digest value to encode a DigestInfo value.

Encode a DigestInfo Value

The message digest obtained from the ContentInfo value is used to encode a DigestInfo value. This encoded DigestInfo value can be represented as:

```
20 30
20 0a
digestAlgorithm
04 02 3b 48 64 48 c4 0b 01 01                    algorithm = md2
04 00                                            parameters = NULL
05 20
     digest
2c 23 ac 11 7e 3a 63 dc 67 48 c2 2b cd ea dc b2
```

The Components of the DigestInfo value are:

♦ DigestAlgorithm identifier: Represents the message digest algorithm that is used to digest the contents.

♦ Digest: Represents the message digest that is a result of the digesting operation.

After encoding the DigestInfo value, this encoded value then needs to be encrypted.

Encrypt the Encoded DigestInfo Value

Bob uses his private key to encrypt the encoded DigestInfo value. This resultant encrypted value is a 64-octet string, which is

```
02 de 4b 76 2f b3 ac 3b d2 c4 32 50 02 f1 2d 48
5d 22 d2 a5 30 dc 30 02 cd 4 30 cd ab b2 45 32
48 46 ba 16 g2 32 c4 6a 16 34 3a 16 8f 3a b1 8a
6a 88 ca b7 a2 4c ef 2a 33 42 67 23 12 75 a1 d2
```

This encrypted DigestInfo value and the first ContentInfo value are then used to generate a SignedData value.

Encode a SignedData Value

After encoding the DigestInfo value, Bob then needs to encode a SignedData value by using the encoded DigestInfo value, the first ContentInfo value, and some more information such as his certificate, his certificate's serial number and issuer, and message digest algorithm identifier. The resulting encoded SignedData value can be represented as:

```
20 78 01 2c
02 01 01
      version = 1
20 0a
04 02 3b 48 64 48 c4 0b 01 01                          algorithm = md2
04 00                                                  parameters = NULL
34 84 45 65 ....... 30 5d 77 88 2f          content = inner
ContentInfo
b0 78 02 4f                                                certificates
20 78 24 4a ... 34 8f 2c 14                         Bob's certificate
42 86 9b
      signerInfos
20 86 94
02 01 01                                                     version = 1
```

```
20 26
        issuerAndSerialNumber
20 3c 32 0a ... 44 64 6d 3e
        issuer
01 03 17 01 00 35                                serialNumber = 17010035
20 0a
04 02 3b 48 64 48 c4 0b 01 01                         algorithm = md2
04 00                                                 parameters = NULL
20 0c
        digestEncryptionAlgorithm
03 04                               digestEncryptionAlgorithm = rsaEncryption
3b 78 54 78 e4 0a 01 01 01
04 00                                                             parameters
= NULL
04 40
        encryptedDigest
02 de 4b 76 2f b3 ac 3b d2 c4 32 50 02 f1 2d 48
5d 22 d2 a5 30 dc 30 02 cd 4 30 cd ab b2 45 32
48 46 ba 16 g2 32 c4 6a 16 34 3a 16 8f 3a b1 8a
6a 88 ca b7 a2 4c ef 2a 33 42 67 23 12 75 a1 d2
```

After Bob has encoded the SignedInfo value, he then encodes another ContentInfo value as per PKCS#7 from the encoded SignedInfo value. Suppose the object identifier value for this content is:

{3   2   520   126731 3   6   3}

The resultant encoded ContentInfo value can be represented as:

```
30 82 02 50
03 06 1b 76 84 78 d6 0c 03 06 02                        contentType =
signedData
b1 72 03 54                                              [0] EXPLICIT
20 46 01 4c ........ 46 24 d2 a2      content = SignedData value
```

LIMITATIONS OF PKCS#7   Similar to PKCS#10, PKCS#7 does not define any syntax for certificate revocation messages. However, combining PKCS#7 with PKCS#10 results in the formation of a complete and secure transaction model. Both of these protocols can be implemented easily since their formats are supported by most systems. PKCS#7 is highly extensible. Any information can be added to the format by using the authenticated and unauthenticated attributes.

Two other protocols that are also often discussed are PKCS#11 and PKCS#12. Let us look at a brief description of these protocols.

The request for comments for PKCS#10 is included in RFC 2315.

PKCS#11

PKCS#11 was introduced to implement cryptography with the use of portable computing devices such as smart cards, PCMCIA cards, and smart diskettes as they provide a way to store the private key component of a public key/private key pair securely, under the control of a single user. In this protocol, the cryptographic application utilizes the device to perform the operations rather than performing cryptographic operations so that sensitive information such as private keys are never revealed. As more applications are developed for public key cryptography, a standard programming interface for these devices becomes increasingly valuable.

This standard is used for a lower-level programming interface that abstracts the details of the devices and presents a common model of the cryptographic device to the application. These cryptographic devices are known as *cryptographic token*. There are different kinds of tokens, namely:

- ◆ **Signing tokens:** These tokens consist of a signing certificate and are used for signing objects, messages, and for SSL authentication.

- ◆ **External key distribution tokens:** These are used for distributing private keys.

- ◆ **Signing and decryption tokens:** Signing tokens do not support encrypted S/MIME, as they cannot decrypt messages. Hence, signing and decryption tokens are used for encrypted messages over the Internet.

- ◆ **Multipurpose tokens:** These tokens can perform several cryptographic functions and are similar to cryptographic accelerator cards.

PKCS#11 can be used for the resource sharing if needed and is also termed as *cryptoki*.

 For more information on PKCS#11, visit the Web site at `http://www.rsasecurity.com/rsalabs/pkcs/pkcs-11`.

PKCS#12

This is a standard, which describes the syntax for the transfer of personal identity information, including private keys, certificates, miscellaneous secrets, and extensions. Applications, browsers, and machines that support PKCS#12 allow users to import, export, and exercise a single set of personal identity information through them.

This standard supports direct transfer of personal information under several privacy and integrity modes.

There are four combinations of *privacy modes* and *integrity modes*. The privacy modes use encryption to protect personal information from exposure, and the integrity modes protect personal information from tampering. The privacy modes are:

♦ **Public key privacy mode:** Personal information is enveloped on the source platform by using a trusted encryption public key of a known destination platform. The envelope is opened with the corresponding private key.

♦ **Password privacy mode:** Personal information is encrypted with a symmetric key derived from a user name and a privacy password. If password integrity mode is used as well, the privacy password and the integrity password may or may not be the same.

The integrity modes are:

♦ **Public key integrity mode:** Integrity is guaranteed through a digital signature on the contents of the PFX Protocol Data Unit (PDU), which is produced using the source platform's private signature key. The signature is verified on the destination platform by using the corresponding public key.

♦ **Password integrity mode:** Integrity is guaranteed through a Message Authentication Code (MAC) derived from a secret integrity password. If the password privacy mode is used as well, the privacy password and the integrity password may or may not be the same.

The most secure of the privacy and integrity modes require the source and destination platforms to have trusted public/private key pairs usable for digital signatures and encryption, respectively. PKCS#12 also supports lower-security, password-based privacy and integrity modes for those cases in which trusted public/private key pairs are not available.

Certificate Management Protocol (CMP)

Certificate Management Protocol, also known as CMP, is required for on-line inter-actions between different PKI entities. These entities can either be users to whom the certificates are issued or the CA that is responsible for issuing the certificates to the users. A CMP can function between two CAs for cross-certification and can also function between a user and an issuing CA. CMP also supports the participation of an RA. CMP has been widely adopted by PKIX vendors, including IBM and Lotus, due to its interoperability features. Baltimore sells the CMP toolkit as a part of their key Tools Pro for Java. Cryptlib has completely automated its process of certificate management by using CMP. CMP allows online issuance, enrollment, and revoca-tion of certificates at Cryptlib. Implementation of CMP has helped users by elimi-nating the needs of the users to have any technical knowledge about certificate management, as the CA now handles all certificate management.

The CMP is composed of four components:

◆ **Header:** This component contains the sender and recipient names, time of message, and the cryptographic algorithm that is used. Apart from this information, the header contains some optional fields such as key identi-fier and transaction identifier. It also contains two more fields, one for extra processing information and another for user information other than the general information field.

◆ **Protection:** This component typically contains a hashed message authenti-cation code. It is used for securing the integrity of the header and body. This is an optional component.

◆ **Extra certificates:** This component contains extra certificates. The sub-scriber might require these extra certificates.

◆ **Body:** This component contains the message types. Some of these message types are:

■ Certificate request and response messages: These request and response messages are required for the purpose of request and delivery of certificates to users. The different message types can identify the type of certificate request.

■ Cross certification request and response messages: These request and response messages are required for the purpose of request and delivery of certificates to CAs.

■ Revocation request and response messages: These request and response messages are required for requesting the revocation of a certificate and its response.

- **Key recovery request and response messages:** These request and response messages are required for transferring the private key for backup purposes.

- **Proof of possession challenge and response messages:** These request and response messages are required as proof of owning the private key during key negotiation.

- **Certificate and CRL distribution messages:** These messages are used as an indication of certificate or CRL issuance.

- **Miscellaneous messages:** These messages could indicate an error, confirmation, request, and nested message types.

According to CMP, there are three major components of a certificate request message, namely:

- Certificate Request Message Format (CRMF)

- Proof of Possession (POP)

- Registration information

Let's discuss each of these in detail.

CERTIFICATE REQUEST MESSAGE FORMAT (CRMF)

CRMF comprises a request identifier, a template that contains information about the certificate, and some optional controls. The template not only consists of all fields of a certificate but also contains certificate extensions.

PROOF OF POSSESSION (POP)

Proof of Possession (POP) allows an entity that is to be associated with a certificate to prove that it possesses the private key that corresponds to the public key for which a certificate request has been made. You can accomplish POP in many ways, such as by using any of the out-of-bound methods or PKIX-CMP in-band messages, depending on the type of key for which a certificate request has been made. For example, if the certificate request is made for signing a key pair then POP of the private signing key is established by using the POPOSigningkey structure. However, if a key is used for multiple purposes, such as an RSA key, then you can choose any method.

REGISTRATION INFORMATION

Registration information consists of some supplementary information such as an entity's contact information and billing information, which are used while requesting a certificate.

Evaluating CMP

CMP provides a complete security solution for PKI transactions. It also facilitates the involvement of RA. However, implementing CMP involves complex processes and requires the establishment of new software since CMP does not support existing format. Let us now look at a few features of CMP.

- ◆ You can use CMP with any transaction model.

- ◆ CMP supports tools for proof of possession. These tools provide a proof of owning the private key during key negotiation, by using a challenge response mechanism.

- ◆ A CMP might not always be clear in indicating which message or transaction is used in a given situation. A CA always needs to maintain the state information in transactions and message flow.

- ◆ Extensibility is achieved in a CMP with the help of the general information field. You can include a type and value in this field, which helps in recognizing the data at the recipient end.

- ◆ CMP protects all messages by using cryptographic techniques, starting from the initial certificate request and the responses from the CA. These signed responses can be archived by the user or RA.

 This management protocol is discussed in detail in RFC 2510.

Certificate Management Using CMS (CMC)

CMC provides all the important functionality of CMP, such as key archiving, certificate issuance, and certificate revocation. This protocol uses cryptographic message syntax and the PKCS#10 and PKCS#7 standards.

Unlike the complexities involved in CMP such as transactions taking too many rounds and it having defined too many messages, CMC transactions (enrollment transaction) can be completed in a single round-trip. The message formats used for requesting and receiving certificates as well as methods involved in this protocol are different for both the protocols.

 The CMC protocol is discussed in detail in RFC 2797.

The content of the transactions in CMC management protocol is of two types, PKI Data and PKI Response. A request message from the entity to the CA is called *PKI Data,* and the response message to the request is called *PKI Response.* However, CMC transaction messages don't need to be confidential; but there is a mechanism to encapsulate the PKI data or PKI response messages in CMS signed data with CMS enveloped data. PKI data and response messages are controlled with control attributes. Every attribute has its object identifier, and while processing, this object identifier is processed first and then the message body processed. These attributes, with identifiers, control the flow of messages. If the PKI data or PKI response messages contain some unrecognized attributes, then the message is rejected. CMC as such has 24 control attributes. Some of the control attributes are extensions, transactions, and proof –of possession. These attributes are used to define the type of request and response.

In short, CMC is less complicated than CMP but more complex as compared to PKCS#10 and PKCS#7. This management protocol can be used in an architecture where RA participation is not mandatory.

Simple Certificate Enrollment Protocol

Simple Certificate Enrollment Protocol (SCEP), which was developed by Cisco Systems, is a communication protocol that is used by PKI. This protocol was designed for issuing certificates to the various network devices (by using whatever technologies were available) in a secure and scalable environment. Several vendors, including Verisign, Entrust Technologies, and Microsoft, support SCEP. SCEP is used by client products, such as Cisco routers and SSH Sentinel and VPN gateway. SCEP is also used by RSA Keon Certificate Server 5.5 product to provide integration with Cisco routers, firewalls, and other products.

Some of the technologies used by SCEP are PKCS#7, PKCS#10, DES algorithm, HTTP, LDAP, and RSA algorithm.

SCEP supports the following transactions:

- ◆ Distributing CA and RA public keys

- ◆ Revoking certificates

- ◆ Enrolling certificates

- ◆ Querying certificates

- ◆ Querying CRLs

Working of SCEP

According to SCEP, the entities should include the following information as a prerequisite for performing any PKI activity:

♦ The Fully Qualified Domain Name (FQDN) of the CA or the CA's IP address

♦ The CA HTTP script path and the proxy information in case no direct connection to the server is available

♦ The URL of the certificate and CRL queries

A PKI transaction process starts with the generation of a key pair by an entity. To accomplish this, the entity can use any algorithm, such as RSA, that is supported by SCEP. Next, it obtains a CA public key using the standard HTTP Get operation after which the entity trusts the CA. After the identity of a CA has been established, the entity uses PKCS#10 to issue a certificate request and PKCS#7 to send the request to the CA. At this point the certificate enrollment process is initiated. SCEP supports two enrollment processes:

♦ **Manual:** In manual authentication, the entity has to wait for the CA's request until the time the CA manually authenticates the identity of the entity.

♦ **Challenge password:** In this type of enrollment, the entity provides a password to the CA. The CA authenticates the request based on this password.

After establishing the authenticity of the entity, the CA issues the certificate.

Certificate Revocation in SCEP

The process of certificate revocation by using SCEP is manual. When an entity requests the revoking of a certificate, the entity contacts the CA over phone. The CA asks for the challenge password. If the password is authentic, the certificate is revoked.

Accessing Certificates and CRLs

To query a certificate, the entities can use either the LDAP protocol or query messages as defined in the SCEP. These query messages consist of a GetCert PKI message and a CertRep PKI message.

To access a CRL, an entity can use the following three methods:

♦ By using a simple HTTP Get request.

♦ By using LDAP. This assumes that the CA server supports CRL LDAP publishing and issues the CRL Distribution Point in the certificate. The CRL Distribution Point is encoded as a DN.

♦ By creating messages that contain the issuer CA's name and CA's certificate serial number. This method is deprecated because it does not scale well and requires the CA to be a high-availability service.

Evaluating SCEP

Unfortunately, SCEP suffers from the following limitations:

◆ It does not define messages for revocation requests. It only supports messages for certificate requests.

◆ It is very algorithm-specific and supports only RSA algorithm.

◆ It can be used only for issuing certificates to network devices. Therefore, it is very specific to an application.

The X Series Standards

International Telecommunication Union (ITU) and International Standards Organization (ISO) has proposed several standards for defining protocols, information, and authentication. These standards are commonly referred to as the X series standards. As part of this series of standards, the two most widely used standards are X.500 and X.509. The X.500 standard is an online, distributed, public directory that is designed to provide services to a global network. The X.509 standard is an authentication framework, which is designed to support the X.500 global directory service.

In addition, these standards are also used to ensure interoperability between the products of multiple vendors offering PKI and have become one of the major international standards for PKI. Let's now examine each of these standards in detail.

X.500

The X.500 directory acts as the repository for certificates and for the Certificate Revocation List (CRL) into which all CAs have published their certificates. The first version of X.500 was released in 1988. X.500 is a distributed global directory service. This means that the information in an organization can be stored locally in one or more databases referred to as *Directory Service Agents* (DSAs). DSAs are not specific to an organization, and one DSA can contain information about one or more organizations. Also, information about a large organization can be stored in more than one DSA. The DSA database maintains information in a hierarchy as per the X.500 information model so that information can be exchanged with other DSAs.

In a X.500 directory service, you can interoperate between the DSAs through the *Directory Information Tree* (DIT). The DIT is organized in a hierarchical tree structure and represents a global directory. It consists of entities in which the entity at the top is referred to as "root," followed by the "countries." The level that appears below the countries are "organizations." Each organization is comprised of "individuals" or "organizational units." Figure 6-2 explains the DIT. Each DSA contains only a part of the database that concerns its employees and processes, but it can find rest of the information from other DSAs by traversing through the DIT. The X.500 standard defines how these DSA should be interconnected to form a global information base.

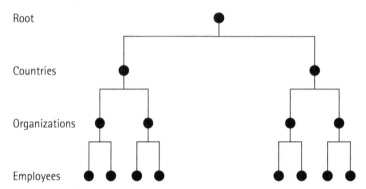

Figure 6-2: An example of a Directory Information Tree

Organizations can define their own DIT structure along with object classes and attributes. This ensures that the attributes are available only for the organization that defines them. The object class, attributes, and DIT follow the definition standard of X.500. This means that one infrastructure can be used to provide infor- mation inside the organization. The same can be used for the outside world by making use of the access control mechanism that is defined in the 1993 standard.

THE DIRECTORY SERVICE INFORMATION MODEL

The Information model in the directory service is defined by the X.500 standard. This information is stored in the form of entries inside the directory; each entry belongs to an object class. The object class can be a country, organization, or user or organizational unit.

The information that pertains to an entity cannot be distributed among different nodes and resides in one node of the DSA part of DIT. The information that pertains to an organization can be distributed in more than one DSA depending on the size of the organization. This process of information distribution or replication among the DSAs is transparent to users. In a distributed directory service, it is important that the information contained in one DSA be replicated to other DSAs. This is to prevent a single point of failure in case the DSA that contains the information is unavailable. It also improves the response time and quality of service.

To access a directory in the directory service, you use a *Directory User Agent* (DUA). The DUA acts as an intermediary between the user and the directory database. To retrieve information from the directory, the DUA contacts its nearby DSA and looks for the requested information. The DUA can be implemented in a platform- independent user interface, or it can be integrated with the application that requires the information to be stored in the DIT.

To search for information that is stored in the X.500 directory, you can query at any level of the DIT by specifying the attribute and its corresponding value. The DSA controls the search capabilities by specifying who can search and to which level of the DIT. However, the search process of X.500 is quite tedious because a user has to browse through the directory of many DSAs. This affects the network performance as well as the DSAs. Secondly, since the DIT structure is not uniform across the entire globe, the person who doesn't know the structure would not be able to search it. This problem is addressed by index services and defined in Whois++, in which the index server stores pointers to servers that contain the address of the organization for a given category.

The Yellow pages directory service uses index servers based on the Whois++ model to enable easy search. The Whois++ model is based on the Whois model. In the Whois model, a single directory database is used to store information, while in the Whois++ model there are several databases. The Whois++ directory is not a hierarchical structure; instead it is a space of interconnected index servers in which every Whois++ server has a pointer stored in one of the index server. Figure 6-3 shows the arrangement of Index and Whois++ servers.

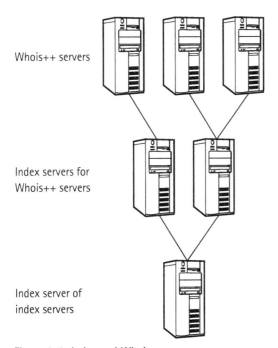

Whois++ servers

Index servers for
Whois++ servers

Index server of
index servers

Figure 6-3: Index and Whois++ servers

The request for comments that is related to this standard is found in RFC 1491 and RFC 2256, respectively.

All the features that we have discussed until now have helped make X.500 a globally accepted directory service. To provide authentication to the X.500 directory entries, the X.509 authentication framework was defined. The following section discusses how this authentication is supported by the X.509 standard.

X.509

PKI has come to be recognized globally as a security solution. Many countries and organizations can now benefit from PKI-based solutions. PKI provides certificate-based authentication. Therefore, to ensure global compatibility between these certificates, you need to define some standards governing the format of these certificates. X.509 defines what information can go into certificates and various standards for certificates and CRLs.

X.509 is a PKI standard accepted globally by the companies involved in producing PKI products. The standard describes a hierarchical model for cross-certification of certificates from multiple CAs. X.509 certificates authenticate the identity of a person by using cryptographic mechanisms and store information and privilege about entities in the form of attributes in the certificate. The X.509 standard is supported by a number of protocols, including PEM, PKCS, S-HTTP, and SSL.

As you already know, the X.509 certificates consist of the following information:

◆ **Certificate Version:** This describes the version of the certificate. The latest version is version 3.

◆ **Certificate serial number:** The CA associates an integer with each certificate. It is unique for each certificate.

◆ **Signature Algorithm ID:** The CA signs the certificate by using an algorithm and the public key of the certificate holder.

◆ **Issuer name:** The issuer name identifies the CA that has signed and issued the certificate.

◆ **Validity Period:** This contains two dates, the date from which the certificate validity period begins and the date when the certificate validity period ends.

◆ **Subject (user) name:** The subject identifies the entity to which a private key is issued. This private key is associated with the public key stored in the subject's public key field.

◆ **Subject public key information:** This field contains the public key along with the identifier of the algorithm with which the key is used.

◆ **Digital Signature:** It contains the digital signature (signature with the private key) of the issuer.

Although the information that is contained in the certificate identifies the entity, it does not guarantee the uniqueness of the subject and issuing CA name. There can be a situation when a single subject name can be associated with two entities. To help resolve such a situation, X.509 version 2 was introduced.

X.509 VERSION 2

X.509 version 2 is the next version of X.509, which, in addition to the preceding information, contains two new fields:

◆ **Issuer unique identifier:** This field contains a unique ID of the certificate issuer. Although the issuer name field also exists, this field ensures that the identifier is unique to the issuing CA and doesn't identify some other CA.

◆ **Subject unique identifier:** This field is similar to the issuer unique identifier. This field ensures the uniqueness of the subject of the certificate.

Figure 6-4 describes the information contained in the X.509 version 2 certificates.

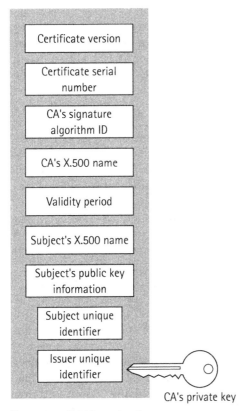

Figure 6-4: X.509 version 2

X.509 versions 1 and 2 are used primarily for intra-organizational purposes. These versions faced some limitations with respect to the type and amount of information they contained. X.509 version 3 incorporates significant changes into version 2. The next section describes this standard.

X.509 VERSION 3

X.509 introduced the concept of *extensions*. This is the latest version and was introduced in 1996. Extensions are fields that contain information in addition to the fields available in earlier versions. By using X.509 version 3 extensions, an organization can define certificate content, depending on their requirements. For example, an organization can include the employee code in the certificate apart from the common name. The different X.509 version 3 extensions are discussed here in detail.

ALTERNATE NAME   An alternate name can be an e-mail address or any other name that is created by an entity or an organization to identify the entity in a user-friendly manner. In addition, the use of alternate names in X.509 version 3 certificates helps to identify the entity without needing to refer to the X.500 directory.

SUBJECT DIRECTORY ATTRIBUTES   This extension can contain the attribute values of an entity, in addition to the subject's name, as defined in the X.500 directory.

CERTIFICATE POLICIES   The CA can include the policies based on which the certificates are issued. These policies indicate the usability of a certificate under different conditions. An associated object identifier that is referred to as policy OID identifies each policy.

Policy mapping is used in situations when more than one CA exists in a hierarchy. In order for the policy of one CA to be recognized by the entity of another CA, the policy of the first CA should be mapped with the policy of the second CA. The policy mapping extension facilitates the inclusion of policy mapping information.

CERTIFICATION PATH CONSTRAINT   The Certification Path Constraint extension was introduced to restrict the certification path in a trust model. A constraint is a kind of condition applied as a restriction to the certification path. To understand certification path constraint better, let's analyze the following example.

CA1 and CA2 are two Certification Authorities, and Alice, Bob, and Charlie are the users under them. CA1 is the certification issuing authority for Alice. The certificate that is issued to Alice by CA1 authenticates Bob for various purposes, such as e-commerce-related transactions, normal code signing, and so on. Furthermore, CA1 authorizes another CA, CA2, for issuing certificates. However, CA1 puts a constraint that CA2 can issue certificates to users only and not to other CAs. CA2 issues a certificate to the user Charlie based on the constraint that Charlie can use the certificate only for normal code signing. After acquiring Charlie's certificate, Alice learns that Bob's certificate can be used only for normal code signing.

Code signing is the process of digitally signing software and macros for secure delivery over the Internet. Digitally signing Active X controls, Java applets, dynamic link libraries, .cab files, .jar files, or HTML content increases the confidence of a customer who downloads such objects from a Web site, secure in the knowledge that the code has an authentic source and hasn't been altered or corrupted since it was created and signed. If signed code is tampered with in any way, the digital signature will break, and the user will be notified that the code has been altered and is not trustworthy.

X.509 client certificates are currently supported by Netscape in its Navigator 3.0 browser. Microsoft has also announced support for X.509 certificates in its client applications. X.509 server certificates are currently used in server products from IBM, Microsoft, Netscape, OpenMarket, and Oracle.

The different RFCs of the X.509 standard are:

- **RFC 2459:** Internet X.509 Public Key Infrastructure Certificate and CRL Profile.

- **RFC 2510:** Internet X.509 Public Key Infrastructure Certificate Management Protocols.

- **RFC 2511:** Internet X.509 Certificate Request Message Format.

- **RFC 2527:** Internet X.509 Public Key Infrastructure Certificate Policy and Certification Practices Framework.

- **RFC 2528:** Internet X.509 Public Key Infrastructure. Representation of Key Exchange Algorithm (KEA) Keys in Internet X.509 Public Key Infrastructure Certificates.

- **RFC 2559:** Internet X.509 Public Key Infrastructure Operational Protocol LDAPv2.

- **RFC 2560:** X.509 Internet Public Key Infrastructure Online Certificate Status Protocol OCSP.

- **RFC 2585:** Internet X.509 Public Key Infrastructure Operational Protocols FTP and HTTP.

- **RFC 2587:** Internet X.509 Public Key Infrastructure LDAPv2 Schema.

- **RFC 3029:** Internet X.509 Public Key Infrastructure Data Validation and Certification Server Protocols.

- **RFC 3039:** Internet X.509 Public Key Infrastructure Qualified Certificates Profile.

Summary

In this chapter you learned about the evaluation criteria for PKI management protocols. You learned about the different PKI management protocols.

You learned that PKCS#10 or Certificate Request Syntax Standard defines syntax for certificate requests. You learned that PKCS#7 or Cryptographic Message Syntax defines syntax for cryptographically signed data, such as digital signatures.

Next, you learned about CMP. CMP is required for online interactions between different PKI entities. You also learned that CMC is less-complex protocol than CMP, which specifies sufficient messages and transaction to meet our requirement or online transaction. You learned about the Cisco-developed SCEP. This protocol is used specifically for issuing certificates to network devices. Finally, you learned about the X series of standards in PKI, including the X.509 and X.500 standards.

Chapter 7

PKI-Enabled Services

WITH THE ADVENT OF THE INTERNET, the process of communication has been redefined. Days when you had to wait for a letter to arrive are long over. Now, all you need to do is click a button or press a few keystrokes, and your message is communicated within no time. Although the Internet has speeded up communication, several questions relating to the security of these messages transmitted over the Internet remain unanswered. How do you ensure that the communication between two entities is not intruded by a third entity, or the message that you send is not read or altered during transit?

These questions are answered by applications that are designed specifically to provide secure communication channels. All these applications, such as SSL/TLS, S/MIME, and IPSec, are based on the concept of PKI and perform specific functions. For example, S/MIME is used specifically for securing e-mail messages.

In this chapter, we'll discuss the applications that are supported by PKI, such as SSL/TLS, S/MIME, and IPSec.

SSL

All data transmission that takes place over the Internet uses the Transmission Control Protocol/Internet Protocol (TCP/IP). Various other application-specific protocols, such as HyperText Transport Protocol (HTTP), Lightweight Directory Access Protocol (LDAP), and Internet Messaging Access Protocol (IMAP), also use TCP/IP to perform some of their functions such as running exchange servers or displaying Web pages. To use TCP/IP these protocols need to work over and above the TCP/IP layer. However, the most important concern for data transmission, irrespective of the source or destination of data, is data security. It is to address this concern that Netscape developed the Secure Socket Layer (SSL) protocol in the early 1990s. SSL is a protocol that has been developed to provide a secure communication channel for data in transit. SSL operates between TCP/IP and other higher-level protocols.

In today's Internet society, SSL is primarily used to secure communication between a user's Web browser (client) and a Web server. In doing so, SSL performs the following functions:

◆ Allows an SSL-enabled server to authenticate to an SSL-enabled client

◆ Allows an SSL-enabled client to authenticate to an SSL-enabled server

◆ Establishes an encrypted communication channel between both the SSL-enabled server and the SSL-enabled client

Let's now look at each of these functions in detail.

Authentication of Servers

SSL allows a Web client to authenticate the Web server with which it is interacting. Any SSL-enabled server is issued an SSL server certificate by a trustworthy CA. This SSL server certificate indicates the integrity and authenticity of the server while the server is communicating with a client. An SSL-enabled client can verify the validity and authenticity of the server's SSL certificate and the public key by using various public key cryptography techniques. To authenticate an SSL-enabled server, an SSL-enabled client performs the following steps:

1. The SSL-enabled client checks for the validity of the date of the server's certificate and compares it with the current date and time. If the current date and time are not within the validity period of the server's certificate, the authentication process does not proceed further, else the authentication proceeds.

2. The SSL-enabled client then matches the distinguished name of the CA that has issued the server certificate with its list of trusted CA certificates. The clients accept only those CA certificates that are included in their list of trusted CA certificates. If the distinguished name of the CA that has issued the server certificate matches with that in the list, then the authentication proceeds further.

3. The issuing CA's digital signature on the server certificate is then validated by using the public key that is present in the CA's certificate (in the list of trusted CA certificates of the client). In this way the SSL-enabled client verifies the information on the server certificate and whether or not any information on the server certificate has changed since its signing by the issuing CA.

4. The SSL-enabled client also checks whether the SSL-enabled server is located in the same network address as specified in the server certificate. This step ensures that no man-in-the-middle attacks take place. If both the domain names match, then the client can authenticate the server.

A man-in-the-middle attack refers to a situation when the network communication between two entities is intercepted in between by an unauthorized entity. This third entity might also be able to intercept the keys when they are transmitted and exchanges them with its own keys.

Finally, after performing all the preceding steps the SSL-enabled client authenticates the SSL-enabled server.

Authenticating a Web server is quite relevant especially when you are making online payments and are required to provide your credit card number. To validate the authenticity of the recipient on the network or the Web server with which you are interacting, your SSL-enabled client application examines the Web server certificate and checks for the validity of its public key and whether the CA who has issued the CA is in your trusted list of CA certificates or not. If this validity is proved positive, you can be assured that the transaction will be secure.

Authentication of Clients

The authentication of a client is as important as the authentication of a server. Just like a client authenticates the server by using various public key cryptography techniques, similarly a server also uses these techniques to authenticate clients. Certification Authorities provide server certificates to individuals, organizations, organizational units, and Web sites. These CAs use extensive authentication procedures to identify valid users. Most Web browsers, such as Netscape Communicator and Internet Explorer, are shipped with a CA's self-signed SSL digital certificate. As a result, installing digital certificates on the Web server enables SSL services. An SSL-enabled server can verify the validity of the client's certificate and also validate whether the CA who was issued the client certificate is in the server's trusted list of CAs. To authenticate an SSL-enabled client, an SSL-enabled server performs the following steps:

1. The SSL-enabled server verifies whether the public key of the client's certificate can validate the digital signature of the client. You already know that digital certificates are generated by using the private key, and therefore if the public key in the certificate can validate the digital certificates it proves that the client possesses the corresponding private key. However, the authentication process does not end here, in fact it starts here. One important factor that you need to take into account is establishing the binding between the distinguished name in the certificate and the public key. It might so happen that an intruder creates a certificate and impersonates the client. To overcome this situation the server needs to perform the following steps:

1. The SSL-enabled server checks for the validity of the date of the client's certificate and compares it with the current date and time. If the current date and time are not within the validity period of the client's certificate, the authentication process does not proceed further.

2. The SSL-enabled server then matches the distinguished name of the CA that has issued the client certificate with its list of trusted of CA certificates. The server accepts only those CA certificates that are included in their list of trusted CA certificates. If the distinguished name of the CA that has issued the client certificate matches with that in the list, then the authentication proceeds further.

3. The issuing CA's digital signature on the client certificate is then validated by using the public key that is present in the CA's certificate (in the list of trusted CA certificates of the server). In this way, the SSL-enabled server verifies the information on the server certificate and whether or not any information on the server certificate has changed since its signing by the issuing CA.

2. After all the preceding steps have been performed, the client is then authenticated and is allowed to access the required resources.

In real life, client authentication is very important in the banking scenario. For example, when a bank wants to send some confidential information to a customer over the Internet, the bank needs to ensure that the information is sent solely to the intended person and not to anyone else. The bank can ensure the authenticity of the customer by requesting the client's certificate. On receiving the client's certificate, the server software then verifies the certificate. Only after the server has verified that the client's certificate is authentic does the bank proceed with the transaction with the client.

Encryption of Data in Transit

When an SSL connection is established between an SSL-enabled server and an SSL-enabled client, all the data that is exchanged between them is encrypted. Just like any other encryption method, an SSL connection also requires that the software that is sending the message encrypts the message and the software at the receiving end decrypts the same. Also, any tampering of the data being transmitted through an SSL channel can be detected automatically.

SSL can be used in any situation where you want to secure the communication between two computers or applications. SSL works on the principle of a public key, which encrypts the data that is transmitted over the SSL connection.

To learn more about installing and configuring SSL, refer to Chapter 9.

The SSL protocol is made up of the following two layers:

◆ **SSL Record Protocol:** The SSL Record Protocol operates on a reliable transport medium, such as TCP. SSL Record Protocol encapsulates higher-level protocols.

◆ **SSL Handshake Protocol:** The SSL Handshake Protocol allows a user's Web browser and a Web server to authenticate each other. After authentication, it negotiates an encryption algorithm and cryptographic keys before the application protocol transmits or receives any data.

Let us look at both these layers in detail.

SSL RECORD PROTOCOL

The record protocol uses the negotiated session key to encrypt data in transit. This protocol fragments the data into non-empty blocks. These blocks of data can be of any size and can undergo the following stages:

◆ Fragmentation

◆ Compression

◆ Record Payload protection

Let's now discuss each of these stages in detail.

FRAGMENTATION   In the fragmentation stage, the data is fragmented into records. These records exist in the plaintext format. The size of each record should be 16,384 bytes or less. Messages with the same content type can be combined into a single record; alternately, one single message can be broken down into multiple records.

COMPRESSION   Before encryption, the data that you want to transmit is compressed by using a compression algorithm. The compression algorithm should ensure that during compression no data is lost. After the data is compressed and transmitted, a decompression algorithm is used to decompress the data at the receiver's end.

RECORD PAYLOAD PROTECTION   After the data is compressed, an integrity check value is computed. This check value is known as the Message Authentication Code

(MAC). The compressed data and MAC value is then encrypted and transmitted. At the receiving end, the data is decrypted and decompressed. The MAC value is recomputed to verify data integrity.

Let's now discuss SSL Handshake Protocol.

SSL Handshake Protocol

An SSL session starts with an exchange of messages between the client and server. This exchange of messages is called *SSL handshake*. The SSL Handshake Protocol uses the SSL Record Protocol to exchange a series of messages between the server and the client when they establish a connection. The SSL Handshake Protocol is primarily responsible for authenticating the server and the client. It operates on top of the SSL Record Layer. A handshaking mechanism allows the interacting entities to establish an SSL session between them. In SSL handshake, the server authenticates itself to the client by using a public key.

The following steps are involved in establishing an SSL session between a client and a server:

1. The client sends its SSL version number, cipher settings, and other information to the server. This information is used by the server to communicate with the client that uses SSL.

2. The server sends its SSL version number, certificate, cipher settings, and other information. This information is used by the client to communicate with the server. If the client needs to be authenticated for accessing a resource, the server sends a request for the client certificate.

3. The client authenticates the server, based on the information sent by the server, and an SSL session is established.

4. The client creates a pre-master secret for the current session. The client then encrypts the pre-master secret using the public key of the server and sends the encrypted pre-master key to the server. If the server has requested client authentication, the client also sends its certificate and signed data along with the encrypted pre-master.

5. The server authenticates the client based on the certificate and the signed data sent by the client. If the client is authenticated, the server decrypts the data sent by the client by using its private key. The server uses the decrypted data to generate a master secret. The client also uses the same data to generate the master secret.

6. The client and the server use the master secret to create *session keys*. These session keys are symmetric and are used to encrypt and decrypt the data transmitted during the SSL session.

7. The client informs the server that all future messages, which it will be sent during the SSL session to the server, will be encrypted using the session

key. It also sends an encrypted message to the server to indicate that the client-side handshake is over.

8. The server also informs the client that all future messages from the server will be encrypted by using the session keys. It also sends an encrypted message to the client to indicate that the server-side handshake is over. After the SSL handshake is over, the client and server use the session keys to encrypt and decrypt the information that they send to each other.

SSL uses a number of algorithms to carry its functions. In the following section we'll look at the different cryptographic algorithms used with SSL.

Cryptographic Algorithms Used with SSL

To authenticate servers and clients, SSL uses a number of cryptographic algorithms. These algorithms can also be used for distributing certificates and establishing session keys. Depending on organizational policies set and the version of SSL, clients and servers support different cryptographic algorithms. The cryptographic algorithms commonly used by SSL are:

◆ Key Exchange Algorithm (KEA)

◆ Data Encryption Standard (DES)

◆ Triple-DES

◆ Digital Signature Algorithm (DSA)

◆ Message Digest Algorithm (MD5)

◆ Secure Hash Algorithm (SHA-1)

 To learn more about cryptographic algorithms, refer to Chapter 1.

SSL is now a universally accepted encryption protocol used over the Internet. Some of the areas where SSL can be used are described below.

◆ Financial institutions that use remote banking programs with strong cryptography to secure online banking transactions

◆ E-commerce sites that accept online payments from their customers

◆ Defense services to ensure data integrity

◆ Major research and development organizations to secure data in transit

TLS

The TLS protocol, developed by IETF, is intended to replace the SSL protocol. The TLS Working Group was established in 1996 to standardize Transport Layer Security Protocol. The focus of this working group is to enhance the TLS Protocol to Internet Standard. The working group based TLS on SSL version 3.0. In 1999, the TLS Protocol version 1.0, RFC 2246, was published as a proposed standard.

TLS ensures privacy and data integrity between two applications that are communicating with each other. TLS is a combination of two protocols:

- ◆ TLS Record Protocol
- ◆ TLS Handshake Protocol

The following sections discuss these protocols in detail.

TLS RECORD PROTOCOL

TLS Record Protocol is composed of various sublayers that:

- ◆ Process application protocol data by fragmenting the data into manageable blocks
- ◆ Verify data integrity
- ◆ Output encryption from previous sublayers and further transmit the result

TLS Record Protocol is layered over a transport protocol, such as TCP. The TLS Record Protocol has the following features:

- ◆ It ensures a secure, reliable, and private connection between the communicating applications.
- ◆ It uses symmetric cryptography for encrypting data. For each new connection, unique keys are generated. These keys are based on a session key negotiated by another protocol, such as TLS Handshake Protocol.

The TLS Record Protocol is used to encapsulate a variety of higher-level protocols, such as TLS Handshake Protocol.

TLS HANDSHAKE PROTOCOL

TLS Handshake Protocol allows clients and servers to authenticate each other, as shown in Figure 7-1. It also allows them to negotiate an encryption algorithm and cryptographic keys before the application layer starts the transmission of data.

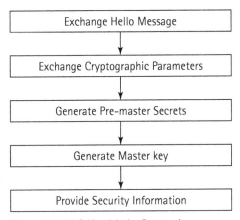

Figure 7-1: TLS Handshake Protocol

TLS Handshake Protocol has the following features:

◆ It provides connection security. The identity of the peers is authenticated by using asymmetric cryptography. However, this authentication can be made optional.

◆ It ensures secure and reliable negotiation of the session key.

The primary function of the Handshake Protocol is to negotiate a session. While negotiating a session it uses the following fields:

◆ **Session identifier:** A random byte sequence chosen by the server to recognize a current session/sessions or to resume a closed session.

◆ **Peer certificate:** It refers to X509version 3 [X509] certificate of the peer.

◆ **Compression method:** The algorithm used to compress data prior to encryption.

◆ **Cipher spec:** Specifies the algorithm by which bulk data encryption can happen (such as 3DES) and an HMAC algorithm (such as SHA-1). It also defines cryptographic attributes, such as the hash size.

◆ **Master secret:** A large secret value shared between the client and server.

The following steps are performed by the TLS Handshake protocol to complete the handshake:

◆ Exchange of an initial Hello message to negotiate algorithms and exchange random values.

◆ Exchange of cryptographic parameters to agree to the pre-master secret.

- ◆ Exchange certificates and cryptographic information for authentication. This can be a two-way process in which the client authenticates the server and the server authenticates the client, if required.

- ◆ Generate master secret from pre-master secret and exchange random values.

- ◆ Provide security information to Record Protocol Layer and verify that both server and client have calculated the same security parameters confirming that handshake occurred without any tampering.

S/MIME

Today, e-mail is one of the most efficient, effective, and fast means of communication. E-mail has completely revolutionized our communication. E-mail messages, which contain personal information and sensitive business information, are regularly sent over the Internet or the intranet. All the standard Internet e-mail that we exchange over the Internet is sent as plaintext without any security. In such a situation, anyone can easily intercept and tamper the content of these plaintext messages, or even spoof the IP address of the sender and send false or junk mail. To address this problem of security, most of today's e-mail security solutions are based on an open standard, known as Secure Multipurpose Internet Mail Extension (S/MIME).

The S/MIME standard is a specification for secure e-mail and was designed to solve the problem of interception of e-mail messages.

The two most important security features of S/MIME are:

- ◆ Authentication: S/MIME uses digital signatures to verify the authenticity of the sender and receiver of an e-mail message.

- ◆ Privacy: S/MIME provides privacy by encrypting e-mail messages.

Need for S/MIME

In 1982, e-mail format was defined in Internet Standard RFC 822. However, this format had some limitations. For example, it supported only plaintext messages and restricted the length of the messages to a maximum of 1000 characters. As the Internet became widely used, it was felt that a much more flexible and extensible standard for e-mail was needed.

In 1992, the Internet Engineering Task Force (IETF) developed a standard for e-mail messages. This standard is known as Multipurpose Internet Mail Extensions (MIME). It defines a specification for formatting e-mail messages with non-ASCII characters. The MIME format allows you to include text, graphics, and audio in normal e-mail.

However, it does not ensure security of e-mail messages. To provide security to e-mail messages in MIME format, RSA Data Security Inc. designed Secure

Multipurpose Internet Mail Extensions (S/MIME) version 2.0. S/MIME protects against tampering and spoofing of messages by combining the cryptographic methods with e-mail systems. The sender digitally signs the messages. Digital signatures provide authenticity to the message. The sender can also encrypt the messages by using the public key in the X.509 version 3 certificate thus preventing it from being tampered.

Cryptographic Algorithms Used with S/MIME

To safeguard against tampering and spoofing of messages, S/MIME recommends the use of cryptographic algorithms, such as DES, Triple-DES, and RC2. These cryptographic algorithms are based on symmetric key encryption, in which the same key is used for encryption and decryption.

For a recipient to be able to read the message encrypted by using the symmetric key, the symmetric key must be transmitted with the message. Every user should have a key pair consisting of a public key and private key. This key pair is used to encrypt and decrypt the symmetric key. The sender uses the public key of the recipient to encrypt the symmetric key,-and the recipient uses his private key to decrypt the key. Both public and private keys are mathematically related.

To prevent the tampering of messages during transit, S/MIME based e-mail systems use the following process.

◆ A hash algorithm is used on the message text to generate a unique digest. The hash algorithm recommended to perform this task is SHA-1.

◆ The digest is then encrypted using the sender's private key and is sent along with the message and the sender's public key. This public key is used by the recipient's e-mail program to decrypt the hash.

◆ The recipient's e-mail program decrypts the message by using the recipient's private key and computes the digest.

◆ If the computed digest matches the digest that was transmitted with the message, it implies that the message is not manipulated.

For S/MIME to work each mail client should have a secure mail certificate. In addition, each mail client should also trust the root CA that is in the certification path of the mail certificate of the other mail client. However, since S/MIME is a client-based standard for secure e-mail it does not define any requirements for key management or recovery. Without a proper key management or recovery mechanism in place, however, it would become very difficult to deploy secure e-mail in an organization. This is because an encrypted message can only be decrypted with the corresponding private key. In case the recipient's private key is lost due to any reason, such as crashing of the hard disk of the recipient, then the recipient cannot read the encrypted message. Hence, it is always recommended that the keys are always stored in a secure database until the validity period of the corresponding secure mail certificate. After the validity period of the certificate expires, the public key cannot be used to send secure mail.

To learn more about configuring S/MIME, refer to Chapter 9, "Installing and Configuring a Windows 2000 Certificate Server for SSL, IPSec, and S/MIME."

The latest version of S/MIME is version 3, which was developed by IETF. The following fields were added in S/MIME version 3:

◆ Mailing lists

◆ Security labels

◆ Key management flexibility

◆ Digitally signed receipts

Let us look at these in detail.

MAILING LISTS

Mailing lists are used when an e-mail message has to be sent to a large number of recipients. The sender can send the encrypted message to a server, which, on behalf of the sender, distributes the message to all recipients. When the message is received from a sender, the server does not need to decrypt the message.

SECURITY LABELS

S/MIME version 3 allows the sender to attach a security label with an e-mail message. This security label defines the handling specifications for the message on the basis of its content. For example, the handling specifications for a message that is encrypted with 128-bit encryption would be different from a message that is encrypted with 40-bit encryption.

KEY MANAGEMENT FLEXIBILITY

To enable the transfer of keys from the sender to the receiver, S/MIME version 2.0 supports only the RSA key transfer mechanism. S/MIME version 3.0 not only supports RSA key transport mechanism but it also supports out-of-band distribution of symmetric key-encryption key and key negotiation processes. The servers that use a mailing list to distribute these key-encryption keys to receivers use the out-of-band key-encryption keys distribution.

DIGITALLY SIGNED RECEIPTS

S/MIME allows a sender to request a digitally signed receipt of the message from the recipient. A receipt enables the sender to know that the intended person received the message and that the message was not tampered with during transit. The recipient, however, cannot send the receipt until the sender has digitally signed the message and the recipient has validated the signature. The digitally signed request uses the PKCS#7-MIME message format.

Advantages of Using S/MIME

The advantages of using S/MIME are the following:

◆ S/MIME, which is primarily used for e-mails, can be used with other mechanisms that transport MIME data, such as HTTP.

◆ All e-mail or messaging applications that implement S/MIME provide the basic security features, such as privacy, data integrity, and authentication.

◆ S/MIME is interoperable and thereby allows secure messages to be exchanged between users using different e-mail applications.

◆ S/MIME is endorsed as a secure means of e-mail communications by different vendors such as Microsoft and Lotus.

IPSec

Internet and large corporate networks have been using the Internet Protocol (IP) to transmit data. IP transmits data in the form of manageable chunks called packets. However, just like e-mail messages, these packets are also susceptible to security threats, such as spoofing, sniffing, session hijacking, and the man-in-the-middle attacks. To take care of these security threats, IP Security (IPSec) protocol suite was developed by Internet Engineering Task Force (IETF). IPSec is an extension of IP that takes care of the security issues at the network level. Hence, IPSec ensures the security of the network rather than the security of applications that use it. As IPSec provides security to the network, all applications that use the network are also secured.

IPSec is a set of extensions to the IP protocol family, which supports authentication, integrity, access control, and confidentiality of data packets at the network layer, unlike TLS/SSL that operates at the transport layer. The operation is completely transparent to the application, and the application does not have to be an IPSec-aware application.

IP Security Overview

The increasing use of the Internet and the ever-increasing risk of network security threats have heightened the need for IP security solutions for all businesses. Security protocols, such as SSL and S/MIME, provide security for only specific functions. For example, S/MIME is used only for messaging applications and SSL is primarily used for secure communication with Web servers. There are applications over the Internet which do not have security mechanisms. This creates a need for a security protocol that can benefit applications that are not security aware.

A typical usage of IPSec is illustrated in Figure 7-2.

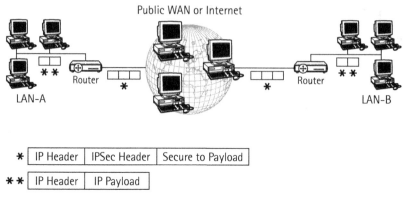

Public WAN or Internet

Router   Router

LAN-A   LAN-B

| * | IP Header | IPSec Header | Secure to Payload |

| ** | IP Header | IP Payload |

Figure 7-2: Usage of IPSec

As shown in the figure, an organization has LANs at two separate locations. Non-secure traffic is flowing in the respective LANs and the secured IP traffic is flowing through the WAN. IPSec protocols are used on the networking devices connecting LAN to WAN (typically routers). For a secure communication to take place, these IPSec networking devices will compress and encrypt the traffic going from LAN to WAN and will decompress and decrypt the traffic coming back to the other end from WAN to LAN. The important thing is that the whole process is transparent to end devices like workstations and clients.

To learn more about configuring S/MIME, refer to Chapter 9.

Components of IPSec

IPSec consists of separate protocols or components:

```
IPSec = AH + ESP + IPcomp + IKE
```

Secure connections already exist for applications, such as HTTP, FTP, Telnet, and SMTP. IPSec adds security to other transport layer-based protocols in TCP/IP, such as TCP and User Datagram Protocol (UDP). It works with all network topologies like Ethernet and token-ring. IPSec provides confidentiality, integrity, authenticity, and replay protection by using the following protocols:

◆ **Authentication Header (AH):** Is a protocol that adds a header to the IP datagram. This header ensures the integrity and authenticity of the data.

◆ Encapsulating Security Payload (ESP): Provides data confidentiality by encrypting the data as well as the IP address in the IP datagram. ESP also ensures data integrity and authenticity.

◆ Internet Key Exchange (IKE): Is a protocol that ensures secure and authenticated transmission of data packets. It defines a *security association* between two peer devices. A security association is a policy that outlines the data handling mechanism between any two devices. IKE consists of Internet Security Association and Key Management Protocol (ISAKMP) and Oakley. ISAKMP and Oakley are the protocols that manage the creation of encryption keys.

These components allow for secure TCP/IP communications in both private and public networks. The following sections describe these protocols in detail.

AUTHENTICATION HEADER (AH)

Authentication Header ensures data authentication by applying a one-way hash function to the data packets. It provides connectionless integrity with origin of data authentication for IP datagrams. When a hash function is applied to a packet, a message digest (MD) is created. This MD is used to build an Authentication Header, which is then attached to the packet. The packet is transmitted to the IPSec peer device. The receiver peer hashes the packet. It extracts the transmitted hash received from the sender and compares the two hashes for authentication. If even one bit does not match, the hash output changes and is detected by the receiver. An AH ensures that data reaches the correct destination and is not tapped in transit or re-routed to another destination. Authentication Header secures a part of the IP header of the packet, such as the source and the destination addresses. It provides for authentication, integrity, and replay protection but not confidentiality or encryption.

The receiver may select this service when a security association (SA) is established. Authentication Header provides authentication for the IP header. However, few IP header fields may change in transit, and when the packet arrives at the receiver, the value of these fields might not be predictable by sender. Authentication Header cannot protect values of these fields. Hence the protection provided to IP header by AH is piecemeal.

The fields in AH are:

◆ Next Header: This field indicates the higher-layer protocol, which is IP in case of tunnel mode and TCP or UDP in case of transport mode.

◆ Length: Indicates the length or size of the AH protocol header. The value of this field can vary depending upon the hash algorithm used.

◆ Security Parameter Index (SPI): This field along with the destination IP address identifies the AH security association. It contains a 32-bit value that identifies the security association.

◆ **Sequence number:** This is a 32-bit counter that is always sent by the sender. It represents the anti-replay sequence number.

◆ **Authentication data:** This variable length field contains the integrity check value.

Figure 7-3 shows the fields that are included in AH.

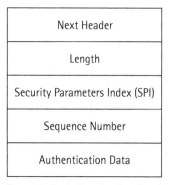

| Next Header |
| Length |
| Security Parameters Index (SPI) |
| Sequence Number |
| Authentication Data |

Figure 7-3: Authentication Header (AH) fields

One of the most important fields in an Authentication Header is authentication data.

AUTHENTICATION DATA   This is obtained by applying the SPI-defined crypto-graphic algorithm to the payload of the packet. The new methods for calculating checksum are a combination of relatively new cryptographic algorithms called Hash-Based Message Authentication code (HMAC) with the MD5 function and HMAC with the SHA-1 function. Both these methods are a result of recent changes to IPSec so as to improve authentication mechanisms. In other words, AH adds strong cryptographic support to packets, thereby ensuring authenticity.

As discussed earlier, Authentication Header applies a one-way hash function to data packets. After the hash function has been applied, a Message Digest (MD) is created. This MD builds an Authentication Header, which is attached to a data packet. The packet is transmitted along with the AH. The recipient computes another hash function by hashing the packets. The two hash functions are then compared to check for authenticity. Even if one bit does not match, the hash output changes and the recipient gets to know that the message has been tampered with in transit.

The process for using HMAC-MD5 or HMAC-SHA-1 is almost the same. In either case, the algorithm operates on 64-byte blocks of data. HMAC-MD5 method produces 128-bit authenticator value, whereas HMAC-SHA-1

produces a 160-bit authenticator value. Since default authenticator length mentioned in AH is 96 bits, any of the authenticator values produced has to be truncated before storing the value in the authenticator field of the Authentication Header.

AH can be used in two modes, transport mode and tunnel mode. Figure 7-3 shows the transport and tunnel mode.

◆ Transport mode: In this mode, the entire data packet except the *mutable fields* is authentication. Mutable fields refer to the fields in the IP header that cannot be predicted by the receiver, such as the type of service and header checksum.

◆ Tunnel mode: In this mode, a new header is created and used as the outermost header of the data packet. It is after this new header that the authentication header is placed. The original data packet (the payload and the IP header) is placed after the authentication header. In the tunnel mode, AH authenticates the entire data packet, and hence any changes made to the data packet during transition can be easily identified.

As both payload and datagram are authenticated, this mode is more secure when compared to the transport mode. As the header is also authenticated, the hackers cannot trace the actual source and destination of the packets and hence cannot perform traffic analysis.

 Authentication is described in RFC 2402.

AH does not encrypt the data. Therefore, the data is sent as cleartext. To encrypt the data Encapsulated Security Payload (ESP) is used.

ENCAPSULATED SECURITY PAYLOAD (ESP)

Encapsulated Security Payload (ESP) is responsible for packet encryption. Similar to the AH, the ESP header is inserted into the packet between the IP header and the packet contents. ESP is responsible for encrypting data packets to ensure that the data is not read or copied, thereby guaranteeing the confidentiality of data. It can provide authentication, integrity, replay protection, and confidentiality of the data. Replay protection requires authentication and integrity. Confidentiality or encryption can be used with or without authentication or integrity. Also, authentication or integrity may be used with or without confidentiality.

The strength of an encryption algorithm determines the level of confidentiality. ESP hides details, such as the number of packets and size. It supports several encryption algorithms. By default, the 56-bit Data Encryption Standard (DES) is used by ESP.

An ESP header comprises the following two fields:

◆ Security Parameter Index (SPI): This field, along with the destination IP address, identifies the ESP security association. It contains a 32-bit value that identifies the security association. This tells the receiver about the security associations and about its appropriateness in processing the packet. The sequence number in the ESP header is a counter that gets incremented each time a packet is sent to the same address using the same SPI. This also shows how many packets have been sent with the same group of parameters along with the packets details. The sequence number also provides protection against replay attacks. Prior to transmission across the network, the remaining parts of the packet are encrypted. When the receiver decrypts it, the new packet includes payload data with about 255 bytes of padding.

◆ Sequence number: This is a 32-bit counter that is always sent by the sender. It represents the anti-replay sequence number.

ESP supports numerous encryption protocols. However, IPSec by default specifies basic DES-CBC (DES with Cipher Block Chaining) cipher, and guarantees minimal interoperability among IPSec networks. The DES-CBC requires a 56-bit DES secret key. Cipher block chaining needs a 64-bit initialization vector, and the data is processed in 64-bit blocks. Figure 7-4 shows the ESP header fields.

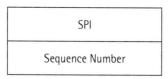

Figure 7-4: ESP header fields

An ESP trailer (Figure 7-5) is composed of the following fields.

◆ Padding: This field ensures that data to be encrypted is in multiples of the cryptographic block size. This field also ensures that the next header comprises 32 bits.

◆ Pad length: This field specifies the size of the padding field that depends on the encryption algorithm used.

- ◆ Next Header: This field indicates the higher-layer protocol, which is IP in case of tunnel mode and TCP or UDP in case of transport mode.

- ◆ Authentication data: This variable length field contains the integrity check value.

Padding
Pad Length
Next Header
Authentication Data

Figure 7-5: ESP trailer fields

ESP is described in RFC 2406.

Like AH, ESP can also be used in two modes, the transport mode and the tunnel mode. In the transport mode, ESP encrypts and optionally authenticates only the payload. However, in the tunnel mode, ESP encrypts and optionally authenticates entire original data packet.

There are some significant differences between AH and ESP. The following list spells these differences.

- ◆ ESP encrypts the entire or a part of the data packet, while AH does not encrypt data.

- ◆ In the transport mode, ESP authenticates only the data and not the IP header. However, AH in the transport mode authenticates an entire data packet except the *mutable fields*.

- ◆ In the tunnel mode, ESP authenticates an entire original data packet (without the newly added outer IP header). However, in the tunnel mode AH authenticates the entire packet.

Internet Key Exchange

In an IPSec framework, IKE authenticates the peers and handles the creation and management of encryption keys. IKE also manages the hashing algorithms between the peer devices and outlines the security association.

Although you can configure IPSec without IKE, it is preferable to configure IPSec with IKE as IKE provides enhanced features and flexibility.

IKE allows you to specify the lifetime of an IPSec SA. Also, when you use IKE, you do not need to manually specify the IPSec SA parameters for the peer devices. The features of IKE are listed below:

◆ Provides anti-replay services

◆ Allows encryption keys to change during an IPSec session

◆ Enables dynamic authentication of peer devices

◆ Generates session keys that are used by the peer devices

The algorithms and mechanisms that are used by IKE are:

◆ **DES:** Is an encryption algorithm, which is used to encrypt data in the packets. IKE uses 56-bit DES and 3DES.

◆ **MD5:** Is a hash algorithm that is used to authenticate the data in packets.

◆ **SHA:** Is a hash algorithm used during IKE exchanges to authenticate packet data.

◆ **Diffie-Hellman:** Is a protocol that enables the creation of shared secret keys over an insecure channel. IKE uses this protocol to generate session keys.

◆ **RSA signatures and encrypted nonces:** Are used by IKE to authenticate the peer devices. While RSA signatures provide non-repudiation, nonces provide repudiation.

Nonce is a random value, which is used in encryption algorithms.

AH and ESP also provide a service called Security Association (SA).

SECURITY ASSOCIATION (SA)

Security Association or SA is a basic parameter in the authentication and confidentiality mechanism for IP. The service is a security standard for network traffic between two computers and specifies how the data should be protected when it is transferred between them. SA specifies the following:

♦ The keys of authentication and algorithm used in AH and ESP

♦ The keys and SA lifetime

♦ The source address of SA

A unique SPI and the destination IP address identify an SA. Before transmitting a data packet, the sender examines the SA database and applies security to the packet. An SPI is also inserted in the IPSec header. On receiving the packet, the recipient looks into the SA database and matches the SPI and the destination IP address. If the values are the same, then the packet is processed.

There are two types of relationship under SA:

♦ One-way Relationship: An association is a one-way relationship between a sender and a receiver that affords security services to the traffic carried on it.

♦ Peer Relationship: Under this, two SAs are required for a two-way secure exchange.

The following parameters identify an SA:

♦ Security Parameters Index (SPI): This index enables the receiving end to select the SA under which a received packet will be processed.

♦ IP Destination Address: This address represents the endpoint of the SA, which could be an end user or network device such as firewall/router. Only unicast addresses are allowed.

♦ Security Protocol Identifier: This indicates if the association provides authentication/encryption.

Hence, in any packet, the security association is uniquely identified by the Destination Address in IPv4 or IPv6 header and the SPI in enclosed extension header (AH or ESP).

SA PARAMETERS

The following parameters define a Security Parameter:

♦ Sequence Number Counter: This 32-bit parameter generates Sequence Number fields on AH/ESP headers.

♦ Sequence counter overflow: This is a flag indicating if the overflow sequence number counter generates an auditable event and prevents further transmission.

♦ Anti-Replay Window: This determines if an inbound packet is a replay.

♦ Authentication Header Information: This includes the authentication algorithm and keys and keys lifetimes.

- ◆ ESP Information: This information includes encryption and authentication algorithm, keys, initialization values, and key lifetimes.

- ◆ Lifetime of this SA: This represents the time interval/byte count after which the existing SA is to be replaced by a new SA.

- ◆ IPSec Protocol Mode: This indicates tunnel mode versus transport mode.

- ◆ Path MTU: As the name suggests, this represents maximum size of a packet that can be transmitted without any fragmentation.

IPSec Modes

IPSec has integrated encryption methods. It supports two modes of encryption, the *transport mode* and the *tunnel mode.*

- ◆ Transport mode: In this mode, only the data (or payload) portion of the packet is encrypted. The IP headers are left unencrypted. This mode is not safe as the hackers can trace the origin of the packet and its destination and hence can perform traffic analysis.

- ◆ Tunnel mode: In this mode both the header as well as payload are encrypted. In the tunnel mode instead of the host, a network device such as a router performs encryption. This network device then forwards the packets in the tunnel. The peer network device at the receiver's end decrypts the entire packet before forwarding it to the destination device.

As both payload and datagram are encrypted, this mode is more secure as compared to the transport mode. As the header is also encrypted, the hackers cannot trace the actual source and destination of the packets and hence cannot perform traffic analysis.

Each host uses a policy database to make decisions on what kind of traffic to encrypt and what kind of traffic can be sent without IPSec being applied. The top two IP packets show how IPSec encrypts sensitive information, and an extra security header is inserted between the original payload and the IP header.

The additional IPSec header is added at the transmitting client for packets that need to be secured, and the original payload is encrypted. The receiving end actually removes the IPSec ESP header and decrypts the payload before passing the original IP packet and payload to the client TCP/IP stack. Since the encryption provided by Interpeak IPSec is very strong, it is impossible for anybody to snoop and decipher the information passed between the two clients. It does not matter how many insecure routers the packets pass through, they remain protected the entire path. This setup requires IPSec on both the end systems but does not require any IPSec on any of the devices between the two clients. The bottom IP packets show normal IP communication where no IPSec header is inserted. The bulk data actually travels in unsecured manner between the two clients.

Working of IPSec

As discussed earlier, IPSec ensures secure transmission of data over the IP layer by using a variety of protocols and technologies. Figure 7-6 shows the inter-communication of two IPSec clients over the Internet using the IPSec transport mode. The clients can get sensitive information by encrypting it using IPSec and sending the unencrypted bulk data.

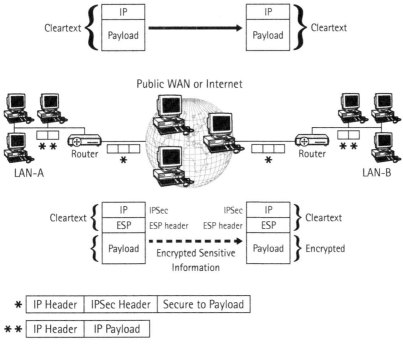

Figure 7-6: Working of IPSec

The steps involved in the working of IPSec are:

1. Process initiation

2. IKE Phase 1

3. IKE Phase 2

4. Data transfer

5. Tunnel termination

The following sections discuss these steps in detail.

PROCESS INITIATION

In this step, the traffic that needs to be sent through the IPSec client is checked for the type of security it needs. If the packets need to be encrypted, the IPSec client initiates the next step in the process.

IKE PHASE 1

In IKE Phase 1, the IPSec peer devices are authenticated. Then, an IKE SA policy is negotiated between the IPSec peers to secure the IKE exchange. In this phase, an authenticated Diffie-Hellman exchange is performed. Diffie-Hellman exchange is a secure method of creating public keys that are further used to create shared secret keys. Subsequently, these shared keys are used by IPSec encryption algorithms. Finally, in this phase a secure channel is set up for exchange of IKE parameters.

There are two modes of IKE:

♦ Main mode

♦ Aggressive mode

Let us discuss these modes in detail.

MAIN MODE   In this mode, three exchanges take place between the sender and the receiver. These exchanges are two-way exchanges. In the first exchange, each IPSec peer agrees upon the algorithms that would be used to secure the IKE transactions. In the second exchange, shared keys are generated by using Diffie-Hellman exchange. In the third exchange, identities of the sender and the receiver are verified. This verification is done by checking the identity value, which is the IP address of the IPSec peer in an encrypted form.

The final result of the main mode is matching IKE SAs between the IPSec peer devices. These IKE SAs are bidirectional and specify the authentication methods used, encryption algorithms, the lifetime of SA in seconds, and the shared keys.

AGGRESSIVE MODE   In the aggressive mode, the establishment of an IPSec session takes comparatively less time as fewer exchanges take place. Hence, this mode is faster than the main mode. In the first exchange, the Diffie-Hellman public key, an identity packet, and the nonces are put into the proposed IKE SA and sent to the destination device. The destination device sends back all information that is required to complete the transaction. After this, the source device just needs to confirm the exchange.

In the aggressive mode the exchange of information between the source and the destination devices takes place without setting up a secure channel. Hence, in this mode there is a threat of hackers discovering the source of SA.

IKE PHASE 2

In IKE Phase 2, IPSec SAs are negotiated and established to create an IPSec tunnel. After IKE establishes a secure tunnel in Phase 1, the IKE Phase 2 enters the quick mode. In this mode, IPSec policy is negotiated. The keying material that is used for creating the IPSec security algorithm is also derived. Finally, IPSec SAs are established. Then, nonces are exchanged. These nonces ensure protection against replays. It is the quick mode that renegotiates an IPSec SA when the lifetime of an IPSec SA is over.

 To ensure the security of the keying material, you need to specify the Perfect Forward Secrecy (PFS) option in the IPSec policy.

DATA TRANSFER

In the data transfer phase, the IPSec tunnel that was created in the IKE Phase 2 is used to transfer the data between the IPSec peer devices. This data is transferred in the form of packets, which are encrypted and decrypted by using encryption algorithms and keys. These encryption algorithms and keys are specified in the IPSec SA.

TUNNEL TERMINATION

An IPSec SA terminates when it is deleted or when its lifetime is over. Usually, when the lifetime of an IPSec SA is about to expire, IKE renegotiates the SAs. This ensures that new SAs are established before the termination of the existing SAs. As a result, an uninterruptible data flow is maintained. Since, with the termination of IPSec SA, the keys also terminate, the renegotiation results in a new SA and new keys. However, if IPSec SAs terminate, the IPSec tunnel is terminated.

Advantages of IPSec

Some of the advantages offered by IPSec are:

♦ IPSec is a network (IP) layer technology. Encryption and authentication occurs in the TCP/IP stack, thus there is no need to modify applications.

♦ IPSec is a standards-based technology that supports interoperability between different vendors' products. It is well documented on various RFCs.

♦ IPSec protocols operate at Layer 3 of the OSI reference model and output straight IP packets. This eliminates the need for infrastructure upgrades on the part of ISPs who wish to support VPN (Virtual Private Network) technology. Hence if IPSec is implemented in end systems, upper-layer software, including applications, is not affected.

♦ It makes the communication secure, without the notice to end user. Hence the end user does not require any special training.

♦ IPSec can also provide the security for end users, if required.

Summary

In this chapter, you learned about the various PKI applications, such as SSL/TLS, S/MIME, and IPSec.

You learned that the SSL/TLS are used for secure transmission of data. The most important security features of SSL are:

◆ Authentication of servers

◆ Authentication of clients

◆ Data encryption

You also learned that SSL comprises two protocols, namely:

◆ Handshake protocol

◆ Record protocol

Then, you learned that Secure Multipurpose Internet Mail Extensions (S/MIME) protocol is one of the most widely used means of providing security to e-mail. You also learned that S/MIME version 3 is the latest version of S/MIME and provides enhancements over S/MIME version 2, such as:

◆ Mailing lists

◆ Security labels

◆ Key management flexibility

◆ Digitally signed receipts

Finally, you learned that IPSec is a set of protocols, which support secure exchange of data packets at the network layer. IPSec consists of the following three components:

◆ Authentication Header (AH)

◆ Encapsulated Security Payload (ESP)

◆ Internet Key Exchange (IKE)

IPSec operates in two modes, namely:

◆ Transport mode

◆ Tunnel mode

Chapter 8

Installing Windows 2000-Based PKI Solutions

IN THIS CHAPTER

♦ Installing a CA

♦ Issuing certificates

♦ Revoking certificates and publishing CRLs

♦ Configuring a public key group policy

♦ Renewing certificates

SO FAR, YOU HAVE LEARNED about the components of PKI, interactions between these components, and applications of PKI. In this chapter you will learn the necessary skills to implement PKI. You will learn to install Certification Authorities (CA), retrieve certificates, and install subordinate CAs. You will also learn how to revoke a certificate and publish CRLs. Next, you will learn how to automatically enroll a certificate by using a Group Policy. Finally, you will learn how to renew a revoked certificate. Let's continue using the example of the company AllSolv Inc., a software company that is based in Atlanta, to explain the steps of installing PKI solutions that we describe in this chapter.

Installing a CA

AllSolv Inc. has decided to work in a secure environment for its daily business transactions. To accomplish this, the company has opted to implement a PKI security solution.

The network of AllSolv Inc. consists of Windows 2000-based computers. As a result, AllSolv Inc. has to implement a Windows 2000 PKI. To implement a Windows 2000 PKI, let us first examine its important features. A Windows 2000 PKI has the following features:

♦ Certificate Services: You can use Certificate Services in Windows 2000 to install, manage, and work with CAs. You can also use Certificate Services to issue certificates. These Certificate Services need to be configured while installing a CA.

163

- ◆ Windows 2000 Active Directory: Windows 2000 Active Directory is used for publishing certificates and CRLs. All certificates that are issued by the CA are stored and published in the Active Directory. The Certificate Revocation List is also stored in the Active Directory.

- ◆ PKI-enabled applications: Applications such as Internet Explorer and Netscape Navigator use certificate-based security. Certificates are issued for various purposes, such as secure transmission of data by using IPSec, securing e-mail by using S/MIME, and securing Web sites by using SSL.

Let us examine the types of CAs that can be implemented in Windows 2000.

Types of CAs in Windows 2000

Windows 2000 includes the following types of CAs:

- ◆ Enterprise CA
- ◆ Standalone CA

Let us look at each of these CAs in detail.

ENTERPRISE CA

Enterprise CA is a CA that requires an active directory to issue certificates. When an active directory is installed, it automatically gets added as the Trusted Root Certificates Authorities repository for all computers and users in a domain. An Enterprise CA issues certificates for various purposes such as digital signatures, authenticating to Web server by using SSL or TLS, or secure e-mail by using S/MIME.
Enterprise CA

- ◆ Issues certificates to users and computers that are part of an organization.

- ◆ Verifies the identity of the requester.

- ◆ Can be installed only by a domain administrator.

- ◆ Issues or denies certificate requests immediately. It never sets the request status to pending.

- ◆ Can use smart cards to issue certificates for logging on to a domain.

- ◆ Uses certificate templates to define certificates that are meant for a specific purpose. Some defined templates are Administrator, Domain Controller, User, and Web Server. Every template has a security permission, which has been set in Active Directory. It helps in determining if the requester has sufficient access rights to retrieve the certificate.

STANDALONE CA

Although a standalone CA also issues certificates just like an enterprise CA, a standalone CA does not use an active directory to issue certificates. When you submit a certificate request to a standalone CA, you need to provide complete information about yourself and the type of certificate you want. This is because when you request a certificate from an enterprise CA, the CA obtains all the information from the active directory. However, since a standalone CA does not use an active directory, you need to provide all the information to the standalone CA. The features of standalone CA are the following:

♦ Issues certificates to users and computers that are not part of your organization.

♦ Does not need Active Directory services. Therefore, the requester has to supply all the information that is required for identification.

♦ Does not use certificate templates.

♦ Sets the default behavior for all certificate requests to pending, until verified by a standalone CA administrator.

♦ Requires local administrative rights for its installation.

♦ Publishes certificates into Active Directory if the domain administrator or an administrator who has the write permission to the Active Directory installs a standalone CA.

The enterprise CA or standalone CA can be established either as root CA, subordinate CA, or issuing CA. These root CAs and subordinate CAs together form a trust model where parent–child relationships are established between these CAs. The root CA is at the top most level of this hierarchy and is the most trusted CA. Its certificate is self-signed and therefore it does not need a certificate issued by some other CA. A root CA is typically used for issuing certificates to subordinate CAs. A subordinate CA is the one that has been certified by the root CA to issue certificates to users on behalf of the root CA. It can also issue certificates to other subordinates CAs. Generally, subordinate CAs issue certificates for specific uses such as authentication of smart cards, secure e-mail, or Web-based authentication.

 To learn more about the trust model in PKI, refer to Chapter 3.

Selecting a Role for the CA

While installing certificate services on a computer running Windows 2000, you are prompted to choose a role for the CA. You can select from the following options:

- Enterprise root CA
- Enterprise subordinate CA
- Standalone root CA
- Stand-alone subordinate CA

A description of these options follows.

ENTERPRISE ROOT CA

This is the top most level in the CA hierarchy. To issue a certificate, an Enterprise Root CA requires Active Directory to be configured. It signs its own CA certificate and thus it does not need to obtain a certificate from any other CA. The certificate of the Enterprise Root CA is published to the trusted root Certification Authority store of all computers running Windows 2000 Server and workstations in the domain.

ENTERPRISE SUBORDINATE CA

You can select this role for a CA if you already have an Enterprise Root CA installed. It can also issue certificates within an organization. An Enterprise Subordinate CA requires a certificate from another CA.

STANDALONE ROOT CA

It is a top-level CA in a certification hierarchy. This role should be selected if you plan to issue certificates outside your organization. A Standalone Root CA does not need to be a member of the domain and does not require Active Directory. However, this CA can use Active Directory, if it is configured.

STAND-ALONE SUBORDINATE CA

A Stand-alone subordinate CA needs to obtain its CA certificate from another CA. The CA that issues a certificate to the Stand-alone subordinate CA can either be a Standalone Root CA, an Enterprise Root CA, or an external commercial CA. Standalone CA doesn't need to be a part of the domain and does not need the presence of Active Directory.

 If setup does not detect the presence of Active Directory, the options for installing enterprise CAs are disabled.

Installing an Enterprise Root CA

An Enterprise Root CA makes use of certificate template information, user account information, and security group information that is stored in Active Directory to approve or deny certificate requests. The requirements for installing an Enterprise Root CA are:

◆ Windows 2000 Server

◆ Windows 2000 DNS installed and configured

◆ Active Directory Services installed and configured

 The account used for installing the certificate services must be a member of the Domain Administrator group.

You can install an Enterprise Root CA either when you are installing Windows 2000 Server or when the Windows 2000 Server installation is complete. When you want to install enterprise CA along with Windows 2000 installation, select Certificate Services from the optional components list that is displayed during the Windows 2000 setup. The CA setup begins only after the Windows 2000 setup has completed and you log on to the computer.

To install the Enterprise Root CA, you need to complete the Windows 2000 Server installation and perform the following steps:

1. Log on as an enterprise administrator.

2. Select Start → Settings → Control Panel. The Control Panel window appears.

3. In the Control Panel window, click Add/Remove Programs to open the Add/Remove Programs dialog box.

4. In the Add/Remove Programs dialog box, select the Add/Remove Windows Components tab to start the Windows Components wizard.

5. In the Windows Components wizard, select Certificate Services. This wizard is displayed in Figure 8-1. A message appears stating that after installing certificate services, the computer cannot be renamed and the computer cannot join or be removed from a domain. Click Yes.

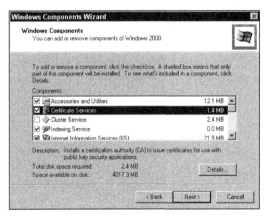

Figure 8-1: The Windows Components Wizard

6. Click Next. The wizard prompts you for the type of Certification Authority you need to install. Select Enterprise root CA since you will install an Enterprise root CA. The other types of CAs that you can install are Enterprise subordinate CA, Standalone root CA, and Standalone Subordinate CA.

7. To change the default cryptographic settings, check the Advanced option on the Certificate Authority Type screen. This screen is displayed in Figure 8-2.

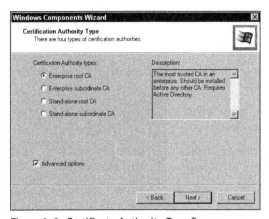

Figure 8-2: Certificate Authority Type Screen

8. Click Next. The Public and Private Key Pair screen of the wizard appears. This screen is displayed in Figure 8-3. On this screen, you can select the following options:

- Cryptographic Service Provider (CSP) that you need to use. The CSP is required for generating the public and the private key pair and for performing all the cryptographic operations for the CA.

- Key length for the public and private key pair. The longer the key the more secure it is. The recommended key length for an enterprise CA is 1024 or 2048. The "Use Existing Keys" option allows you to use previously generated keys or reuse keys from a previously installed CA.

- The hash algorithm you want the CA to use, such as MD2, MD4, MD5, and SHA-1. You can also import keys by specifying the location of a PKCS#12 file and also the password for the file.

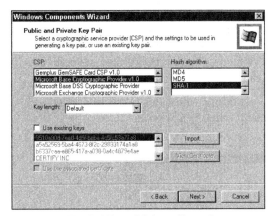

Figure 8-3: The Public and Private Key pair screen

To learn more about PKCS #12, refer to Chapter 6.

9. Retain the default settings and click Next. The CA Identifying Information screen appears. You need to specify the CA identification information on this screen. This screen is displayed in Figure 8-4. The fields that need to be specified in the identification information are given below:

- CA name: This is the name of the Certification Authority that you'll install. In addition, this CA name will also be the common name of the CA's distinguished name in Active Directory. You can designate any name to your CA such as Enterprise CA or AllSolv CA.

- Organization: The organization name that has been registered with the state or country authorities. In our case we'll use AllSolv, Inc.

- Organizational unit: The division within an organization, such as IT or Security Solutions Division.

- City: The city in which the organization is located. In this case it is Atlanta, as AllSolv Inc. company is based in Atlanta.

- State or province: The state in which the organization is located. In our case it is Georgia.

- Country: A two-character code required by the X.500 naming convention. For example, the code for the United States is US.

- E-mail: The e-mail address of the person responsible for managing the CA, such as Caadmin@allsolv.com.

- CA description: This string describes the role of the CA. For example, you can mention that the enterprise CA will be the enterprise CA for AllSolv Inc. In addition, you can also mention some specific functions performed by the CA such as issuing certificates, revoking certificates, or renewing certificates.

- Valid for: The time period for which this CA is authorized to issue certificates. The default value is two years.

Figure 8-4: CA identifying information

10. Click Next. The Data Storage Location screen appears. This screen is displayed in Figure 8-5. In this screen, you specify the storage location for the certificate database and certificate database log. By default, the location for the certificates that are issued by CA and the certificate database log is \<systemroot>\system32\certlog. You can also choose a location of your choice where you want to store the certificate database and certificate database log. To do this click the Browse button and select the appropriate location.

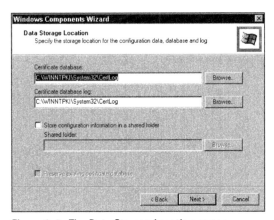

Figure 8-5: The Data Storage Location screen

 You can also specify a shared folder as the storage location, which identifies the location in which the configuration information would be stored. This shared folder contains all the information about certification authorities, which is generally published in the Active Directory. However, when an Active Directory has not been configured, you can obtain all the information about Certification Authorities from this shared folder. Furthermore, the Active Directory contains information about Certification Authorities only and does not contain information about certification services. All information about certification services is stored locally.

11. Accept the default values and click Next. If Internet Information Services (IIS) are running on the system, you will be prompted with a message to stop the IIS. Click OK to stop the IIS.

12. You'll be prompted to insert the Windows 2000 Server CD. After the required files are copied, the installation is complete.

13. The Completing the Windows Components Wizard screen appears. This screen is displayed in Figure 8-6. Click Finish to close the wizard.

After installing the Enterprise root CA, you need to verify whether the installation was successful or not. You can accomplish this by verifying the installation of the certificate services.

Figure 8-6: The Completing the Windows Components wizard screen

Verifying the Installation of Certificate Services

To verify that the installation of the certificate services was successful, you need to perform the following steps:

1. Choose Start → Run.

2. In the Run dialog box, type **cmd** and click OK.

3. The Command Prompt window opens. In this window, type **net start**. If the certificate services have started, an entry for the same appears in the list of services.

TIP If you are not able to view the complete list, type **net start |more**.

Alternatively, you can also check if certificate services are running from the Services window. To do this, select Start → Programs → Administrative Tools → Services. The status column against the certificate server displays "Running" to indicate a functional certificate server, or it will appear blank if the service is not running.

In some organizations, you might want to delegate certain responsibilities of the root CA, such as issuing or revoking certificate of the root CA. This might be required if the geographical separations between the different organizational units might be quite large for a single CA or you might want to apply different issuing standards or policies to different organizational units. For this, you can install a subordinate CA on a Windows 2000 server and delegate the responsibility of the root CA. Let us examine the procedure to install a subordinate CA.

Installing a Subordinate CA

To install a subordinate CA, you need to perform the following steps:

1. Log on as Enterprise Administrator.

2. Select Start → Settings → Control Panel. The Control Panel window appears.

3. In the Control Panel Window, click Add/Remove Programs to open the Add/Remove Programs window.

4. Select the Add/Remove Windows Components tab to start the Windows Components Wizard.

5. Select the Certificate Services option. A message appears stating that after installing certificate services, the computer cannot be renamed and the computer cannot join or be removed from a domain. Click Yes. The Windows Components screen with the Certificate Services option selected is displayed in Figure 8-7.

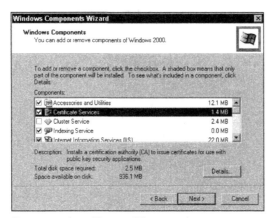

Figure 8-7: Installing certificate services

6. Click Next. The Certification Authority Type screen appears. This screen is displayed in Figure 8-8. On this screen, you specify the type of CA you need to install. Choose Stand-alone subordinate CA. The options for Enterprise Root CA and Enterprise Subordinate CA are not available because Active Directory is not installed.

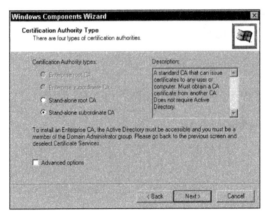

Figure 8-8: Choosing the type of CA

7. To retain the default settings, click Next. The wizard prompts you for the CA Identifying Information. The CA Identifying Information screen is displayed in Figure 8-9.

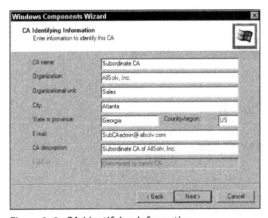

Figure 8-9: CA Identifying Information

8. Click Next. The Data Storage Location screen appears. This screen is displayed in Figure 8-10. Specify the location here. The default location for the certificate database and certificate database log is <SystemRoot>\System32\CertLog. The location for the shared folder is \\<machinename.domainname>\CertConfig. Click Next.

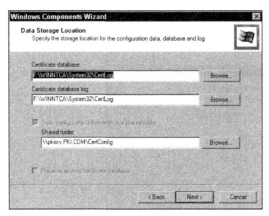

Figure 8-10: Data Storage Location

9. The CA Certificate Request screen appears. This screen is displayed in Figure 8-11. By default the option, Send the request directly to a CA already on the network, is selected. In the Computer name text box, type the computer name of the root CA and press the Tab key. The name of the parent CA appears in the Parent CA list. You can also choose the option Save the request to a file. This option will save your request to a Request file. Click Next.

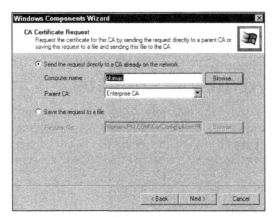

Figure 8-11: CA Certificate Request

10. The Completing the Windows Components Wizard screen appears. Click OK to stop the Internet Information Services. You'll be prompted to insert the Windows 2000 server CD. The installation is complete after the required files are copied from the CD.

11. The Completing the Windows Component Wizard dialog box appears. This dialog box is displayed in Figure 8-12. Click Finish to close the Wizard.

Figure 8-12: Completing the Windows Component Wizard

 Subordinate CA installation can be verified in the same manner as the Enterprise root CA.

After the Enterprise Root CA and the Subordinate CA have been installed, the Subordinate CA needs to retrieve the enterprise CA certificate.

Retrieving an Enterprise CA Certificate

The subordinate CA needs to retrieve the enterprise CA certificate, to add to its list of trusted CAs. The enterprise CA can then act as a trusted CA for the subordinate CA. A certificate can be retrieved through the Web. You need to perform the following steps to retrieve the enterprise CA certificate and include the certificate in the list of trusted CAs:

1. Launch your browser window.

2. In the Address bar, type `http://<enterprise CA server name>/certsrv`.

3. The Microsoft Certificate Services window appears, prompting you to select a task. This screen is displayed in Figure 8-13. Select Retrieve the CA certificate or certificate revocation list to retrieve the certificate of the enterprise CA that has just been installed. The other two options available are Request a certificate (which sends a request to the CA for issuing a certificate) and Check on a pending certificate (which provides you with the status information of the required certificate).

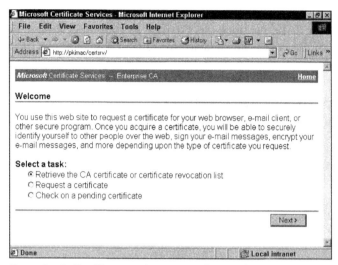

Figure 8-13: Certificate services options for certificate retrieval

4. Click Next. The next screen enables you to specify the file to download. This screen is displayed in Figure 8-14. On this screen, click the Download CA certificate link to download the enterprise CA certificate. The other two links that are available are Download CA certification path (which gives you the complete CA certification path) and Download latest certificate revocation list (which provides you with the latest CRL).

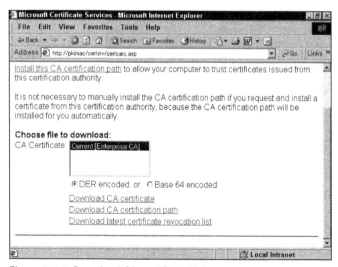

Figure 8-14: Download CA certificate link

5. The File Download dialog box appears. This dialog box is displayed in Figure 8-15. Select the Open this file from its current location option and click Next. To save the downloaded file to your computer you can choose the other option, which is Save this file to disk.

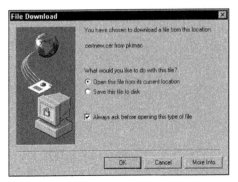

Figure 8-15: File Download dialog box

6. Click OK. A sample certificate is displayed in Figure 8-16.

Figure 8-16: A sample certificate

7. Click Install Certificate to install the CA certificate. The Certificate Import Wizard appears, which helps you to store your certificates and CRLs from your computer to a certificate store. The Certificate Import Wizard screen is displayed in Figure 8-17. Click Next.

Figure 8-17: The Certificate Import Wizard

8. The Certificate Store screen appears. This screen is displayed in Figure 8-18.
   Ensure that the option Automatically select the certificate store based on the
   type of certificate is selected. This ensures that all the certificate information
   is stored in an appropriate location on the basis of the type of certificate. To
   specify your own certificate store, you can choose the other option, which is
   Place all certificates in the following store. Click Next.

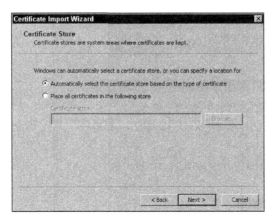

Figure 8-18: The Certificate Store screen

9. The Completing the Certificate Import Wizard screen appears. This screen
   is displayed in Figure 8-19. Click Finish.

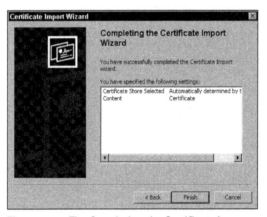

Figure 8-19: The Completing the Certificate Import
Wizard screen

10. A message box appears informing you that the import was successful.
    Click OK to close the message box.

11. On the Certification Services screen, click the Install this CA certification
    path link. This link is displayed in Figure 8-20. This will install the
    certificate path of the Enterprise Root CA.

Figure 8-20: Installing the CA Certification path link

12. A screen appears stating that that CA certificate is installed. This screen is
    displayed in Figure 8-21.

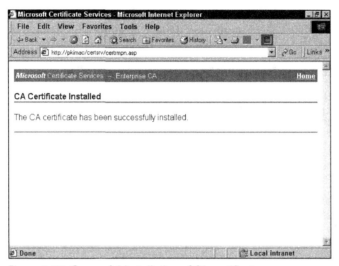

Figure 8-21: Successful installation of CA certificate

After the Enterprise Root CA has been installed, you can then start using it. However, before you start using this certificate it is always preferred that you verify whether the certificate was successfully installed or not.

Verifying Enterprise Root CA Certificate Retrieval

You can verify the retrieval of the Enterprise root CA certificate by performing the following steps:

1. Choose Start → Run.

2. Type **mmc** and click OK.

3. The Console1 – [Console Root] window appears. Choose Console → Add/Remove Snap-in.... The Standalone tab is active.

4. Click Add. The Add/Remove Snap-in dialog box appears.

5. From the Available Standalone Snap-ins, select Certificates.

6. Click Add. The Certificates snap-in dialog box appears. Select Computer account.

7. Click Next. The Select Computer dialog box appears. Local computer: (the computer on which this console is running) is selected.

8. Click Finish. Click Close.

9. In the Add/Remove snap-in dialog box, observe that Certificates [Local Computer] appears. Click OK.

10. In the left pane of the window, under Console Root, expand Certificates (local Computer). The Console 1 window is displayed in Figure 8-22.

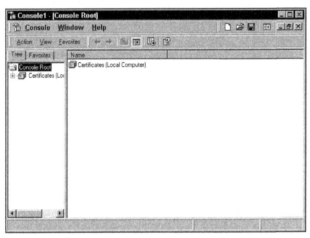

Figure 8-22: Console 1 window

11. Expand the Trusted Root Certification Authority and select Certificates.

12. In the right side pane, a list of Root CAs appears. Scroll down to view Enterprise CA. The list is displayed in Figure 8-23.

Figure 8-23: Root CAs list

13. Choose Save. To save at the default location, type Certificate as the certificate name. Click Save.

14. Close the mmc.

You have successfully installed an Enterprise root CA, a subordinate CA, and retrieved a CA certificate. Let us now look at how to issue certificates to the different entities such as users and CAs.

Issuing Certificates

On the basis of the entity that you want to authenticate, certificates can be issued to:

♦ Root CA: Root CA certificates are usually self-signed by the CAs.

♦ Subordinate CA: Subordinate CAs are issued CA certificates from a root CA.

♦ Users: User certificates are issued to users to prove their authenticity.

Let's now discuss the process of requesting a certificate.

Certificate Requests

Certificates are issued to the entities on the basis of the certificate requests that are submitted by them. A certificate request can be made in the following two ways:

♦ Using the Certificate Request Wizard, which requires an enterprise certificate authority

♦ Using certificate services Web pages through the Web

In this section, we examine how you can use Web pages to request certificates. These Web pages are stored at http://*servername*/certsrv, where *servername* is the name of the CA server. Web pages are used if a standalone CA requests a certificate. You can also request these certificates by using Web pages from an enterprise CA and make use of the additional options available with certificate Web pages, which are not available with Certificate Request Wizard. A few of these options are:

♦ Certificate template: Identifies the templates on which the certificate is based. The templates that are available are Administrator, Basic EFS, EFS recovery agent, User, Subordinate Certification Authority, and Web Server.

When you are requesting a certificate from a subordinate CA, the certificate template options are different. Some of the certification template options are Code Signing, User Signature Only, IPSec, IPSec (Offline request), Smart Card logon, Smart Card User, and Trust List Signing.

◆ Cryptographic Service Provider (CSP): You can select a CSP from the list of available CSPs.

◆ Key Size: The size of the public key appears in bits. The larger the size, the stronger the protection. For example, in case of a 32-bit long key, the number of steps required to break the cipher are about 2^{32} or 10^9. Similarly, a 40-bit key requires about 2^{40} steps to break the cipher. Today, 128-bit encryption is considered to be the safest and most reliable means of encrypting messages.

◆ Hash algorithm: Specifies the hash algorithm to be used with a certificate. You can choose from any of the specified algorithms such as MD4, MD5, or SHA1.

◆ Create a new key set or use an existing key set: Enables you to create a new key pair or keep using the existing one.

◆ Enable strong private key protection: Enables you to provide a password every time the private key is used.

◆ Mark keys as exportable: Keys can be marked as exportable and can be saved in a PKCS#12 file. This file is used in case you want to move the key pair to another machine.

◆ Use the local machine store: This option is used to generate the keys in the local machine store. It is required if the private key needs to be stored on the local server, such as in the case of a Web server.

◆ Save the request to PKCS#10 file: This option is used if you intend to save the certificate request in a file and then later submit the file to a CA for certificate generation.

Requesting and Installing a User Certificate

Let us now look at the steps to request and install a user certificate from an enterprise CA:

1. Open the Web browser window.

2. In the Web browser address bar, type `http://servername/certsrv`, where servername is the name of your enterprise CA server, and press enter.

3. Under Select a task, select the Request a certificate option. This option is displayed in Figure 8-24. The other available options are Retrieve the CA certificate or certificate revocation list (which gives you the requested CA certificate or the CRL) and Check on a pending certificate (which provides you with the status information of any requested certificate that has still not been issued).

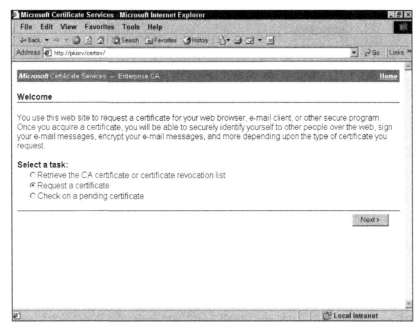

Figure 8-24: The Request for a certificate option

4. Click Next. A window appears prompting you for the type of request that you want to select. You can select User Certificate request or Advanced request. This window is displayed in Figure 8-25. Select Advanced request and click Next. If you choose the other option, that is, User Certificate request, then all the options of Advanced request will not appear. By choosing the Advanced request option, you can view all other options and request a certificate as per your requirements.

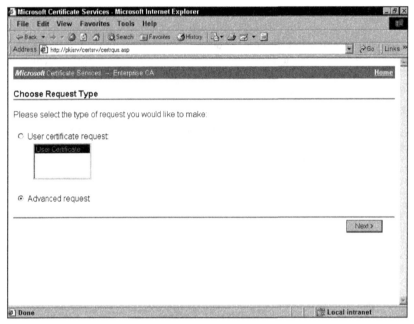

Figure 8-25: Advanced request for a certificate

5. On the Advanced Certificate Requests screen, select the Submit a certificate request to this CA using a form option. This option is displayed in
   Figure 8-26. To request a certificate for another user or a computer, you
   can choose the option Request a certificate for a smart card on behalf of
   another user using the Smart Card Enrollment Station. Click Next.

6. The Advance Certificate Request window appears. This window is
   displayed in Figure 8-27. In this screen, from the Certificate Template
   list, select User. Scroll down and check the Use local machine store
   option.

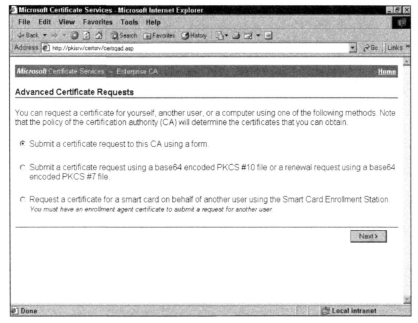

Figure 8-26: The Advanced Certificate Requests option

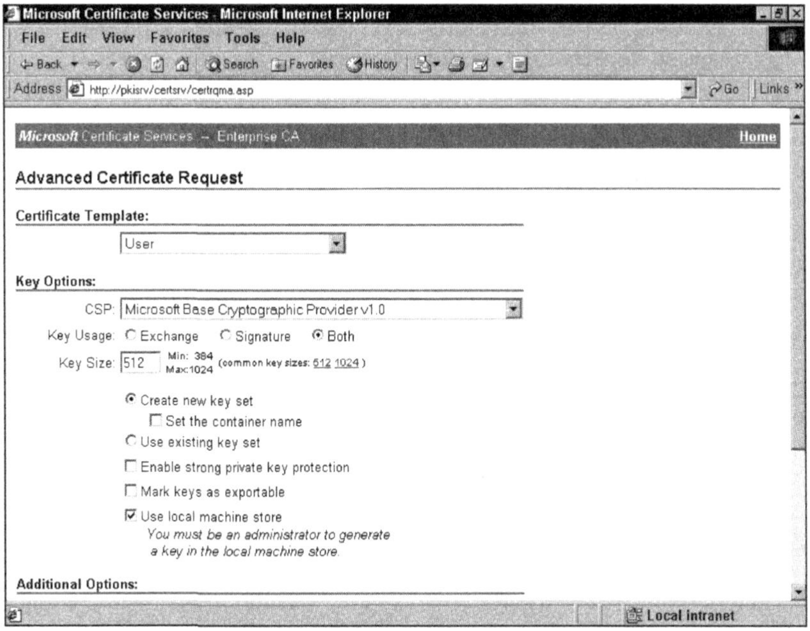

Figure 8-27: The Advance Certificate Request window

7. Click Submit. A window appears stating that the certificate has been issued. This window is displayed in Figure 8-28.

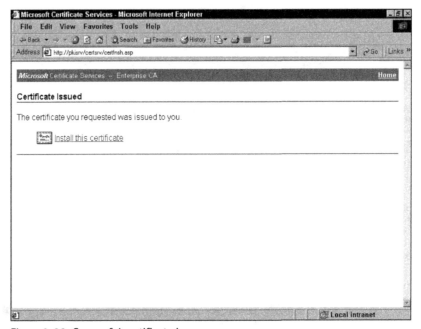

Figure 8-28: Successful certificate issuance

8. Click the Install this certificate link option. A window appears stating that the certificate you requested has been installed. This window is displayed in Figure 8-29.

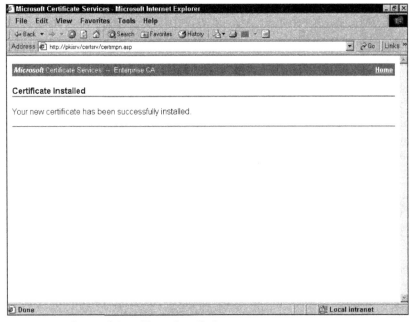

Figure 8-29: Successful certificate installation

The certificate that is issued can now be used to authenticate users. As you already know, when a certificate is issued, a new key pair must be generated for the entity to whom the certificate has been issued and who will possess the corresponding private key of the key pair. The certificate contains the public key, the subject name, expiration date of the certificate, operations to be performed by the public key, the issuer's digital signature, serial number, and encryption method of the entity to which the certificate has been issued. This private key is used by the entity to create a digital signature.

You have already learned about the process of creating digital signatures in Chapter 2.

The corresponding public key in the certificate verifies the authenticity of the digital signature. On the other hand, the authenticity of the digital certificate is verified by the issuing authority. In this way, a certificate is used to authenticate a user.

You have already learned about the complete certification process in Chapter 2.

However, while every certificate has a validity period, a certificate can also lose its authenticity before its validity period expires due to reasons such as key compromise and a change in affiliation. In such cases, you need to revoke the certificates. Let us now look at the process of revoking a certificate and publishing a CRL.

Revoking Certificates and Publishing CRLs

The reasons for revoking a certificate and the entities involved in certificate revocation have already been discussed. If the certificate has become invalid for one reason or another, it has to be revoked. Once the certificate is revoked, the revocation information is published in the form of a CRL.

For more information on certificate revocation and CRLs, refer to Chapter 5.

Revoking a Certificate

To revoke a certificate, you need to perform the following steps:

1. Choose Start → Programs → Administrative Tools → Certification Authority. The Certification Authority window appears.

2. In the left pane of the window, under Certification Authority [Local], expand Enterprise CA.

3. Select Issued Certificates. The list of issued certificates appears. This list is displayed in Figure 8-30. The right pane lists all issued certificates. The enterprise CA has issued only one certificate to the user administrator. Only one certificate appears with Request ID 2. However, if a subordinate CA has been issued a certificate, the Request ID can differ.

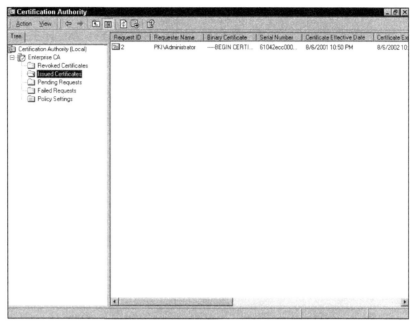

Figure 8-30: List of issued certificates

4. Right-click the certificate and select All Tasks → Revoke Certificate from the shortcut menu. The Reason Code dialog box appears. This dialog box is displayed in Figure 8-31. It prompts you to specify the reason for revoking the certificate. From the Reason code list, select Key Compromise.

Figure 8-31: The Reason code list dialog box

5. Click Yes to revoke the certificate.

6. In the right pane, you can see that the certificate you revoked no longer exists in the Issued Certificates list. This pane is displayed in Figure 8-32.

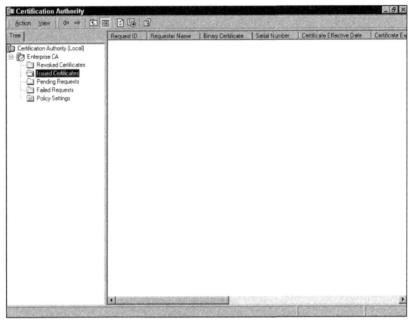

Figure 8-32: Transfer of certificate from issued to revoked certificate list

7. In the left pane, select Revoked Certificate. In the right pane, the certificate you revoked now appears in this list, as shown in Figure 8-33.

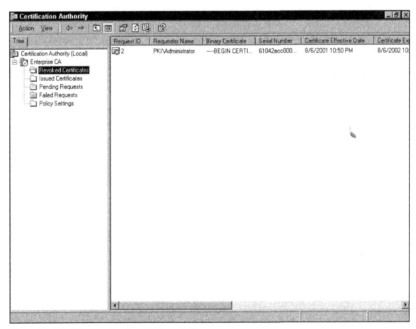

Figure 8-33: The revoked certificate list

After revoking a certificate, you need to publish the CRL. The CRL consists of a list of all the revoked certificates.

Publishing a CRL

You should publish CRLs frequently because they need to have updated information each time a certificate is revoked. To publish a CRL, you need to perform the following steps:

1. In the left pane of the Certification Authority window, right-click Revoked Certificates → All Tasks → Publish.

2. A message box appears stating that the last CRL is still valid and can be used by the clients. It asks you whether you still want to publish the new CRL?

3. Click Yes to publish the CRL.

The CRL has now been published. To confirm that the CRL has been published, you need to view it.

Viewing a Published CRL

To view a published CRL, you need to perform the following steps:

1. Select Start → Programs → Administrative Tools → Certificates. The Certificates window appears.

2. In the left pane, expand Certificates if it is not already expanded and view the entries under Certificates.

3. Under Certificates, expand Intermediate Certification Authorities.

4. Select Certificate Revocation List. In the right pane, double-click CRL to open Certificate Revocation List. The Certificate Revocation List Information is displayed in Figure 8-34. Look at the value of the Effective date field in order to confirm that this is the latest CRL you published.

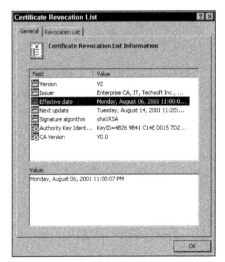

Figure 8-34: Certificate Revocation List Information

5. Select the Revocation List tab. This tab is displayed in Figure 8-35. Under Revoked certificates, you will see that the certificate that you revoked now appears.

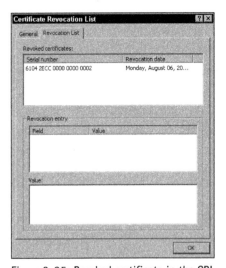

Figure 8-35: Revoked certificate in the CRL

You have examined the manual process for enrolling or requesting a certificate. You can also enroll for a certificate automatically. You can accomplish this task by using group policies. The next section examines this in detail.

Configuring a Public Key Group Policy

You can use a Group Policy to configure automatic certificate settings so that computers associated with Group Policy can enroll automatically for certificates. These automatic requests can be used for computer certificates, IPSec certificates, and Web server certificates. The automatic certificate settings can only be configured in the enterprise CA. To configure Group Policy, perform the following steps:

1. Select Start → Run.

2. Type mmc. The mmc window appears.

3. Choose Console → Add/Remove Snap-in. The Add/Remove Snap-in window appears.

4. Click Add. From the list of Available Standalone Snap-ins, select Group Policy.

5. Click Add. The Select Group Policy Object dialog box appears.

6. Click Browse. The Browse for a Group Policy Object appears.

7. Under Domains, OUs, and linked Group Policy Objects, select Default Domain Policy. Click OK.

8. Click Finish. The Default Domain Policy is added to the Add/Remove Snap-in window.

9. Click Close. Click OK.

10. In the left pane, under Console Root, expand Default Domain Policy.

11. Expand Computer Configuration → Windows Settings → Security Settings → Public Key Policies. The expanded console is displayed in Figure 8-36.

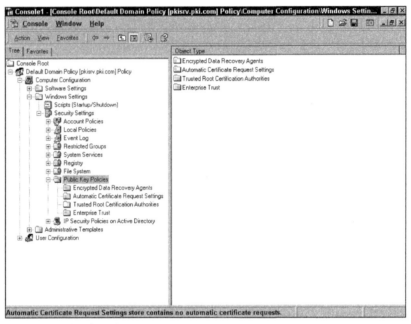

Figure 8-36: The Console root tree

12. Right-click Automatic Certificate Request Settings. Select New →
    Automatic Certificate Request. The Automatic Certificate Request Setup
    Wizard appears.

13. Click Next. Under Certificate templates, select Computer. The Certificate
    Templates list is displayed in Figure 8-37. You can also choose other types
    of certificate templates, such as Domain Controller, Enrollment Agent
    (Computer), and IPSec, depending on your requirements. Click Next.

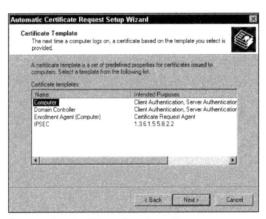

Figure 8-37: Certificate Templates list

14. Ensure that under Certification Authorities, Enterprise CA is selected. The CA list is displayed in Figure 8-38. Click Next.

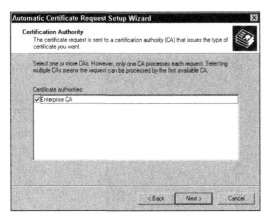

Figure 8-38: CAs list

15. Click Finish to complete.

Renewing Certificates

Every certificate that is issued has an expiration date. If the certificate has not been revoked, before the expiration date, the certificate should be renewed. Certificates can be renewed by generating a new key pair or by using the existing key pair. In this section, we will examine the steps for renewing a certificate.

Renewing a Certificate

To renew a certificate, you need to perform the following steps:

1. Choose Start → Programs → Administrative Tools → Certificates. The Certificates window appears.

2. In the left pane of the Certificates window, to view the objects under Certificates, expand Certificates if it is not already expanded.

3. Under Certificates, expand Personal and select Certificates. The right pane displays a list of certificates issued by Enterprise CA. The list of issued certificates is displayed in Figure 8-39.

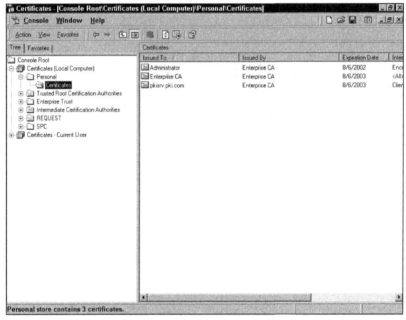

Figure 8-39: Issued certificates list

4. Under Certificates, right-click the certificate <servername.domain name> and select All Tasks → Renew Certificate with the Same Key from the shortcut menu. The Certificate Renewal Wizard appears. Click Next.

5. In the Certificate Renewal Options dialog box, ensure that the option Yes, use default values is selected. This dialog box is displayed in Figure 8-40. Click Next.

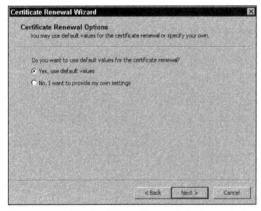

Figure 8-40: The Certificate Renewal Options window

6. Click Finish. A message box appears informing that the certificate request was successful.

7. Click OK.

After renewing a certificate, you can verify whether it was successfully renewed or not.

Verifying Certificate Renewal

To verify the renewal of a certificate, perform the following steps:

1. Under Certificates, double-click certificate <servername.domain name>. The Certificate window appears.

2. Click the Details tab to verify that the certificate contains new dates.

If the dates correspond to the dates when you renewed the certificate, it indicates that the certificate was successfully renewed.

By performing the tasks mentioned in this chapter, you can complete the implementation of PKI in AllSolv Inc. All the data transactions conducted by AllSolv Inc. can now be made over a PKI-enabled network.

Summary

In this chapter, you learned about installing CAs. You also learned about the different types of CAs in Windows 2000. These CAs are listed below:

◆ Enterprise Root CA

◆ Enterprise Subordinate CA

◆ Standalone Root CA

◆ Stand-alone subordinate CA

You learned about installing Enterprise root CA and subordinate CA. You also learned about retrieving and installing a CA certificate.

Next, you learned about issuing certificates. Certificates can be issued to:

◆ Root CAs

◆ Subordinate CAs

◆ Users

You learned about revoking a certificate and publishing a CRL. You learned that the CRL needs to be published frequently, and that you can view the latest revoked certificates in the CRLs. You also learned that Group Policies allow you to enroll for a certificate automatically. Finally, you learned how to renew a certificate that is due for expiration.

Chapter 9

Installing and Configuring Windows 2000 Certificate Server for SSL, IPSec, and S/MIME

IN THIS CHAPTER

- ◆ Installing and configuring SSL
- ◆ Installing and configuring IPSec
- ◆ Configuring S/MIME

IN THE PREVIOUS CHAPTER, you learned how to install a CA, retrieve certificates, and install subordinate CAs. You also learned how to revoke a certificate and publish CRLs. These components form the basis for implementing PKI-enabled applications, such as SSL and IPSec.

The most commonly used PKI-enabled applications are SSL, IPSec, and S/MIME. SSL uses PKI to ensure a secure communication with a Web server. On the other hand, IPSec uses PKI to implement a security solution for transmission of data over a network. In this chapter, you'll learn to install and configure SSL. You'll also learn to make a Web site SSL-enabled. Next, you'll learn to install and configure IPSec. You'll learn to create and test an IPSec policy. Finally, you'll learn to configure S/MIME. To reiterate, S/MIME is a standard that allows you to add digital signatures and encrypt your e-mail messages.

Installing and Configuring SSL

Let's consider the case of AllSolv, Inc. that we had in the previous chapter. With an increase in the traffic over the network, the security of data in transit has become a major concern at AllSolv. Therefore, AllSolv, Inc. has now decided to make its Web site SSL-enabled. To enable SSL for a Web site, the first step is to install a server certificate for SSL. The following section describes the process of installing a server certificate for SSL.

Installing a Server Certificate for SSL

SSL enables secure communication between a Web site and a client. The first step in enabling SSL for a Web site is to acquire a certificate for the Web site. This certificate is then associated with the Web site. To install a server certificate for SSL, you need to perform the following steps on the Windows 2000 server on which the server certificate for SSL will be installed:

1. Launch your Web browser. In the Address bar, type `http://<enterprise CA server name>/certsrv`. A Microsoft Certificate Services window appears. In the Select a task section, select the option Request a certificate. The Microsoft Certification Services window with the required option is displayed in Figure 9-1. Click Next.

Figure 9-1: Request a certificate option on the Welcome screen

2. A window appears prompting you to select the type of request. This window is displayed in Figure 9-2. Select the Advanced request option. This option allows you to select the type of certificate request you want to submit. In addition, you can also select the key option and additional options later on by choosing the Advanced request option. Click Next.

3. The Advanced Certificate Requests window appears. This window is displayed in Figure 9-3. In this window, select the Submit a certificate request to this CA using a form option and click Next.

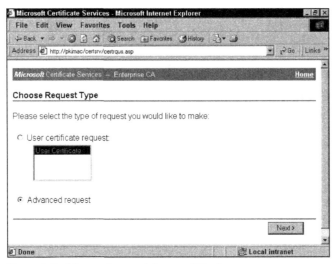

Figure 9-2: Advanced request for a certificate

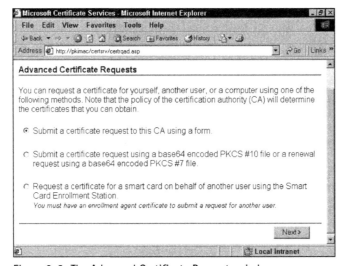

Figure 9-3: The Advanced Certificate Requests window

4. The Advanced Certificate Request window appears. This window allows you to select various options such as Certificate Temple, Key options, and some additional options as displayed in Figure 9-4. Under Certificate Template, select the Web Server option. Specify the required information. You need to give your identifying information for submitting a certificate request. Scroll down and check the Use local machine store option. You'll store the certificate information locally in your machine.

Figure 9-4: The Advanced Certificate Request window

5. Click Submit. The Certificate Issued window appears, stating that the certificate you requested was issued to you. This window is displayed in Figure 9-5.

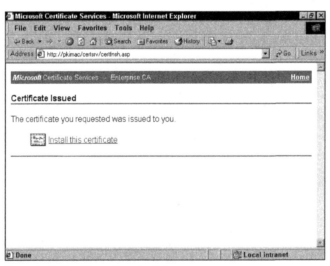

Figure 9-5: Certificate Issued window

6. Next, click on the link Install this Certificate. A window stating that the certificate has been installed appears. This window is displayed in Figure 9-6.

Figure 9-6: Successful certificate installation

7. Close the Web browser window.

After you have installed a certificate for a Web site, you need to verify that the certificate has been installed successfully.

Verifying the Installation of Server Certificates for SSL

You can verify that the Server certificate was installed successfully by using the Certificate Manager. To do so, perform the following steps:

1. Select Start → Run.

2. In the run dialog box, type **Certmgr.mmc** and click OK.

3. In the left pane of the console, under Console Root, expand Certificates (Local Computer).

4. Expand Personal and select Certificates.

5. In the right pane, ensure that the certificate you installed appears. In this case, observe that pkisrv certificate is listed in the Issued To list and Enterprise CA is listed in the Issued By list.

6. Close the Certificates console.

After the server certificate for SSL has been acquired, it has to be associated with the Web site to enable SSL communication. The next section discusses how to associate a server certificate with a Web site.

Associating the Server Certificate with the Web Site

Associating the server certificate with a Web site enables communication with clients by using SSL. To associate a server certificate with a Web site, you need to perform the following steps:

1. Choose Start → Programs → Administrative Tools → Internet Services Manager. The Internet Information Services window appears.

2. In the left pane of the window, under Internet Information Services, expand your computer. For example, in our case the computer name is pkisrv.

3. Right-click Default Web Site and select Properties. The Default Web Site dialog box appears.

4. Click the Directory Security tab. The Default Web Site dialog box with the required tab selected is displayed in Figure 9-7.

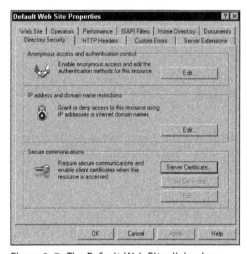

Figure 9-7: The Default Web Site dialog box

5. On this tab, in the Secure communication section, click Server Certificates, as you will install a server certificate. The Welcome to the IIS Certificate Wizard appears.

6. Click Next. In the Server Certificate screen, select the option Assign an existing certificate. You'll assign the server certificate you just installed. In this case, the certificate was issue to pkimac1 by Enterprise CA, as displayed in Figure 9-8.

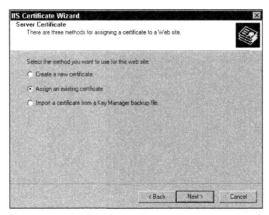

Figure 9-8: The Server Certificate screen

7. Click Next. The Available Certificates screen appears that shows the available certificates. This screen is displayed in Figure 9-9.

Figure 9-9: The Available Certificates screen

8. In the Available Certificates screen, from the Select a certificate list, select the pkisrv certificate and click Next.

9. The Certificate Summary screen appears displaying the summary for the certificate. The certificate summary consists of information such as the entity to whom the certificate was issued, the entity who issued the certificate, the expiry date of the certificate, and the intended purpose of the certificate. This screen is displayed in Figure 9-10. Click Next.

10. The Completing the Web Server Certificate wizard appears. Click Finish to complete the wizard.

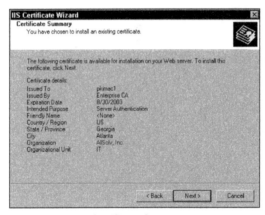

Figure 9-10: The Certificate Summary screen

After the certificate has been associated with the Web site, SSL communication has to be enabled. This is the final step in making a Web site SSL-enabled.

ENABLING SSL COMMUNICATION WITH A WEB SITE

To enable SSL communication with a Web site, you need to perform the following steps:

1. In the Default Web Site Properties window, under Secure communication, select View Certificate. Check the details of the certificate associated with the Web site. A sample certificate is shown in Figure 9-11.

Figure 9-11: A sample certificate

2. Click OK. Under Secure Communication, click Edit.

3. In the Secure Communication dialog box, check the Require secure channel (SSL) option. This option allows you to set a secure communication channel. The Secure Communications window is displayed in Figure 9-12.

Figure 9-12: The Secure Communications dialog box

4. Click OK.

5. Click Apply and click OK.

6. Restart IIS.

The certificate is associated with the default Web site. After the certificate has been associated with the Web site, clients can communicate with the Web server using SSL.

VERIFYING SSL COMMUNICATION BETWEEN THE CLIENT AND THE WEB SITE

After a client establishes a connection with an SSL-enabled Web site, it can verify that a secure connection was established. To verify that a secure SSL channel has been established, the client needs to perform the following steps:

1. Launch the Web browser. In the Address bar type, `http://<Subordinate CA server name`. A message is displayed, stating that the page must be viewed over a secure channel.

2. Now, in the address bar replace http with https. The Web page is now displayed.

Installing and Configuring IPSec

As you already know, IPSec is a set of extensions to the IP protocol family, which supports authentication, integrity, access control, and confidentiality of data packets at the network layer. IPSec provides security for data in transit. Unlike SSL, IPSec is not application-specific. You can implement IPSec on a TCP/IP host or a network device such as a router.

To learn more about IPSec, refer to Chapter 7.

For implementing IPSec, you first need to acquire a certificate for the host. IPSec uses this certificate for secure communication between the host and other IPSec-enabled hosts or devices.

To see the working of IPSec communication between two computers, you need to perform all IPSec configuration activities on two computers simultaneously.

Installing a Certificate for Implementing IPSec

To install a certificate for implementing IPSec, you need to perform the following steps:

1. Launch your Web browser. In the Address bar type, `http://<enterprise CA server name>/certsrv`. A Microsoft Certificate Services window appears.

2. In the Select a Task section, select the option Request a certificate.

3. Click Next. A window appears prompting you to choose a request type. Select the Advance request option.

4. Click Next. The Advanced Certificate Requests window appears. This window is displayed in Figure 9-13. In this window, select the Submit a certificate request to this CA using a form option.

Figure 9-13: Submitting a certificate request

5. Click Next. The Advanced Certificate Request window appears. This window is displayed in Figure 9-14. In this window, under the Certificate Template section, select Administrator. The Administrator template can be used for various purposes, such as code signing, Certificate Trust List (CTL) signing, Secure E-mail, and Client Authentication. Next, under Key Usage, select Signature and under Key Size type select 1024. A 1024-bit key size is considered as the safest. Fill in the information as displayed in the figure below. Scroll down and check the option Use local machine store. You'll store all certificate information locally in your machine.

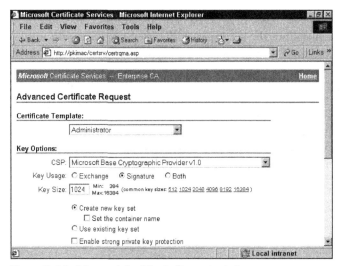

Figure 9-14: Advanced Certificate Request window

6. Click Submit. A window appears, stating that the certificate you requested was issued to you.

7. Click the Install this Certificate link. A new window appears, stating that the certificate has been installed.

8. Close the browser window.

After you have installed a certificate for implementing IPSec, you need to verify its successful installation.

VERIFYING THE INSTALLATION OF A CERTIFICATE FOR IMPLEMENTING IPSEC

You can verify that a certificate was installed correctly by using the Certificate Manager console. To do so, perform the following steps on two Windows 2000-based computers:

1. Select Start → Run.

2. In the Run dialog box, type **Certmgr.mmc** and click OK. The Certificate Manager console appears.

3. In the left pane of the console, under Console Root, expand Certificates (Local Computer).

4. Expand Personal and select Certificates.

5. In the right pane of the window, you will see that in the Issued To list, Administrator certificate is listed, and in the Issued by list, Enterprise CA is listed.

6. Close the Certificates console.

Remember that all the steps need to be performed on two Windows 2000-based computers. After installing the certificate to be used by IPSec, you need to define the policy for IP security. The IP security policy defines the security rule for IPSec. This security rule helps in managing IPSec-enabled communication between two computers. You can configure the IP Security Policy by using the IP Security Policy Snap-in. To use this snap-in you need to add it to the MMC window.

ADDING IP SECURITY POLICY SNAP-IN TO THE MMC WINDOW

The MMC window interface allows you to add and use different tools or snap-ins. To add IP Security Policy snap-in in the MMC window, you need to perform the following steps:

1. Choose Start → Run.

2. Type **MMC** and click OK.

3. In the Console menu, Click Add/Remove snap-in. The Add/Remove snap-in window appears. Ensure that the Standalone tab is selected. Click Add.

4. Scroll down and select IP Security Policy Management from the Available Standalone Snap-ins. Click Add.

5. Under Select Computer ensure that the Local Computer is selected.

6. Click Finish.

7. Click Close.

8. Click OK.

After adding the IP Security Policy snap-in in the MMC, you need to create an IPSec policy.

Creating an IP Security Policy

The IPSec policy defines the security rule for IPSec. This security rule governs the communication between two computers, the authentication method used, and the type of network to which the rule is applied. It is also used to create an IP Filter List. An IP Filter List segregates IP traffic on the basis of the source, destination, and type of IP traffic. This segregation helps administrators to find out which IP traffic will be secured.

To create an IP policy, you need to perform the following steps (all 31 of them):

1. In the left pane of the MMC console window, under Console Root (see Figure 9-15), double-click IP Security Policies on Local Machine. In the right pane, you'll see that the IP security policies appear.

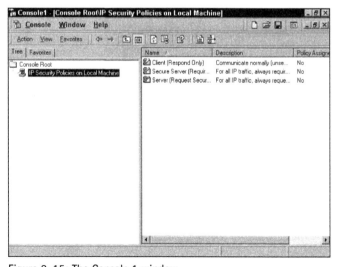

Figure 9-15: The Console 1 window

2. Right-click on the IP Security Policy on Local Machine and select the Create IP Security Policy option from the shortcut menu. The IP Security Policy Wizard appears. Click Next.

3. The wizard prompts you for the IP Security Policy name. This IP Security Policy Name screen is displayed in Figure 9-16. By default, the name of the IP security policy is New IP Security Policy. Click Next.

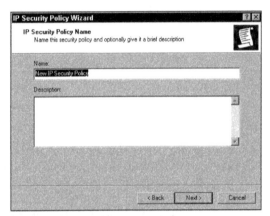

Figure 9-16: The IP Security Policy Name screen

4. In the Requests for Secure Communication screen, deselect the Activate the default response rule option. You'll specify your own response rules when a security request is made. The default rules apply only when other response rules are not specified. This screen is displayed in Figure 9-17. Click Next.

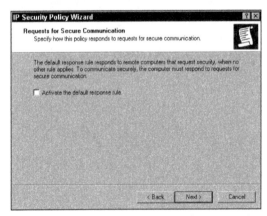

Figure 9-17: The Requests for Secure Communication screen

5. On the Completing the IP Security Policy Wizard screen, ensure that the option Edit properties option is selected. This screen is displayed in Figure 9-18. Click Finish.

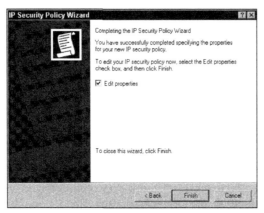

Figure 9-18: The Completing the IP Security Policy Wizard screen

6. The New IP Security Policy Properties dialog box appears. This dialog box is displayed in Figure 9-19. Ensure that the Use Add Wizard option is selected.

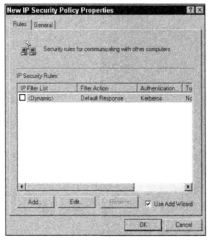

Figure 9-19: The New IP Security Policy Properties dialog box

7. In the New IP Security Policy Properties dialog box, click Add. The Security Rule Wizard appears. This first screen of this wizard is displayed in Figure 9-20. Click Next.

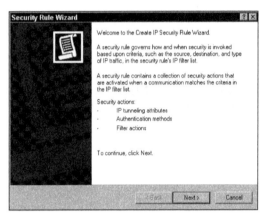

Figure 9-20: Security Rule Wizard

8. The Tunnel Endpoint screen appears. On this screen, under Specify the tunnel endpoint for the IP security rule, ensure that the option, This rule does not specify a tunnel, is selected. You'll set a security rule that does not specify a tunnel endpoint. Tunnel end-point refers to the tunneling computer that is closest to the destination of the IP destination. The Tunnel Endpoint screen is displayed in Figure 9-21. Click Next.

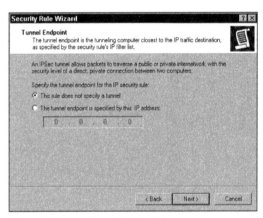

Figure 9-21: The Tunnel Endpoint screen

9. The Network Type screen appears. This screen displays the type of net-work to which you want to apply the security rule. On this screen, under Select the network type, ensure that the option All network connections is selected. This option allows you to apply security rules over all types of network connections including LAN and Remote access. The Network Type screen is displayed in Figure 9-22. Click Next.

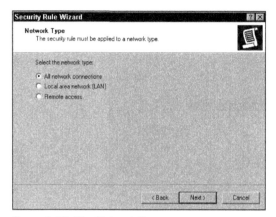

Figure 9-22: The Network Type screen

10. The Authentication Method screen appears. This screen prompts you for the initial authentication method for this security rule. Select the option Use a certificate from this Certificate Authority (CA).

11. Click the Browse button. Scroll down, and under the Issued To column, select Enterprise CA.

12. Click OK. The completed Authentication Method screen is displayed in Figure 9-23.

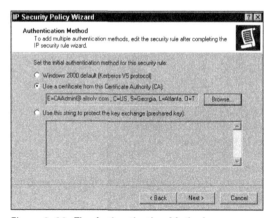

Figure 9-23: The Authentication Method screen

13. Click Next. The IP Filter List screen appears. This screen is displayed in Figure 9-24. By using IP Filter list, you can specify the protocol to be monitored between the two hosts and the action to be performed. Click Add.

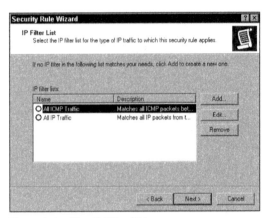

Figure 9-24: The IP Filter List screen

14. The IP Filter List dialog box appears that prompts you for the name of the IP filter list. This dialog box is displayed in Figure 9-25. Retain the default name and ensure that Use Add Wizard is checked. Click Add.

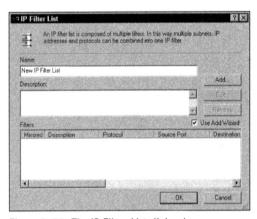

Figure 9-25: The IP Filter List dialog box

15. The IP Filter Wizard appears. The welcome screen of this wizard is displayed in Figure 9-26. Click Next.

Figure 9-26: The Welcome screen of IP Filter Wizard

16. The IP Traffic Source screen appears. In this screen, you'll specify the source of the data. On this screen, from the Source address list, ensure that the My IP Address option is selected. In this case, since you'll be sending the data, you select the source as MY IP Address. This screen is displayed in Figure 9-27. Click Next.

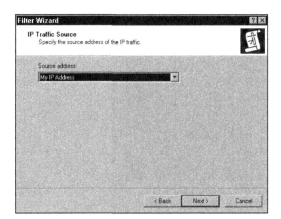

Figure 9-27: The IP Traffic Source screen

17. The IP Traffic Destination screen appears. In this screen, you'll specify the destination of the data. On this screen, from the Destination address list, select the A specific IP Address option and specify the IP address of the other computer for IP Address. In this case, specify the IP address of the other computer. The IP Traffic Destination screen is displayed in Figure 9-28. Click Next.

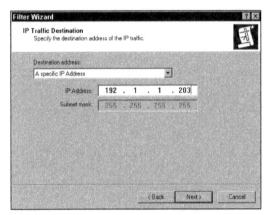

Figure 9-28: The IP Traffic Destination address

18. The IP Protocol Type screen appears. On this screen, from the Select a protocol type list, select the Any option. This screen is displayed in Figure 9-29. Click Next.

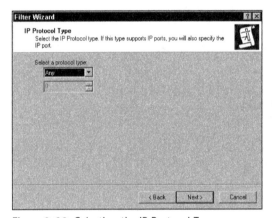

Figure 9-29: Selecting the IP Protocol Type

19. The Completing the IP Filter Wizard screen appears. On this screen, ensure that Edit properties option is unchecked and click Finish. The screen is displayed in Figure 9-30.

20. Click Close to close the IP Filter List window.

Figure 9-30: The unchecked Edit properties option

21. The Security Rule Wizard reappears. On the IP Filter List screen, from the
    IP Filter List, select the New IP Filter List option. The IP Filter List screen
    with the required option selected is displayed in Figure 9-31. Click Next.

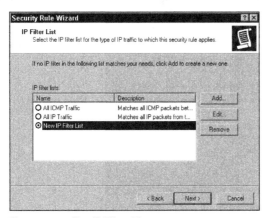

Figure 9-31: The IP Filter List screen

22. The Filter Action screen appears. On this screen, ensure that the Use
    Add Wizard option is selected. The Filter Action screen is displayed in
    Figure 9-32. Click Add.

Figure 9-32: The Filter Action screen

23. The Welcome screen of the Filter Action Wizard appears. This screen is displayed in Figure 9-33. Click Next.

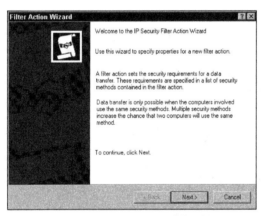

Figure 9-33: The Welcome screen of the Filter
Action Wizard

24. The Filter Action Name screen appears. On this screen, retain the default name of the filter action. The Filter Action Name screen is displayed in Figure 9-34. Click Next.

25. The Filter Action General Options screen appears. This screen allows you to define the security settings for data transmission. On this screen, ensure that the Negotiate security option is selected. The permit option does not allow any negotiation of communication. The block option simply ends all communication from an authorized computer. The Negotiation security

policy allows you to negotiate secure communication. This screen is
displayed in Figure 9-35. Click Next.

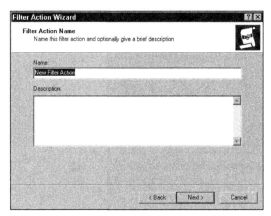

Figure 9–34: The Filter Action Name screen

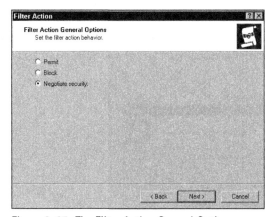

Figure 9–35: The Filter Action General Options screen

26. The Communicating with computers that do not support IPSec screen
    appears. This screen gives you an option of whether you want to commu-
    nicate with a non-IPSec enabled computer or not. It is recommended that
    you do not communicate with computers that do not support IPSec. This
    screen is displayed in Figure 9-36. In this window, ensure that the Do not
    communicate with computers that do not support IPSec option is selected.
    Click Next.

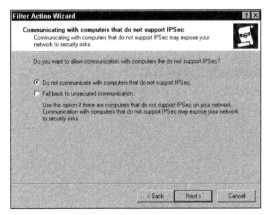

Figure 9-36: Ensuring communication only between
IPSec-enabled computers

27. On the IP Traffic Security screen, select the Medium (Authentication
   Header) option. You'll be setting medium security for your message. When
   you set a medium level security, the transmitted data remains authentic
   and unmodified. However, it does not get encrypted. However, in case
   of a high-level security, in addition to the data remaining authentic and
   unmodified, it also gets encrypted. This screen is displayed in Figure 9-37.
   Click Next.

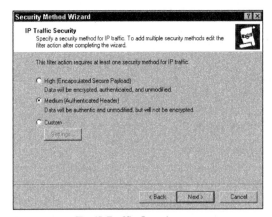

Figure 9-37: The IP Traffic Security screen

28. The Completing the IP Security Filter Action Wizard screen appears, as
   shown in Figure 9-38. On this screen, ensure that the Edit properties
   option is not checked and click Finish.

Figure 9-38: The Completing the IP Security Filter
Action Wizard screen

29. The Security Rule Wizard reappears. On the Filter Action screen, select the New Filter Action option. The Filter Action screen is displayed in Figure 9-39. Click Next.

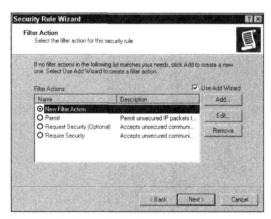

Figure 9-39: The Filter Action screen

30. The Completing the New Rule Wizard screen appears (see Figure 9-40). On this screen, ensure that the Edit properties option is unchecked and click Finish.

Figure 9-40: The Completing the New Rule Wizard screen

31. In the New IP Security Policy Properties dialog box (see Figure 9-41), click OK to complete the process of configuring IP Security Policy on both the computers.

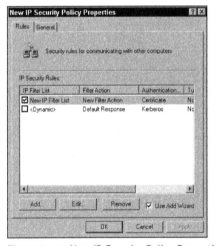

Figure 9-41: New IP Security Policy Properties dialog box

 You should confirm that you have completed all the steps described in the previous section on both computers.

After you have configured the IPSec policy, you need to verify it.

Testing the IPSec Policy

To verify that the IPSec policy was successfully installed, you need to perform the following step on both computers:

1. In the console window, right-click the New IP Security Policy and select Assign from the shortcut menu. The Console 1 Window is displayed in Figure 9-42. Notice that the value of Policy Assigned is Yes.

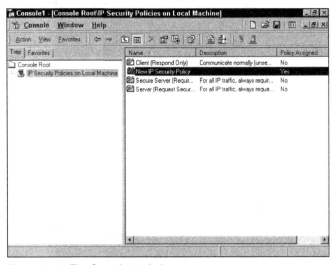

Figure 9-42: The Console 1 window

2. On one of the computers, start the IP Security Monitor tool. To do so, perform the following steps:

   1. Select Start → Run. In the Run dialog box, type **ipsecmon** and click OK.

   2. The IP Security Manager window appears. Click Options to change the default value of refresh from 15 to 1. This refreshes the IPSec monitor after every 1 second. Click OK.

   3. Minimize the IP Security Manager window.

   To check whether IPSec negotiation is working as per the defined policy, perform the following steps on either of the two computers:

1. Open the command prompt window and ping the other computer.

2. You should receive four responses of Negotiating IP Security. The responses of the other computer are displayed in Figure 9-43. This indicates that IPSec is working as per the security policy.

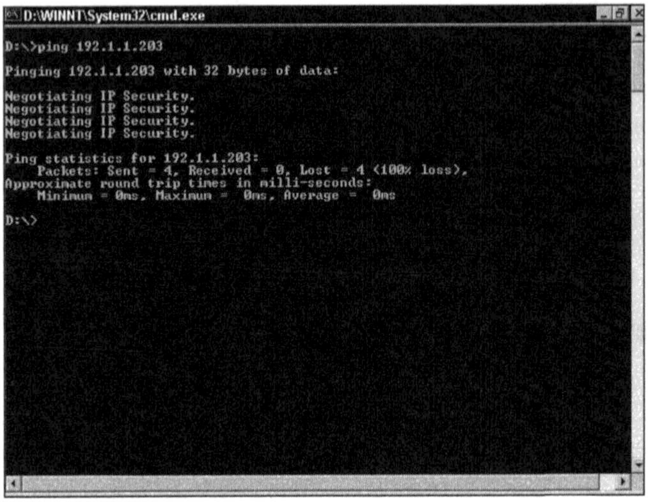

Figure 9-43: Negotiating IP Security

3. Again, ping the other computer and you will get four successful replies. These responses are displayed in Figure 9-44.

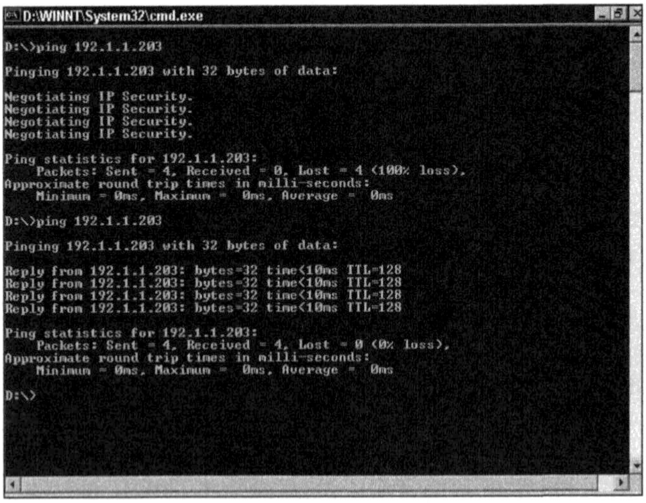

Figure 9-44: Successful pinging

4. Restore the IP Security Monitor window and observe the details, such as Security Association, Statistics on the number of Authenticated and Confidential bytes transferred.

5. You have now successfully configured and tested IPSec on the two Windows 2000 hosts.

After installing and configuring IPSec, let's now look at how you can configure S/MIME to send signed and encrypted e-mail messages.

Configuring S/MIME

You would already be aware that S/MIME allows you to digitally sign and encrypt mail. S/MIME ensures the integrity of the messages that you send and also ensures that only the intended recipient can decrypt the message. On the other hand, the recipient is also assured that the sender of the message is authentic and also that the message is genuine.

To learn more about S/MIME, refer to Chapter 7.

For S/MIME to work, each mail client should have a secure mail certificate. In addition, each mail client should also trust the root CA that is in the certification path of the mail certificate of the other mail client. In Windows 2000, secure mail certificates are published to the Active Directory in the user account of the user who has been issued a certificate.

This book assumes that you already have Microsoft Outlook installed and it is configured to send and receive mails.

In this case, we will configure Microsoft Outlook 2000 to send signed and encrypted e-mail messages by using S/MIME.

Configuring Microsoft Outlook 2000 for S/MIME

To configure Microsoft Outlook 2000 for S/MIME, you need to perform the following steps:

1. Select Start → Programs → Microsoft Outlook to start Microsoft Outlook.

2. Choose Tools → Options. The Options dialog box appears as displayed in Figure 9-45.

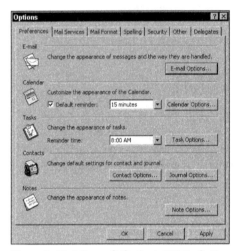

Figure 9-45: Microsoft Outlook 2000's Options dialog box

3. In the Options dialog box, click the Security tab. You can see the different security options that are available. You can choose the following options, as illustrated in Figure 9-46:

   ■ Secure e-mail: Allows you to secure your e-mail by enabling you to choose a Signing Certificate, a Hash Algorithm, an Encryption Certificate, and an Encryption Algorithm.

   ■ Secure Content: Allows you to customize the security for different attachments and links in your messages. It also allows you to customize security of zones that might contain your Web content. You can choose from different zones such as Internet, Local intranet, Trusted sites, and Restricted sites.

   ■ Digital IDs (Certificates): Allow you to either import/export a digital ID or get a Digital ID to prove your identity.

4. In the Options dialog box, under the Secure e-mail section, click the Setup Secure E-Mail button. The Change Security Settings dialog box appears, as displayed in Figure 9-47.

Figure 9-46: Security options in Microsoft Outlook 2000

Figure 9-47: Change Security Settings dialog box

5. Outlook 2000 automatically determines which certificates are issued for encrypting e-mail and digital signatures and then chooses a certificate for each one of them. You can also change the certificates that Outlook 2000 has selected. To do so, under the Certificates and Algorithms section click the Choose button in the Signing Certificate section. You can then select a certificate that you want to use for applying digital signatures on your e-mail messages, as shown in Figure 9-48.

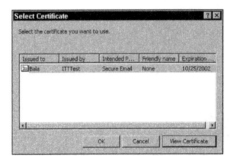

Figure 9-48: The Select Certificate dialog box

6. Similarly, to select an encryption certificate other than the one chosen by default, you can click the Choose button in the Encryption certificate section. The Select Certificate dialog box appears, as shown in Figure 9-49.

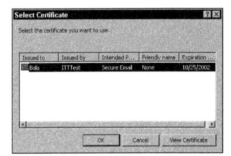

Figure 9-49: The Select Certificate dialog box

7. After you have selected a certificate for adding digital certificates to your e-mail and encrypting your e-mail, click OK to close the Change Security Settings dialog box.

8. In the Options dialog box, as displayed in Figure 9-50, check the Encrypt contents and attachments for outgoing messages option. This allows you to encrypt all e-mail messages that you send.

9. In the Options dialog box, check the Add digital signature to outgoing messages option, as displayed in Figure 9-51. This option allows you to digitally sign all e-mail messages that you send.

Figure 9-50: Enabling encryption of e-mail messages

Figure 9-51: Adding digital signatures to
outgoing messages

10. Click Apply to apply the new security settings.

11. Click OK to close the Options dialog box.

By performing all the preceding steps, you can configure Microsoft Outlook
2000 for S/MIME.

However, there might be situations when you want to encrypt or digitally sign only a few messages. To encrypt a particular message, you need to perform the following steps:

1. Start Microsoft Outlook, choose Actions → New Mail Message.

2. In the To field, enter the e-mail address of the recipient. Also enter the Subject and the message body.

3. Choose View → Options, to open the Message Options dialog box, as displayed in Figure 9-52. In this dialog box, you'll configure your Outlook 2000, to encrypt the current outgoing message.

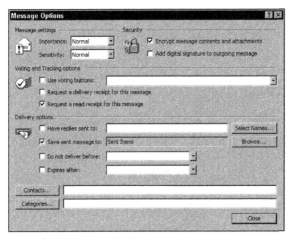

Figure 9-52: Message Options dialog box

4. Check the Encrypt message contents and attachments option. This allows you to encrypt the outgoing message.

5. Click Close.

6. Click the Send button. This sends your plaintext message in an encrypted format.

You cannot send an encrypted message to someone unless you have a copy of the intended recipient's public encryption key or encryption certificate. The simplest way by which you can obtain a copy of an encryption public key of the intended recipient is to first ask the recipient to send you a digitally signed message. You can then save a copy of the digital certificate sent with the signed message in your address book.

If you want to digitally sign only a particular message and not all messages, then you need to perform the following steps.

1. Start Microsoft Outlook, choose Actions → New Mail Message.

2. In the To field, enter the e-mail address of the recipient. Also enter the subject and the message body.

3. Choose View → Options, to open the Message Options dialog box, as displayed in Figure 9-53. In this dialog box, you'll configure your Outlook 2000 to digitally sign the current outgoing message.

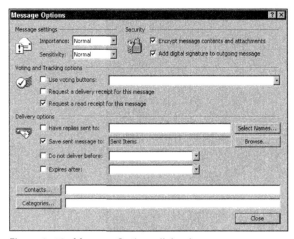

Figure 9-53: Message Options dialog box

4. Check the Add digital signature to outgoing message option. This allows you to add a digital signature to the outgoing message.

5. Click Close.

6. Click the Send button. This sends your digitally signed message.

You can now send digitally signed and encrypted e-mail messages and be assured about the integrity and authenticity of the messages.

Summary

In this chapter, you learned to implement PKI-supported applications: SSL and IPSec. You learned about requesting and installing server certificates and associating them with a Web site to enable SSL.

Then, you learned about requesting and installing a local computer certificate for IPSec. You also learned about confirming that the installation was performed successfully. You also learned about configuring IPSec policies for a secure communication between two Windows 2000-based computers.

Finally, you learned to send encrypted and digitally signed messages by using S/MIME.

Chapter 10

Understanding PGP

ONE OF THE MOST WIDELY USED APPLICATIONS of the Internet is electronic mail (e-mail). More and more people, today, rely on the e-mail system to send messages to other people either within the organization or outside the organization. Messages floating over the Internet – an open, public, and unsecure network – are susceptible to being read or changed without the knowledge of sender as well as the recipient of the message. Considering the wide usage of e-mail messages for communication, there arises the need to secure these messages. This security is provided in e-mail applications by using Pretty Good Privacy (PGP).

In this chapter, you will learn about PGP, the different operations performed in PGP, certificates supported by PGP, PGP keys, and key rings. You'll also look at the working of PGP.

Introduction to Pretty Good Privacy (PGP)

PGP is one of the well-known public key cryptosystems that provides services like authentication and confidentiality and is typically used in securing e-mail messages over the Internet. Developed in the year 1991 by Phil R. Zimmerman, PGP has gained huge popularity and is now being used by masses worldwide. PGP is one of the most powerful encryption techniques being used today as it makes use of some of the best-known cryptographic algorithms used in PKI.

Some features of PGP that have made it such a popular and powerful tool for security are:

- Flexibility to be used across a wide range of platforms
- Speed of encryption that makes it faster than most of the cryptographic systems available today
- Free availability over the Internet

The following sections discuss the working and various components of PGP. However, before moving further let us first look at some uses of PGP:

- Allows you to encrypt files on your computer in such a manner that no one else can decrypt them.
- Allows you to encrypt messages and files so that only the intended recipient can decrypt them.
- Allows you to attach a digital signature with the encrypted message or file to prove your authenticity. A digital signature establishes the identity of the sender.

Let us now discuss how PGP ensures security of not only the data stored in the computer but also of the data in transit.

Operations Performed in PGP

To ensure secure communication, the various steps or procedures performed in PGP are:

- Hashing
- Addition of a digital signature
- Compression
- Message encryption
- Radix 64-conversion
- Segmentation

Let us now look at each of these in detail.

HASHING

PGP performs hashing to convert a message into a fixed-length string. SHA-1 is the commonly used hash algorithm in PGP. SHA-1 outputs a fixed hash value of 160 bits, known as message digest, for an input string of any length. As you have already learned, a hash function is a one-way function, which means that after the original message has been hashed it cannot be derived back from the hash value.

For more information on hash functions and SHA-1, refer to Chapter 1.

DIGITAL SIGNATURE

Digital signatures prove the authenticity of the sender. PGP makes use of the private key of the sender along with a hash function to generate the digital signatures. As you have already learned, a hash function (SHA-1) is first applied to the message and a hash value of fixed length is obtained. The private key of the sender is then applied to this hash value, and finally the digital signature is created.

This digital signature can be verified at the receiving end in the following manner:

1. On receiving the message, the receiver extracts the hash value from the message.

2. After the hash value has been obtained, the receiver decrypts the value by using the sender's public key.

3. When the hash value has been decrypted, the receiver recomputes the hash value by using the original message.

4. If the original and the recomputed hash values match, the digital signature is authentic and the message has not been tampered with.

COMPRESSION

Compression is applied to reduce the size of messages so that the network bandwidth can be saved. PGP deploys a ZIP compression technique to not only reduce the size of the messages but also to provide extra security. Compression in PGP is applied after the digital signature has been verified. This ensures that, if required, users can save the uncompressed messages along with the signature for future verification purposes.

Encryption is performed on this compressed data. Compression applied before encryption enhances security, as it is more difficult for the hacker to decode the compressed ciphertext as compared to the uncompressed ciphertext.

MESSAGE ENCRYPTION

Message encryption in PGP makes use of the secret key encryption method along with public key encryption method. The message is encrypted with the secret key using the symmetric key algorithm like IDEA, Triple-DES, or CAST-128. This secret key is generated during the process of session establishment between the sender and receiver and is valid only for the given session during which it was created. This secret key is then encrypted with the public key of the recipient using the public key algorithm like RSA or Diffie-Hellman. Figure 10-1 depicts the process of encryption in PGP.

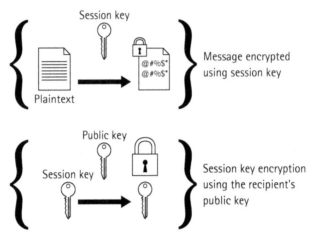

Figure 10-1: Message encryption in PGP

This encrypted secret key along with the encrypted message is then sent to the recipient. This completes the task of encryption performed at the sender-end.

RADIX 64-CONVERSION

Radix 64-conversion is applied to the encrypted blocks for compatibility between different e-mail systems. The output of PGP encryption is a stream of 8-bit octets as compared to many e-mail systems that make use of ASCII blocks. To bridge this difference and make PGP compliant with other e-mail systems, Radix 64-conversion is used. Radix 64-conversion converts a binary stream of 8 bits into ASCII blocks.

Radix 64-conversion increases the size of a message by 33%. This increase in size is compensated by the use of compression. The compression mechanism compresses the given block of data by 50 percent. Thus, the actual message is compressed around by 66 percent. The recipient first converts the Radix 64 ASCII blocks into binary stream, and then the decryption and verification processes take place. Figure 10-2 depicts the Radix 64-conversion process.

SEGMENTATION

The messages that pass through the e-mail systems on the Internet usually have an upper limit on size. If the size of a message is beyond the imposed limit, the message needs to be divided into smaller segments before being sent to the destination. PGP does this by dividing a message into small blocks, if the message is large enough.

Segmentation is performed in the end after Radix conversion and all the above processes are performed. At the recipient end, these small blocks of messages are combined into the original single, large message.

After having discussed how communication is secured in PGP, let us now see the role of certificates in PGP.

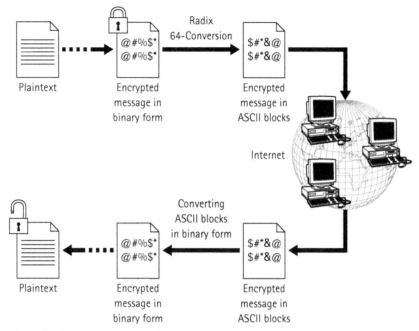

Figure 10-2: Radix 64-conversion

Certificates in PGP

As you have already learned, certificates are the proof of the identity of an entity to which the certificate has been issued. A certificate typically binds the information of the entity to its public key. Only then does a trusted authority or Certification Authority (CA) sign this bounded document. The CA signature on the certificate ensures the integrity of the information enclosed with the certificate.

Apart from this, authentication certificates are required to distribute the public key of the entities that are stored inside the certificate. Otherwise, public keys can also be distributed by using a medium such as a floppy. The floppy can be transferred to the entity that wishes to use the public key for message encryption through snail mail or courier. All these are the methods of manually distributing the public key, which might work in a small base but are not feasible enough in today's environment where communication is not limited to certain geographies.

For certificate distribution, PGP makes use of a PGP certificate server. This certificate server acts as a repository of all certificates that have been published by a CA or another authority empowered to issue certificates. Users, who want to make their certificates available to other entities, publish their certificates into a certificate server. The PGP certificate server also allows users to retrieve certificates that are contained within it.

Let's take an example where Alice wants to make her certificate available globally. For this purpose, she publishes her certificate in the certificate server. Bob wants to send a secure message to Alice, Bob retrieves Alice's certificate from the PGP certificate server, encrypts the message using Alice's public key, which is enclosed within her certificate, and sends the encrypted message to Alice. Figure 10-3 displays the certificate publishing and retrieval process.

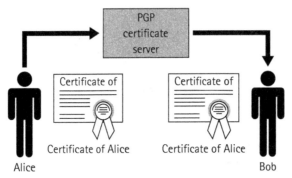

Figure 10-3: Certificate retrieval from PGP certificate server

These certificates used in PGP are based on the well-accepted format of X.509. Apart from this, PGP also has its own certificate format.

CERTIFICATE FORMATS

All the certificates used in PKI have to follow some basic template or format. This template or format defines the structure of the certificate. Moreover, the certificate format has to be recognized among different PKI implementations to support interoperability. PGP supports two formats for the certificates:

♦ X.509 certificate format

♦ PGP certificate format

The next section discusses these two certificate formats in detail.

X.509 CERTIFICATE FORMAT   You would already be aware that X.509 is a standard for certificates and is the certificate format that is widely used by different PKIs because of its high degree of interoperability. X.509 version 3 is the currently used version of X.509 certificate with the main feature of extensions that make X.509 certificate flexible enough to hold information pertaining to an organization's requirement.

For more information on X.509 certificate format, refer to Chapter 6.

PGP CERTIFICATE FORMAT   PGP, apart from supporting the X.509 format, also has its own format for certificates. This certificate format is referred to as PGP certificate format. The unique feature of a PGP certificate format is that any number of people including the certification authority and the owner can sign it. The signature of the owner, in the certificate, is called a *self-signature*. A self-signature is contained in every PGP certificate, which means that every owner will sign his/her certificate thus ensuring non-repudiation on the part of the owner.

The following information is contained inside a PGP certificate:

◆ **PGP version number:** The version of PGP that is used to create the key pair. Some versions of PGP that are available are PGP2.6ui, MacPGP2.3, Atari PGP, and Amiga. The latest version of PGP for Windows is 7.0.3, for Unix is 6.5.8, and for MS-DOS is 5.0i. The public key of this key pair is bound with the certificate.

◆ **Public key of the owner:** The public key part of the key pair, associated with the owner, is contained here. The owner keeps the corresponding private key in safe custody.

◆ **Public key algorithm identifier:** The identifier of the algorithm that is used with the public key for encryption. For example, RSA or Diffie-Hellman.

◆ **Identification information of the owner:** The identification information of the certificate owner is contained here. The identification information includes the name of the owner, his/her e-mail ID, photograph of the owner, and so on.

◆ **Digital signature of the owner:** The owner of the certificate digitally signs the certificate. These signatures, also called self-signature, are contained here.

◆ **Digital signature of the Certification Authority:** The digital signature of the certification authority that has issued the certificate is contained here.

◆ **Validity period:** A pair of dates indicating when this certificate was issued and when it is supposed to expire.

◆ **Symmetric key algorithm identifier:** Contains the identifier of the algorithm that is used with the secret key for encryption. For example, the identifier may have the values IDEA or CAST or Triple-DES.

Figure 10-4 illustrates the PGP certificate format.

As we already discussed, PGP is based on public key encryption. It uses a key pair, public key and private key, to encrypt and decrypt data. The next section discusses the role of keys in PGP and how these keys are stored in PGP.

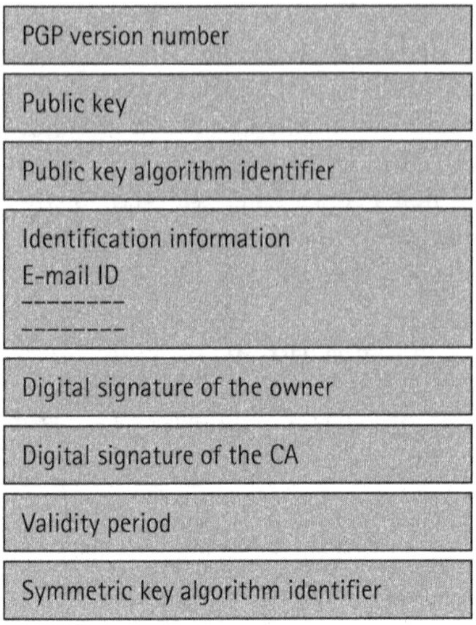

PGP version number
Public key
Public key algorithm identifier
Identification information
E-mail ID

Digital signature of the owner
Digital signature of the CA
Validity period
Symmetric key algorithm identifier

Figure 10-4: PGP certificate format

PGP Keys and Key Ring

Every cryptographic system makes use of some keys. As you have already learned, a key can be a number, word, or phrase which is used with a cryptographic algorithm to encrypt messages. To understand the use of a key, let us take a simple example of symmetric cryptography where Alice wants to send a secure message to Bob. Figure 10-5 depicts the use of a key.

Algorithm
Hello world
lfmmp xpsme
1

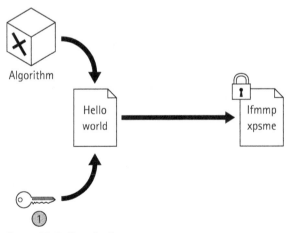

Figure 10-5: Use of a key

Alice and Bob agree upon a key by using some out-of-band mechanism. The value of this key is "1." Both Alice and Bob also agreed upon an algorithm "X." This algorithm "X" states that each character in the input string will be incremented by the value specified in the key. By using this key and algorithm an input string, "Hello world" becomes "Ifmmp xpsme." Alice sends this encrypted information to Bob who retrieves the original message by using the same key and algorithm on the encrypted message.

PGP makes use of a symmetric key and a key pair to provide cryptographic services. The symmetric key is valid only for a single session (that is when a sender sends an encrypted mail and the receiver decrypts that mail) and cannot be used afterward. The key pair comprises a public key and a private key, much the same as public key encryption. This public key is bound with the certificate and is stored inside the PGP certificate server. Any user can retrieve the certificate for making use of the public key for encryption. Private key is used to decrypt all the messages that have been encrypted using the public key.

All three keys are used by PGP for safe transfer of messages. Let us take an example to understand the role of keys in PGP. Suppose Alice wants to send an encrypted message to Bob. When Alice uses PGP to encrypt her message, a symmetric or session key is generated. This session key along with an encryption algorithm, such as SHA1, encrypts Alice's message. After Alice's message has been encrypted, the session key is then encrypted by Bob's public key. The encrypted message is then sent to Bob along with the encrypted session key. Bob, on receipt of the encrypted message and the session key, decrypts the session key by using his private key, which corresponds to the public key used for encrypting the session key. This decrypted session key is then used to decrypt the message.

Now, if Bob has got more than one key pair, how will he come to know which private key to use for message decryption? Then arises a need for some sort of key pair identification. PGP associates a key identifier or key ID with every public key. This key ID consists of the least significant 64 bit from the public key part of the key pair. There is very high probability of this key ID to be unique per user. The digital signature also includes a key ID associated with the public key. This is done so that the recipient can identify the public key to be used to verify the digital signature.

In PGP, keys are stored in their encrypted forms in files known as PGP Key Rings. Let us now discuss PGP Key Rings in detail.

PGP Key Ring

Keys are used to provide confidentiality and authentication in PGP. The keys are always stored at the user end inside the key rings. A *PGP key ring* is a collection of public keys of the entities with whom the owner intends to communicate. Every PGP user maintains two types of key rings:

◆ Private key ring

◆ Public key ring

Let's now discuss each of these key rings in detail.

PRIVATE KEY RING

Each PGP user has one or more associated public/private key pairs. A *private key ring* is required to store these key pairs. The private key is also contained inside the key ring but in an encrypted form. For encrypting a private key a passphrase is supplied by the user at the time of key generation. A hash function like SHA-1 is applied on this passphrase, and a hash value of fixed length is obtained. This hash value is used as a key along with a symmetric algorithm to encrypt the private key. Figure 10-6 displays this procedure.

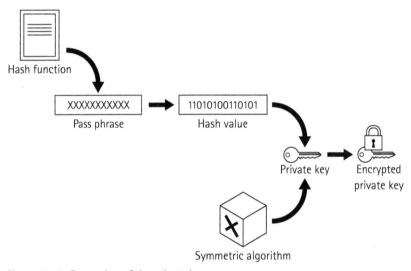

Figure 10-6: Encryption of the private key

The following fields are present in the private key ring of an entity:

◆ **Timestamp:** Date and time on which the key pair is generated.

◆ **Key ID:** It acts as public key identifier that contains 64 bits from the public key part of the key pair.

◆ **Public key:** The public key of the owner.

◆ **Private key:** The private key of the owner encrypted by using the passphrase as mentioned above.

◆ **User ID:** The identification of the owner. This field typically contains the e-mail address.

The private key ring can thus be considered as the store of all description keys. Lets now discuss about the public key ring.

PUBLIC KEY RING

The *public key ring* is a collection of the public keys of the PGP users. These public keys are either sent by the owner through e-mail or by some other means or can be retrieved from a PGP certificate server. Every key introduced in the key ring of an entity has to be signed by that entity.

The following fields are present in the public key ring of an entity:

- ◆ Timestamp: Is the date and time when this record was created.

- ◆ Key ID: Is the key identifier associated with the public key of the key pair owner.

- ◆ Public key: Public key of the entity, which owns the corresponding private key.

- ◆ Owner Trust: This field indicates the level of trust that can be put in the public key owner. This trust will help in determining whether the keys introduced by the owner of this public key can be trusted or not.

- ◆ User ID: The identification of the owner. This field typically contains the e-mail address.

- ◆ Key Legitimacy: This field indicates the level of trust that can be put in the public key for validity. This field is computed by PGP based on the value of the Signature Trust field.

- ◆ Signature(s): The signature(s) of all the entities that have signed this public key.

When a user adds a public key in his/her key ring, he/she also needs to sign it. This way, for example, if Alice has obtained Smith's public key from Bob and added it in her key ring, then in addition to Alice's signature, Smith's public key will also have Bob's signature. This is because Bob already has Smith's public key in his key ring, and Bob has signed this key.

- ◆ Signature Trust(s): This field indicates the level of trust put in the signatory by the key ring owner to certify public keys.

Until now we have discussed the various functions performed in PGP, PGP certificates, keys, and key rings. Let's now look at how PGP works.

How PGP Works

The traditional method of encryption involves only one key that is the secret key as compared to recent cryptosystems, which makes use of a key pair or two keys. In secret key cryptography, only one key is used for both encryption as well as decryption purposes. The dual key pair model, also called public key cryptography, comprises public and private keys, where the public key is used for encryption and the corresponding private key is used for decryption. PGP deploys both these techniques for securing messages.

The working of PGP revolves around two core services of PKI, which include:

◆ Authentication

◆ Confidentiality or integrity

 PGP provides authentication by using digital signatures.

Authentication

Authentication is the primary purpose of any PKI implementation including PGP. Digital signature provides authentication of the sender. Let's take an example to look at how digital signatures works.

Alice wants to send a secure message to Bob. First she needs to establish the identity of Bob. For this reason, Bob creates a digital signature by using his private key and sends it to Alice. Alice can verify Bob's signature by using Bob's public key as stated in the following steps:

1. Bob creates a message and applies a hash algorithm like SHA-1 onto it, which results in a fixed size of hash value.

2. Bob applies his private key on the hash value and the digital signature is created.

3. Bob then sends this digital signature along with the message to Alice.

Figure 10-7 illustrates message hashing and signing.

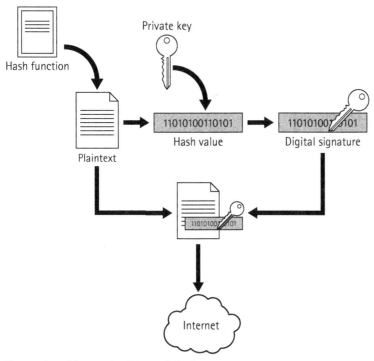

Figure 10-7: Message hashing and signing

The following steps list the tasks performed by Alice when she receives the encrypted message from Bob:

1. Alice, on receipt of the digital signature and message, retrieves the fixed-size hash value by applying Bob's public key on the digital signature.

2. Alice generates another hash value by applying the same hash function on the message.

3. Finally, Alice compares the two hash values. If the two hash values match, it means the corresponding private key of the key pair is in possession of Bob and hence Bob's authentication.

Figure 10-8 illustrates signature validation process.

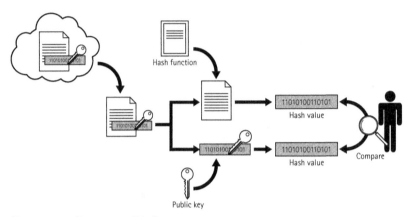

Figure 10-8: Signature validation

The signatures are generally attached to the message and passed to the verifier (or the recipient). But signatures can also be sent separately to the verifying entity without having to attach them to a message. This can be a requirement in a situation when a document is to be signed by more than one entity. Let us assume that there is a legal document that needs to be signed by more than one person. In such a case, the signature of every person must be sent separately.

After authentication PGP needs to provide integrity or confidentiality of the message.

Confidentiality

Confidentiality is another basic service provided by PGP. Confidentiality is achieved in PGP by encrypting the messages before transit, by combining the technique of symmetric and asymmetric cryptography. To understand the process, let us continue with the previous example where Alice had already verified Bob's signature.

1. Alice creates a random session key and encrypts the message using this session key.

2. Alice encrypts the session key using Bob's public key.

3. Alice then attaches the encrypted session key with the encrypted message and sends it to Bob.

4. Bob decrypts the session key using his private key.

5. Finally, Bob decrypts the message using the session key.

Figure 10-9 illustrates steps of decrypting a message.

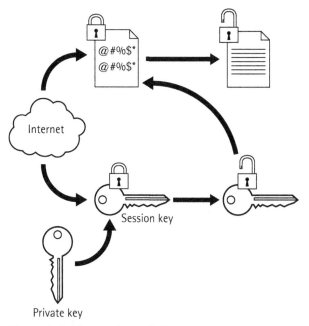

Figure 10-9: Message decryption

After having discussed how PGP works, let us now discuss one of the most unique and widely used features of PGP, Web of Trust.

Web of Trust

You have already learned about the different trust models of PKI in Chapter 3. You also learned that CAs play a pivotal role to establish trust in PKI. All PKI users rely upon the CAs to trust each other. However, PGP is unique in the sense that it relies to a great extent on users for establishing trust in a PKI environment. In PGP, any PGP user can sign the public key and thus can act as a CA. The user who signs the public key is referred to as an introducer. An introducer can be compared to a CA in an X.509 environment. In PGP, "meta" introducer is equivalent to a root CA and "trusted" introducer is equivalent to a subordinate CA.

Every introducer can define another user as an introducer to sign the keys of other users. Let's take the example where Bob wants to make Alice an introducer. Suppose Alice's key is present in Bob's key ring. Bob validates Alice's key and signs it with his public key. Alice can then use her validated key to sign the keys of other users and becomes a CA. When Alice signs the key of some other user, say, Charlie, then Charlie's key appears as valid on Bob's certificate. As this process of signing and validating the public key certificates continues, it establishes a Web of Trust. In this Web of Trust every user can sign the certificate of the other user. The relying party trusts the introducer through personal knowledge. However, the introducer is trusted only to verify whether or not the user who is named in the certificate possesses the secret key corresponding to the public key in the certificate. Bob first makes Alice's key a valid key so that Alice can further sign the keys of other users.

The public key ring of every user includes information that indicates:

◆ The validity of a particular key

◆ The level of trust that can be placed on the key so that the owner of the key can validate other keys

According to PGP, the trust in your own key pair, known as implicit trust, is the highest level of trust that you can put in a key. PGP assumes that if you possess the private key, then you should also trust all the actions performed by the corresponding public key. Hence, in PGP all the keys that are signed by your key pair's public key are valid.

In a PGP environment, you can assign three levels of trust to the public key of the other user. These are:

◆ **Complete Trust:** When you assign complete trust to the owner of the key, you fully trust that user to sign and validate the public keys of other users.

◆ **Marginal Trust:** When you assign marginal trust, this means you only partially trust that user to validate the public keys of other users.

◆ **Notrust:** This means that you do not trust the user to validate the public keys of other users.

On the basis of the level of trust assigned, there are three types of key validity. These are:

◆ **Valid:** A key is considered valid only if at least one completely trusted key or two marginally trusted keys sign it.

◆ **Marginally Valid:** For a marginally valid key to be valid, it needs to be signed by least two keys with marginal trust.

◆ **Invalid:** All certificates that are signed with this key are ignored.

Summary

In this chapter, you learned about PGP. You learned that PGP is one of the most commonly implemented public key cryptosystems that provides services like authentication and confidentiality. PGP is typically used in securing e-mail messages over the Internet. Developed in the year 1991 by Phil R. Zimmerman, PGP has gained huge popularity and is now being used by masses worldwide because of the ease of use and strong e-mail security base that it offers. Then, you learned about different operations performed in PGP transactions, namely:

◆ Hashing

◆ Digital signature

◆ Compression

◆ Message encryption

◆ Radix 64-conversion

◆ Segmentation

Next, you learned about the two certificate formats supported by PGP. These formats include the X.509 format and PGP certificate format. You also learned about PGP keys and key rings. The two types of key rings are:

◆ Public key rings

◆ Private key rings

You looked at the working of PGP and how it provides authentication and confidentiality. Finally, you learned about one of the most unique aspects of PGP, that is, Web of Trust.

Chapter 11

Planning for PKI Deployment

IN THIS CHAPTER

◆ Evaluating PKI solutions

◆ Operational requirements for PKI

IN PREVIOUS CHAPTERS, you learned about the concepts and implementation of PKI. To ensure that you implement a feasible PKI solution that meets your requirements, you need to evaluate the solution first. However, there are no defined rules for implementing PKI because different vendors provide these solutions.

In addition to evaluating PKI solutions, you also need to consider the operational requirements for PKI. These operational requirements can be measured in terms of hardware requirements, client-side PKI components, online/offline availability, and key compromise. This chapter gives you an insight into evaluating PKI solutions. This chapter also explains the operational requirements for PKI. In addition, it provides a brief background to the legal framework that governs PKI.

Evaluating PKI Solutions

Security needs of companies depend on their areas of operation, business processes, and demographic conditions. To meet the security needs, a company can select from a number of available products and services. Before implementing a solution, a company needs to evaluate it.

Although PKI is still in its infancy, it is fast gaining ground as a complete security solution for companies. Therefore, evaluating PKI solutions is important, more so when the number of vendors offering PKI is increasing by the day. The following criteria can be considered as a baseline for evaluating a PKI solution:

◆ Interoperability and compatibility

◆ Ease of deployment and usability

◆ Flexibility

- ◆ CA security

- ◆ Scalability and adaptability

Let us now discuss each one of these parameters in detail.

Interoperability and Compatibility

With new technological advancements taking place in PKI every day, the design of PKI should be such that it is interoperable and compatible with the latest devices and applications. Additionally, it should be compatible with the products and services offered by other PKI vendors.

A PKI solution should be built on open standards and should blend with the existing and planned IT infrastructure of a company. While purchasing a PKI solution, a company should ensure that the product is fully compatible and interoperable with its existing infrastructure.

The interoperability of a PKI solution can be evaluated on the basis of the following factors:

- ◆ PKI standards

- ◆ Products from multiple vendors

Let us now look at these factors in detail.

PKI STANDARDS

The PKI product that you are considering should support PKI standards. Most PKI standards are open and free from any proprietary dependency. The open standards for PKI result in the interoperability of PKI across a wide range of platforms and devices. Some PKI standards that are most commonly implemented are:

- ◆ PKIX

- ◆ X.509 Version 3

- ◆ PKCS #10

- ◆ PKCS #7

- ◆ S/MIME

PKI standards not only allow interoperability between multiple PKIs but also allow multiple applications to interface with a single PKI implementation.

PRODUCTS FROM MULTIPLE VENDORS

A PKI solution should be able to operate on any device or application, independent of its vendor. An organization needs to communicate with other organizations that might have different hardware and software. Therefore, the PKI solution should be such that it allows a seamless communication between companies.

Interoperability in PKI can be segregated into the following three categories:

♦ Interoperability between applications

♦ Interoperability between components

♦ Interoperability between enterprises

Let us now discuss each of these in detail.

INTEROPERABILITY BETWEEN APPLICATIONS

Different applications should be able to interoperate with one another, irrespective of the vendor of the application. For example, two different e-mail applications that support S/MIME should interoperate with each other, regardless of who supplies the application or the supporting software. In a PKI environment, application interoperability assumes larger proportions due to an ever-increasing number of vendors offering PKI solutions. You need to keep into mind the following considerations for developing an application interoperability environment for PKI:

♦ Users should be able to access their private credentials irrespective of the storage of these credentials. For example, some of the common methods of storing credentials are smart cards, token cards, and software. Now different users might adopt different methods of storing their credentials. At times, information stored at one place might need to be accessed from some other application or method. A PKI application should allow users to have access to their credentials irrespective of the application that stores their credentials. It should not restrict or impose a user to choose only a particular application or method. The OpenCard Framework provides smart card users an interoperable and portable environment for using their smart cards. You can use smart cards in diverse fields such as banks, telecommunications, travel, and government. The OpenCard framework provides a common interface for both the smart card application and the smart card reader.

♦ There should be compatibility between various file and message formats. In addition, the key sizes and algorithms should also be compatible between different applications. You have already learned about the certificate request syntax standard, PKCS#10 and Cryptographic Message Syntax Standard, PKCS#7. These standards are applicable to all applications irrespective of the vendors or platform. Hence, next time when you are requesting for a certificate or sending a cryptographic message, by simply following these standards you can put aside the worries of vendor or application compatibility and interoperability.

♦ To enable communication between different applications, the communication protocols that are used for exchanging information should be compatible. One such communication protocol is Simple Certificate Enrollment Protocol (SCEP). SCEP can communicate with various network devices in a secure and scalable environment.

To learn more about Simple Certificate Enrollment Protocol (SCEP), refer to Chapter 6.

Another important aspect of PKI interoperability is the interoperability between the different components of PKI.

INTEROPERABILITY BETWEEN COMPONENTS

As you already know, PKI consists of a number of components, which function together to deliver one complete PKI solution. Each of these components has a defined role to play in a PKI deployment. Hence, interoperability between these components is quite relevant, as a failure in communication with any one component can lead to a disruption in the working of PKI.

You need to keep in mind the following considerations for developing a component interoperability environment for PKI:

◆ There should be common protocols and message formats to enable communication between the different components such as CAs, RAs, and Clients. For example, Public Key Infrastructure X.509 standard Certificate Management Protocol (PKIX-CMP) and Public Key Infrastructure X.509 standard Certificate Request Message Format (PKIX-CRMF) are two standards that are implemented to ensure interoperability.

Entrust Technologies has used PKIX-CMP to demonstrate interoperability with Baltimore Technologies and IBM.

◆ Common mechanisms for certificate revocation mechanism should be supported, such as Online Certificate Status Protocol (OCSP) and Certificate Revocation List Distribution Points (CRLDP). RSA and ValiCert, Inc. have decided to launch a joint effort for ensuring interoperability between the numerous OSCP-enabled applications.

For more information on OSCP, refer to Chapter 5.

♦ Common authentication methods and algorithms should be implemented. In addition, there should be standardized methods for securing data between the different components. For example, implementing S/MIME is one such method. S/MIME, as you already know, not only offers security to messages but it also offers complete interoperability between different S/MIME-enabled applications. You can use S/MIME in any electronic mail environment, and it is not limited only to the Internet.

After having discussed application and component interoperability, let us now look at enterprise interoperability, which is the most complex of the three.

INTEROPERABILITY BETWEEN ENTERPRISES

Interoperability between enterprises involves many issues as compared to the application or component interoperability. In addition to providing solutions to technology-related issues, it requires having answers to solve policy-related issues. The following issues needs to be given due attention for enabling interoperability between enterprises:

♦ Information about the public key in one domain should be available for other domains in order to enable users of domains to communicate and authenticate each other. For example, Alice, a user of the AllSolv domain, is transferred to TotalSolv, Inc., a partner of AllSolv, Inc. Now Alice becomes an authenticated user of the TotalSolv domain. However, her assignment requires her to use information from both the domains. In such a case she should be able to use the public key information of the AllSolv domain while she is a member of the TotalSolv domain.

♦ There should be some common policies that are followed by the enterprises. In addition, each enterprise should agree to abide by a certain set of policies that guides its certification process. For example, a certificate policy can define the use of certificates, that is, for what purpose and under what conditions is a particular certificate valid.

 For more information on Certificate policy, refer to Chapter 4.

♦ The most important aspect of enterprise interoperability is support for CA-CA cross-certification. You can implement CA-CA cross-certification by using PKIX-CMP and other PKCS standards such as PKCS#7 and PKCS#10. For example, IBM generated its certificate requests by using PKIX-CMP. These certificate requests were processed by the Entrust/PKI to issue end-user certificates.

After having discussed interoperability in PKI, let us now discuss how ease of deployment and usability affect the deployment of PKI in an organization.

Ease of Deployment and Usability

The deployment of PKI should be such that any employee of an organization can use it. It should not be so complicated such that only the technical staff can use it. Although PKI is built upon complex mechanisms consisting of digital signatures, cryptographic algorithms, and cryptographic keys, its deployment should support a user-friendly graphical user interface.

Another crucial aspect of using PKI is its management. The management of PKI should be based on an organization's security policy. It should be such that the roles of the CAs, RAs, and certificate users are clearly defined and understood. Management of PKI should also take into account the cost implications. A number of factors that contribute to the cost for managing PKI are maintenance, training, and integrating the PKI solution with the existing infrastructure. You might also incur additional costs in terms of system configuration and enabling the opportunity for future growth.

On comparing these additional costs with the initial implementation costs, the additional costs outweigh the implementation costs. Therefore, the additional cost factor also needs to be kept in mind while evaluating a PKI solution. For example, suppose an organization has many branches and has to authenticate these branches by issuing certificates. Now, for an organization with a 25,000-strong user base, the estimated total cost of ownership, over a period of three years, for the initial investment would be anywhere between $180,000 to $400,00, with an additional cost of $500,000 to $800, 000 for maintenance and support. An organization with a user base of 5,000 would incur similar costs. Over the same period of time, the initial cost would be anywhere between $80,000 to $170,000; additional support and maintenance costs would be between $280,000 to $410,000.

PKI supports various applications, such as VPNs, messaging, and e-commerce applications. The users of PKI should be able to work with these applications without spending much effort and cost.

Flexibility

The PKI solution that you select should be customizable to meet user requirements. It should not be rigid and should have scope for changes suggested by the user. As you already know, there are multiple vendors of PKI. One such vendor for PKI is Entrust, Inc. Some flexibility features that are delivered by Entrust/PKI are the following:

♦ The Entrust/PKI's CA can issue digital IDs to any device or application that supports the X.509 certificate standard.

♦ It offers more flexibility in usage of databases by offering additional support for Oracle 8.1.6 on a Solaris Operating System.

- ◆ Entrust/PKI can now sign certificates by using the elliptic curve algorithm, an attractive choice for certain mobile applications.

- ◆ It offers support for an unlimited number of RAs per CA.

- ◆ In addition, it offers support for the real functions required to maintain a secure infrastructure, such as key backup, key recovery, updating information about your users (and other registered devices), change DN, change CA, automatic certificate update, and certificate revocation.

 You can find more information about Entrust/PKI on the Web at http://archive.entrust.com/entrust/ra.htm

CA Security

The CA is the backbone of all PKI operations. All the important functions of PKI are either carried out by the CA or are facilitated by it. PKI needs to provide a maximum level of security to CA because any breach in the security of the CA can lead to a complete breakdown of the PKI system. PKI can implement the following security measures to secure the CA:

- ◆ **Limit access to CA:** PKI should limit access to the CA by implementing stronger authentication methods, such as smart cards. The certificate management process should be defined so that the RA (Registration Authority) processes the certificate requests.

- ◆ **Secure the CA's private key:** The private key of the CA should be placed in a highly secure location. It should be protected from any unauthorized access.

- ◆ **Digitally sign all certificate requests:** Digital signing of certificate requests would not only ensure that fake certificates are not published but also establish the authenticity of certificates.

- ◆ **Verify CAs:** The identity of the CA should be verified by an external entity.

PKI should also provide the same level of security to RAs as it provides to CAs. This is because RAs also perform functions that are quite similar to CAs and therefore their security is also equally important.

In addition to providing security, PKI systems should also have adequate key backup mechanisms to ensure that there is no loss of data in case a user loses a key.

Scalability and Adaptability

As the business environment changes, so do the organization's needs, policies, and infrastructure. In today's dynamic environment, a PKI solution should be scalable enough to answer all existing and planned requirements. The PKI solution should be able to scale down to the lowest level for meeting the organization's needs. For example, when PKI is implemented initially it caters to only the existing setup and infrastructure, but as the organization grows, PKI should adapt to the growth and support all new devices and applications added to the organization.

With the growth of an organization, the PKI solution implemented by the organization should also grow in its capability. For example, with the increase in the number of employees in an organization, the number of certificates issued or revoked also increases. Therefore, a PKI solution should have provisions for addition of more CAs to manage the increased number of certificates. Also, new services and new types of certificates might be added with the increase in the scope of business and the PKI system. To accommodate these new services and certificates, your PKI system should also be resilient.

In addition, as an organization grows it ventures into newer areas for expanding its business. One such new area of growth potential is mobile Internet. According to Jupiter Communications, November 1999 report, "*The number of users of browser-enabled mobile phones will soar from 1.1 million this year to 79.4 million in 2003, whereas Internet-capable PDA users will only increase from 5.2 million to 12 million in the same period of time.*" However, the security threats in case of mobile Internet or wireless communication are much greater than those of the normal Internet or the wired communication. One reason for security threat to wireless communication is its architecture. The architecture of the Internet access through Wireless Application Protocol (WAP) comprises three tiers, namely:

- ◆ WAP Server
- ◆ WAP Gateway
- ◆ Device for mobile access

On the other hand, when you access the Web through your computer, only two tiers are involved, which are:

- ◆ Web Server
- ◆ Computer

The presence of an extra third layer in wireless communication leaves an additional layer open for security breaches. In this situation, one possible solution that an organization can look for is Wireless PKI (WPKI). WPKI allows organizations engaged in wireless communication to operate in a secure and trusted environment. Organizations such a Baltimore Technologies have already started working with

WAP forum to develop standards and protocols to ensure a trusted environment where wireless communication can boom. While implementing a particular PKI solution for wireless communication, an organization needs to ensure that the solution offers complete scalability, compatibility, and security.

Operational Requirements for PKI

In this section, we will discuss the operational requirements for implementing PKI. These requirements can be measured on the following parameters:

- Hardware requirements
- Client-side PKI components
- Online and offline availability
- Key compromise

These requirements are discussed in detail in this section.

Hardware Requirements

Hardware requirements differ for various PKI implementations. The CA hardware requirements are greater than the end entity or client-side requirements. This is because all the activities performed in a PKI operation are centered around a CA. A CA binds all PKI components. However, PKI implementation for the end entity or client might not involve too much processing and can be implemented on comparatively low-end machines.

While implementing PKI at the client-side, adequate care should be taken, as the client machines can be prone to hackers and worm attacks. To protect the private key of a client against these attacks, the key should be stored in a safe location. Additional components and safety mechanisms, such as smart cards, can be used to store the client's private key. This can help in recovering the private key in case the computer storing the private key becomes unusable.

In addition to smart cards certain biometric devices, such as retina scanners, can also be deployed to enable powerful authentication. All activities performed to strengthen security result in additional costs. Also, as more complex hardware is deployed, there is a greater need for technical expertise to operate it. This might affect the usability, as everyone may not find these tasks easy to perform. This also affects CPU utilizations. For example, DES can encrypt 1160 Kbytes/sec on a P100 and 2467 Kbytes/sec on a P6/200. When 3DES is used, on a P100 the encryption gets reduced to 410 Kbytes/sec and 940 Kbytes/sec on a P6/200. In addition, when SSL is used it might result in a performance degradation of about 40 to –50 percent, and for initiating a 1024-bit key process it requires about 3 CPU seconds per user.

Client-Side PKI Components

The services offered by PKI can be used across a wide range of applications ranging from operating systems and client applications to libraries and protocols. Applications require various services to ensure security. These services include authentication, encryption, non-repudiation, and data integrity. The PKI security system should therefore cater to all these security needs.

However, the present-day software applications may not provide all the features necessary for working with PKI. These features are verifying revocation, managing key and certificate life cycles, and implementing certificate policies while validating entities. These limitations have created a need for client-side PKI components.

The client-side PKI components add to the scalability and flexibility of PKI. For example, if all the security functions of PKI are incorporated in one operating system or application, the scope of these functions gets limited to that operating system or application. Hence, PKI loses its scalability and multi-platform support. To restore this scalability and multi-platform support, you can embed the security functions into client-side PKI components. One such example of the PKI-client-side component is a smart card. A smart card allows users to authenticate themselves by using a PIN. Smart cards have today emerged as vital authentication tools as they offer security, flexibility, and confidentiality.

To quote the United States federal government: "The government's goal is to adopt an interoperable multi-application smartcard that will support a wide range of governmentwide and agency-specific services. This goal sets the target for every federal employee to carry a smart card that can be used for multiple purposes — travel, small purchases, identification, network and building access, and other financial and administrative purposes — by the year 2001."

 For more information on smart card implementation, refer to the Web at `http://egov.gov/committee_docs/scards.htm`.

In addition to scalability and flexibility features, client-side PKI components also provide better management and administration. For example, compare a client-side PKI component with a third-party client application. If you need to update the client-side architecture, it is easier to update one software component and notify the users about this update. But if you have third-party client applications, you need to incorporate the architectural update in all the applications.

After discussing client-side PKI requirements, let us now discuss another parameter for measuring operational requirements for PKI, which is availability of online and offline services.

Online and Offline Availability

While implementing a PKI solution, a security policy should define the scope of online and offline services. It should lay down guidelines to determine the number of services that are available online and offline. There might be instances when users might get disconnected from the Internet. In such situations, the security policy should specify whether the user has access to some of the services or gets disconnected from all the services. For example, for transmitting data, if the policy for offline services has specified that the data can be encrypted and digitally signed offline, then the sender can encrypt and digitally sign the data offline by using locally cached certificates and other related data. But, if the policy does not specify the use of offline content, then the user cannot encrypt or digitally sign the data until the network connection is restored.

While deciding on the offline policy, you need to consider the following points:

◆ **Regular updates:** Information relating to certain dynamic data, such as CRLs and newly enrolled certificates, should be updated regularly in the cache on local computers.

◆ **Access to online-only services:** If the offline services are enabled, some online services cannot be accessed.

For example, if certificates and revocation information have been cached locally, then the user cannot access this information online. The security policy of an organization plays an important role in laying down the operational requirements for PKI. To understand how security policy affects PKI, let us look at the following example of the security policy of AllSolv, Inc.

SAMPLE SECURITY POLICY OF ALLSOLV, INC.

Let us look at the security policy of AllSolv, Inc. The purpose of this policy is to specify and lay down the guidelines for providing a foolproof security to the network resources of AllSolv, Inc. These guidelines are designed to minimize the potential threats to AllSolv, Inc. that might be caused due to improper and unconstitutional use of resources of AllSolv, Inc.

The security policy of AllSolv, Inc. comprises the following sections:

◆ Identification and authentication

◆ Password management

◆ Digital signatures and certificates

◆ Software import control

◆ Protection against viruses

- Control over interactive software

- Software licensing

- Encryption

- System architecture

- Incident handling

- Intrusion Detection System (IDS)

- Internet Usage

- Training

For the purposes of this book, we will discuss only some sections that are relevant to PKI.

DIGITAL SIGNATURES AND CERTIFICATES   If the identification and authentication of AllSolv users involve making use of digital signatures, then certificates need to be issued. Certificates in AllSolv, Inc. can be issued by the AllSolv CA or by a trusted third party. In addition, these certificates can only be issued by the CAs that have been approved by AllSolv, Inc. Three levels of certificates can be issued on the basis of certification requests, namely:

- Level 1 certificate for verifying a user's name, address, and other information against the AllSolv user database.

- Level 2 certificates for verifying e-mail addresses.

- Level 3 certificates are issued to companies.

After these certificates have been obtained, their information should be stored in a Web application. This information should be provided whenever a user or a Web site requests it to verify the identity of the user with whom they are communicating.

Any organization that provides only limited information over the Internet needs to provide digital certificates of both its users and server for validating their identities to AllSolv CA.

To eliminate any risks of session hijacking and provide continuous authentication, all certificates of AllSolv, Inc. must support standard technologies, such as SSL.

All certificates stored on personal computers should be protected by passwords or passphrases. These passwords should follow the password security policy of AllSolv, Inc.

ENCRYPTION   All users of AllSolv, Inc. should ensure that they use only the standard and proven algorithms for encryption. Some of the algorithms that users of AllSolv, Inc. can use are DES, RSA, RC5, and IDEA. The length of the symmetric key should be not less than 56 bits. AllSolv, Inc. does not permit the use of proprietary algorithms for any purpose. Users should make themselves aware of the encryption laws and be aware that the U.S. government restricts the export of certain encryption technologies.

Under any circumstance, if any employee of AllSolv, Inc. is found to have violated this policy then he/she will have to face a disciplinary action.

After having discussed the operational requirements for PKI, let us now look at the process of PKI deployment.

Deploying PKI

Planning is a very key component in the successful execution and deployment of any project. The process of deploying PKI in any organization also involves the same set of steps as would be required for the deployment of any other system.

The process of PKI deployment in any organization comprises the following phases:

- ◆ Planning for the project

- ◆ Analyzing and documenting requirements

- ◆ Installing and testing the system components

- ◆ Deploying the system

- ◆ User Acceptance Test and commissioning the project

Let us look at each of these phases in detail.

Planning for the Project

This phase involves the documentation of business requirements. It also involves the process of identifying the current business case and the advantages that will be gained by deploying PKI in the organization. This phase also involves carrying out a feasibility study to identify the Return on Investments (ROI) on deploying PKI as a solution. The main steps that are carried out in this phase are:

- ◆ Identifying the business case for PKI deployment

- ◆ Identifying the Return on Investments (ROI) on deploying PKI

- ◆ Identifying the number of users for the project

Calculating ROI for a PKI deployment requires that you have a very thorough understanding of the different processes of your organization, which facets of your organization will be affected by PKI, and also the risks involved with PKI deployment. You can take into account the following considerations while calculating ROI for PKI:

- Subtracting the total cost of deploying PKI from the total benefits achieved from the new application, the amount of reduced risk and the total cost savings is equal to ROI. But this is not all; some other points also need to be taken into account.

- You need to estimate the total cost of your PKI by the number of employees in your organization over some specific period of time.

- You need to estimate the benefits in terms of new business and revenue generated as a result of implementing PKI-enabled applications.

- You also need to estimate the costs saved by implementing PKI as against using an Internet-based EDI, or VPN.

However, all this is not so easy as it depends on the setup of your organization and the requirements for PKI. The output of this phase are listed below:

- A project plan with identified milestones and dates

- The system specifications document, which specifies the hardware and software requirements of the system

Analyzing and Documenting Requirements

This phase involves determining the requirements that will be satisfied by the system that is being developed. In this phase, the following activities need to be performed:

- Identifying the security policy that will be followed by the organization.

- Identifying the operational requirements, which includes the hardware platform on which the system is to be deployed.

- Identifying the security requirements of the organization. This includes identifying the Certificate Policy and the Certification Practice Statements.

- Identifying and documenting the requirements of the PKI system.

- Documenting the design of the PKI system.

- Identifying the training requirements for the various individuals in the organization who will be using the PKI system.

- Identifying the risks associated with the system and performing risk analysis.

- Identifying the parts of the system that are most susceptible to attacks and creating the appropriate security system.

For example, you need to secure all computers or servers that store sensitive information, such as information related to keys, from any physical intrusions and place them under locked rooms.

Installing and Testing the System Components

This phase involves installing the PKI components that are a part of the system, which includes the operating system, the network, the firewall, the directory, and the Web server and any additional third-party software that is required.

Deploying the System

This phase involves actually deploying the solution to the end-users in the organization. The deployment of the system can be done in the following modes:

♦ **Piloting the System:** In this method, the system is first deployed to a selected audience, and the findings and the information from the pilot can be used to improve the proposed system.

♦ **Phase-wise deployment of the system in the organization:** This method involves first deploying the system in the division of the organization that most needs the system. The deployment is done based on the priority of the organization. For example, you might want your finance department to be the most secured and the access to this department to be limited. In this case, you need to deploy the system in the finance department before it is installed in any other department.

User Acceptance Testing and Commissioning the Project

This phase involves the actual "real-life" usage of the system by the users in the organization. The purpose of the phase is to find out the flaws (if any) that exist in the system. Any flaws that are identified by the users are fixed in this phase. User Acceptance Testing involves prototype phase and the implementation phase. The prototype phase includes:

♦ Establishing procedures and project controls

♦ Defining data to be tested, file formats, and documents

♦ Testing and validating test data

♦ Tracking user's defect and metrics

♦ Preparing reports and recommendations

On the basis of the prototype phase, the implementation phase takes place. The implementation phase involves:

♦ Defining and mapping end-user requirements with the results of the prototype phase

♦ Preparing the specification design document

◆ Defining and running the prototype to ensure it is free of defects

◆ Preparing a report

According to the Gartner Group, 80 percent of PKI deployments are prototypes. While out of the remaining 20 percent actual deployments, 40 percent implementations fail within two years of their deployment as they do not provide any significant value to the organization. Considering these statistics, it thus becomes imperative for the users to test the usage of the system in real-life conditions and check their performance levels. When the system reaches a zero-defect stage, the final commissioning of the system can take place.

Problems in PKI Deployment

Although PKI is fast gaining ground as a popular system that is being deployed in various organizations, this system still faces a few fundamental problems and issues. This section discusses some of the issues that are involved in PKI deployment.

Key Compromise

Key compromise is a serious security threat for a user as well as for a CA. The impact of key compromise varies depending on the entity whose key is compromised. For example, if only a user's key is compromised, it affects the user and the entities relying on the user. On the other hand, if a CA's key is compromised, it can have a serious impact on the entire PKI system. If a CA's key is compromised, all the users and other subordinate CAs are affected. Let us examine the impact of key compromise on users and CAs.

USER KEY COMPROMISE

In most typical PKI implementations, the user's private key is stored on his local machine. This key can be secured by using a password or a passphrase. However, there is no method to detect if a key has been compromised. Also, there is no method to protect the key from attacks from hackers or viruses. Although smart cards are implemented to protect the user's private key, they are very weak and do not provide too much protection. If a user's key is compromised then any person can forge his identity.

CA KEY COMPROMISE

In every PKI implementation, almost all the entities trust a CA. A CA key compromise will result in the loss of trust by entities trusting the CA. Key compromise can happen because of a private key being known to someone or because of the CA server holding the private key becoming unusable.

Although key compromise and key loss result in new trust establishment by the entities, key compromise is more disastrous as compared to key loss. A key compromise makes all existing certificates that have been signed and issued by the concerned CA unusable.

Also, if someone knows the private key of the CA, the user can issue certificates to users on behalf of the CA. The user can also extend the trust to entities that are not trusted by the CA whose key has been compromised. The entity can also be made a subordinate CA by issuing a CA certificate. All these situations can lead to a complete breakdown of the PKI system.

As soon as a key compromise is detected, the CA should inform all relying parties about the key compromise and instruct them not to rely upon the certificates issued by that CA. This solution can work in a situation where the client base of the CA is small and the CA knows all its relying parties. However, this solution might not work in a situation where CA does not know all of its relying parties. For example, if a CA certificate is embedded in the browser application, the CA does not know all the users using this browser. In such a situation, another way to notify users about CA key compromise is through Authority Revocation List (ARL).

ARL contains a list of compromised CA certificates. While issuing an ARL, the CA uses the same compromised key, therefore making it difficult for the entities to trust the ARL. However, this method also has one disadvantage. If a person has gained access to the private key of the CA, he or she might not make the key untrustworthy by issuing an ARL.

Another way to notify users about a key compromise is by making two signing keys for the CA before the CA issues certificate to other entities. When the certificate is signed and issued by CA, the CA will include the hash of the other key on every certificate it issues. Now, when one key is compromised, the CA can sign and issue ARLs by using the second key. In this solution, to enable users to verify the signature on this ARL, the CA can distribute the public key corresponding to the second signing key to all users. Since the user's certificate already has the hash of the second key, users can easily verify the signature by computing another hash and comparing them.

Management of Encryption Key

Another issue that needs to be taken while deploying PKI is managing the encryption key. Encryption key management assumes larger proportions, especially when an organization considers the need for a key escrow. Here an organization needs to decide whether or not to keep an encryption key in escrow for specific purposes, such as employee termination or departure. It might so happen that an employee who has encrypted the data might leave the organization and take the key with him/her. This data cannot be accessed without the availability of the encrypting keys. In this case, keeping a key in the escrow can prove to be a solution. However, providing security to that key and keeping it a secret then becomes a major issue.

DN Name Duplicity in Certificates

It is not possible to identify by just seeing the key that it belongs to the person with whom you want to interact. Let's take an example, where you get a certificate with a DN name Jack, from a person who wants to communicate with you. You also have a friend called Jack. There could be multiple people called Jack, to whom the CA could have assigned the certificate. As a result, there is no way to find out whether or not the certificate that you received is from your friend John.

Weakness in CA/RA Model

Ideally in a PKI system there should only be one entity for performing verification, issuing, and managing certificates. The involvement of multiple entities leads to multiple security loopholes. The CA/RA model is weaker than either a single CA or a single RA because there is a possibility that an impersonator may pose as a CA or RA.

Certificate Lifetime

Certificate lifetime is one of the factors which should be calculated very carefully. A certificate with a longer lifetime will be prone to attacks in the future because of powerful machines and futuristic software.

Example

For example, let's consider an example to illustrate all the above issues. Alice wants to send a message to Bob. Here is the list of potential threats that this communication can face:

- Any unauthorized person can launch an attack using Alice's machine.
- An unauthorized person can steal Alice's private key or the person can also steal the passphrase to her private key.
- An attacker can replace Alice's key with his key.
- An attacker can replace the root certificate of the Certification Authority and replace these certificates with his certificate.

Legal Considerations

With the growth of electronic commerce and PKI system deployments on the rise, it is of utmost importance to understand the legal framework, which is a critical success factor for any PKI implementation across countries. Most of the legal framework around PKI varies from one country to another. However, there are two main issues that form the core of the legal considerations:

- ◆ Legal invalidity, which includes creating statutes and laws to make electronic documents and signatures as valid as paper signatures.

- ◆ Attribution; this is the most difficult aspect, and it involves proving that the person is who he or she claims to be.

With an unprecedented increase in the use of cryptography, even the ordinary citizens have started using several cryptography techniques, such as encryption. This has put the U.S. government in a catch-22 situation. Users can now use encryption in carrying out illegitimate and illegal activities. Until 1996, cryptography export came under the purview of the International Traffic in Arms Regulations (ITAR). However, in 1996 cryptography export control was transferred to the Export Administration Regulations (EAR) of the Department of Commerce. Every time you export a product that contains strong cryptography, you need to obtain permission (export license) from the Commerce Department.

The U.S. government's policy on encryption allows strong encryption for commercial purposes, yet it ensures that intelligence agencies are able to break the ciphers if need be. Any encryption that uses symmetric algorithms, such as DES or IDEA, with a key length of 40 bits and asymmetric algorithm, such as RSA, with a key length of 512 bits, is considered a strong encryption by the government agencies.

After you have obtained the necessary export license, you can export the following applications that containing strong cryptography:

- ◆ Financial-specific applications

- ◆ Fixed-data compression or coding techniques

- ◆ Decrypt-only licensing applications

- ◆ Personalized smart cards

- ◆ Access control applications

- ◆ Authentication applications

- ◆ Entertainment decoders

- ◆ Anti-virus software

In addition, a permanent export license for a product with strong encryption is provided only if the product will be used by:

- ◆ Financial institutions

- ◆ Overseas branches or subsidiaries of U.S. companies

- ◆ Overseas partners of U.S. companies involved in a joint venture

You can find more information about encryption export acts on the Web at `http://www.cs.uct.ac.za/courses/CS400W/NIS/papers98/ esaul/export/node1.html`.

Electronic Signatures in Global and National Commerce Act

A digital signature is the most important legal aspect of PKI. If a digital signature is not legal then the entire PKI system loses its basic purpose of establishing trust between entities. The Electronic Signatures in Global and National Commerce Act came into effect in October 2000 in the United States. This act is also referred as the E-Sign act. As a part of this act:

◆ All electronic/digital signatures are valid. The signature should uniquely identify and verify an individual. This electronic signature is technology neutral.

◆ Companies can create contracts online to buy and sell products.

 You can find more information about this Act on the Web at `http:// www.whitehouse.gov/omb/memoranda/m00-15.html`.

Uniform Electronic Transactions Act

The purpose of this law was to take care of the following issues in e-commerce:

◆ The enforceability of contract cannot be denied if the original documents for the document are in an electronic form.

◆ In case a law requires a document to be in writing and provides for an alternative, then an electronic document can substitute for a paper document.

◆ An electronic signature should be valid in the absence of a physical record.

This act was approved by the National Conference of Commissioners on Uniform State Laws and came into effect in July 1999. At present, this law has been enacted by 22 states in the United States.

You can find more information about this Act on the Web at `http://www.law.upenn.edu/bll/ulc/uecicta/uetast84.htm`.

Summary

In this chapter, you learned about evaluating PKI solutions. You also learned that there are multiple vendors of PKI and the criteria that can be used to evaluate PKI solutions. The criteria can be based on:

- Interoperability and compatibility

- Deployment ease

- Flexibility

- CA security

- Scalability and adaptability

Next, you learned about the operational requirements for PKI. You can measure PKI requirements on the following parameters:

- Hardware requirements

- Client-side PKI components

- Online/offline availability

- Key compromise

You learned about the impact of an entity key compromise and CA key compromise. Finally, you learned about the legal considerations involved in PKI.

Chapter 12

AllSolv, Inc. Case Study

THE BEST WAY TO CONSOLIDATE your learning of PKI is to examine typical case studies of companies that have deployed a PKI solution. By examining such case studies, you can appreciate the role of PKI in enabling secure transactions and create similar opportunities for deploying the PKI solution in your company.

In this chapter, we will examine the case study of AllSolv, Inc., which has implemented a PKI solution.

In this case study, we examine how AllSolv Inc. has decided to implement a PKI solution to meet its business requirements. Let us begin with the case study.

Introduction

AllSolv Inc. is a U.S.,-based retail chain that has over 200 retailer outlets across the United States. The retailer has revenues of over $200 million. However, the revenues have not grown substantially in the last two quarters. The retailer attributes this lack of growth to market saturation and competition from another retail chain that has taken over major market share from the areas that the retailer had plans to explore.

To boost its revenues, AllSolv Inc. plans to increase its customer base across the globe. The sales team has, on the basis of market surveys and cost analysis, identified Asia-Pacific and Europe as the potential markets. The company plans to make its presence in the European and Asia-pacific markets before the end of the next financial year. The company has estimated a growth rate of 1.5 percent in the next three consecutive quarters if it ventures into these areas. However, to accomplish this AllSolv, Inc. needs to implement such a solution that can suitably meet all its expansion plans.

To devise a solution, the company has conducted extensive market surveys and analyzed the business trends of these regions. On the basis of these analyses, the company has decided that the solution that they implement should have the following features:

♦ It should be implemented in a short duration and should be easily deployable. This is because due to the rapid increase in competition, AllSolv, Inc. plans to start its business operations as soon as possible. This would also help AllSolv, Inc. in gaining an early mover advantage and establish itself in the new territory.

♦ As the company wants to enter territories that are absolutely new to it, the solution should be flexible enough to meet the challenges of the new market and equipment.

♦ It should be able to generate revenues with relatively little investment. This would also ensure that the company's baseline is not affected.

♦ The solution should be scalable so as to meet the projected growth of the company.

♦ The solution should be such that it is interoperable and compatible with the latest devices and applications. The standards and equipments that AllSolv, Inc. would have to work with in the new areas might be quite different from that of its parent country. As a result, to counter these challenges the solution that AllSolv, Inc. implements needs to be quite portable and interoperable.

♦ Finally, the solution should provide complete security not only to the existing setup but also to the projected setup.

After conducting a thorough market analysis and exploring several options, AllSolv, Inc. has decided to implement a PKI-based solution. PKI offers AllSolv, Inc. a complete solution and fulfills all the criteria that AllSolv, Inc. is looking for in the solution. Some of the most elementary yet the most imperative features of PKI are:

♦ Ease of deployment and usability

♦ Interoperability and compatibility

♦ Flexibility

♦ Security

♦ Scalability and adaptability

You can learn more about the features of PKI in Chapter 11.

Let's look at the PKI architecture, which is most basic for any PKI implementation.

AllSolv's Architecture

The company has a hierarchical structure that is based in the United States, the traditional stronghold of the company. The company plans to establish a corporate office in the United States that will be a central location for managing all the other offices of the company. A number of regional offices will fall under the direct purview of the corporate office. The regional offices will be catering to the business requirements of broad geographical locations. Each regional office will have a number of distribution offices in its purview. The scope of distribution offices will be limited to a more specific region than the regional office.

The hierarchy is shown in Figure 12-1.

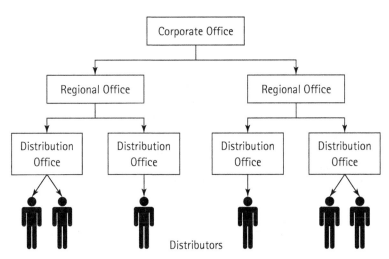

Figure 12-1: Hierarchy in AllSolv, Inc.

Keeping in mind the hierarchy of AllSolv, Inc. Chris, the project manager responsible for implementing PKI at AllSolv, Inc., has decided to implement a hierarchical PKI architecture with the following features:

- ◆ The corporate office in the United States will be the root Certification Authority (CA). It would be responsible for:
  - Issuing certificates to the regional head offices that fall under its direct purview.
  - Creating policies for the regional offices.
  - Acting as the Policy Approval Authority (PAA). As the PAA, corporate office would have the last say in the policies related to issue of certificates.

- ◆ Considering the vast geographical spread of the company and huge number of distributors and customers, the root CA will not be able to handle all the certification requests. Therefore, each regional office would act as a second-level CA. The region-level CA cannot accept direct certification requests. Therefore, any certificate requests must be routed through an RA. It is responsible for:
  - Issuing certificates on receiving certificate requests from RAs.

- ◆ Zonal offices will act as the RAs that forward the certificate requests to the corresponding regional office.

- ◆ Distribution centers also would act as an RA and route certificate requests to the zonal office, which in turn will route these requests to the regional office.

The hierarchical PKI architecture at AllSolv, Inc. will address issues of not only scalability and ease of deployment but also that of a short certification path. Hierarchical PKIs are quite scalable, and to meet the needs of a growing organization such as AllSolv, Inc., the root CA simply needs to establish a trust relationship with the CAs of the entities. In addition, being uni-directional, the hierarchical PKI architecture is quite easy to deploy. The path for the entity to the root or the issuer CA can be determined quickly and easily, and the biggest path in the PKI is equivalent to the CA certificate for each subordinate CA plus the end entity's certificate.

Using Cryptographic Algorithms

To provide authentication, integrity, and confidentiality to data and applications, the following algorithms are used:

- ◆ MD5 for one-way hash functions. MD5 is one of the most widely used algorithms for Internet applications. AllSolv, Inc. can also implement SHA-1, which is the official NIST standard for a data hashing algorithm.

- ◆ RSA for key management and digital signatures.

- ◆ TC. Using Ipv6 is rather impractical for real-world use at this time.

- ◆ RC5 for symmetric encryption.

Digital Certificates

The AllSolv PKI supports only X.509 version 3 certificates. X.509 certificates have now been recognized as the de facto industry standard digital certificates. The user certificate at AllSolv, Inc. has the public key of the user and an X.500 Distinguished Name. While requesting a certificate the users need to follow PKCS#10 or Certificate Request Syntax Standard. The certificate request information is composed of the Distinguished Name (DN) of the user, the public key of the user, and the postal address of the user. After obtaining the certificate, to create a digital certificate the user needs to follow the PKCS#7 or Cryptographic Message Syntax Standard.

The PKI Architecture and Distributor Relationship

The company plans to make its distribution offices the hub of all transactions with its customers. Each distribution office will register distributors that will be responsible for promoting the company products in the market. The distributors will not be regular employees on the company payroll. When a distributor approaches a distribution center, he or she must fill in a registration form. The distribution center then forwards the form to the Distribution Manager (DM). In this manner, the distribution centers act as the first level of check where the identity of the distributors is verified. The DM verifies the information supplied and forwards the form further to the controlling RA. Each RA then verifies the authenticity of the information supplied in the form.

When the RAs at the distribution and zonal levels are sure about the information, the information is forwarded to the country-level CA. The country-level CA then issues a certificate to the distributor and signs the certificate with its private key. The corresponding public key of the certificate is stored on the certificate server. The CA dispatches the X.509 certificate to the RA, which in turn forwards the certificate to the next level. The certificate is forwarded to the next level, until it reaches the distributor who applied for it. The entire process of issuing certificates is shown in Figure 12-2.

In order to keep a firm control on the inter-region transactions, the top management have also decided that any inter-region transaction must be routed through the root CA (i.e., the corporate headquarter). For example, a distributor UK urgently needs to acquire a product. At the given point of time, the product is available only in the Malaysian inventory. Instead of buying the product and investing money unnecessarily into the acquisition of the given product, it makes sense if the company transfers the required amount of product into the inventory of the UK.

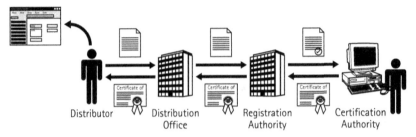

Figure 12-2: Process of registering distributors

As per this scenario, the region-level CAs cannot issue certificates to each other and neither can they validate each other. As a result, for every inter-region transaction the certificate would be issued by the root-level CA – the corporate head office. When the root-level CA issues a certificate to the two concerned regional offices, it must also validate the entire chain from the requesting distributor to the supplier distribution center. The entire transaction is depicted in Figure 12-3.

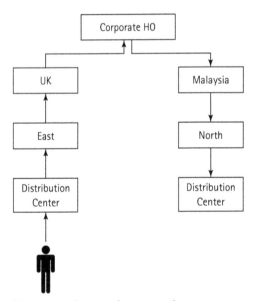

Figure 12-3: Inter-region transaction

The interaction with the distributor will be such that each distributor can place its order at the corporate office directly by its Web site. This will ensure that the distributor need not wait for the order to be routed through the three levels of company hierarchy, thereby saving time for the procurement of the inventory.

Securing AllSolv's Web Site

The Web site will be an important entity in the procurement chain and the failure of the site can causes extensive losses to the company.

The company has consulted security analysts to secure the Web site. During interaction with the security analysts, the following observations were made:

◆ The Web site should be accessible to all distributors so that the distributors can place their orders.

◆ Each distributor must be authenticated before an order can be placed on the Web site.

◆ There should be a reliable mechanism to ensure authenticity of distributors. This is because considering the quantity of orders expected from each distributor; the company stands to lose major revenue on shipment of commodities if they are not ordered.

◆ There should be a reliable mechanism for rejecting orders from distributors if they do not honor company regulations.

To impart maximum security, the company has decided to SSL-enable its Web site. To ensure that only authorized transactions happen on the Web site, the company will issue digital certificates to all its distributors. It will also issue digital certificates to all its employees at the regional offices and the distribution offices because these offices will be connected through the Internet and the authentication will be based on digital certificates.

The company plans to make this Web site available only to its employees and distributors. If a retailer wants to find information about the company and register as a distributor, the retailer can access the promotional Web site of the company that has the details of schemes and benefits available to a distributor. The Web site also enables a distributor to find a distribution center that is nearest to the distributor's geographical location.

Let us now examine a workflow from the registration of a prospective distributor to the transactions made by the distributor. A prospective distributor comes to know about AllSolv Inc. by their promotional Web site of by word of mouth. By using the promotional Web site, the distributor examines the policies of the company and locates a distribution point that is closest to his or her location. The distributor approaches the distribution point and fills the registration form. The distributor then generates a public key/private key pair for itself.

The distribution point implements the first level of checks to assure itself of the identity of the distributor. The form is forwarded to the DM, who submits it to the RA. The RA examines the form and verifies the authenticity of the applicant. When the RA is sure that the request for membership is genuine, it forwards the request to the CA.

The CA issues a certificate to the distributor and signs the certificate with its private key. The public key of the certificate is stored on the certificate server. The CA dispatches the X.509 certificate to the RA. The RA, in turn, sends the certificate to the concerned DM, who hands over the certificate to the distributor. The distributor is now registered with the company.

The workflow is illustrated in Figure 12-4.

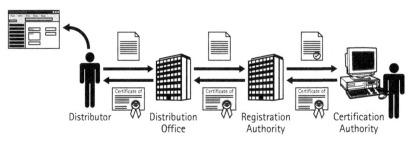

Figure 12-4: Workflow for registering distributors

The company employees also need certificates for secure communication. The company employees need secure communication because, apart from other transactions, they need to update the company databases at the corporate office with the sales revenue that has been generated by each distributor. Certificates are generated for new employees that join the company in the same way as they are generated for distributors. The only difference is that the employees do not need to go through the elaborate verification round. They can directly send their requests to the RAs who, in turn, forward the requests to the CA.

After the certificate is issued to the distributor, the distributor is able to place orders on the corporate Web site. Let us examine the processes involved when a distributor places an order on the Web site.

After the distributor obtains the certificate, he or she installs it in the Web browser. When a user begins a session on the corporate server, the following interactions take place:

1. The client sends information to the server, such as its SSL version number, cipher configuration information, and other information, which the server requires to communicate with the client using SSL.

2. The server in turn also sends the servers SSL version number, cipher settings, and other information, which the client needs to communicate with the server. In addition the server sends also its own certificate. If a situation arises that the client is accessing the resource, which needs to be authenticated, the server asks the client for its client's certificate.

3. The client uses the information provided by the server to authenticate the server. For any reason, if the server is not authenticated, the client is

warned about the ambiguous server and prompted that a secured connection cannot be established. If the server is authenticated successfully, the client can move ahead to establish a SSL session.

4. Based on the encryption algorithm, the client creates a pre-master secret for the SSL session. This pre-master secret is encrypted by using the public key of the server and then sent to the server.

5. If the server requires client authentication, it requests a client certificate. The client signs a fresh piece of data that is unique to this handshake and sends it to the server. Both the client and the server know this data. In addition to the signed data, the client also sends its own certificate to the server along with the pre-master secret.

6. If the server is not able to authenticate the client, the server terminates the session. If the client is authenticated successfully the server uses its private key to decrypt the pre-master secret and generates a master secret.

7. Both the client and the server use the master secret to generate session keys. The session key is a symmetric key, which is used to encrypt and decrypt the data that is transferred over the SSL session.

8. The client informs the server that all the future communications initiating from the client will be encrypted using the session key, then the clients sends the confirmation separately that the client's portion of the handshake is over.

9. The server also responds to the client, informing the client that all the future messages from the server would be encrypted with a session key. Like the client the server also sends a separate message confirming that the handshake is over.

10. At this stage the SSL handshake is complete and the SSL session has begun. Both the client and the server use the session keys to encrypt and decrypt the data they transmit to each other, to validate its integrity.

11. After the session key is available at the server, the distributor can send data to the server in the form of messages. The message that the distributor needs to send to the server is hashed and encrypted with the private key of the distributor to generate the digital signature.

12. The digital signature and the message are further encrypted by the session key and sent to the server.

13. On the server, the session key is used to decrypt the data that is transmitted from the client. The data is decrypted to retrieve a message and a digital signature.

14. The message is hashed to obtain a message digest. The digital signature is also decrypted with the public key of the client to obtain a message digest.

15. If the two message digests are identical, the server is sure of the authentication of the data and the transaction is carried out.

The transactions are summarized in Figure 12-5.

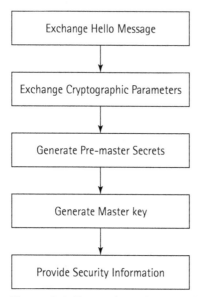

Figure 12-5: Data exchange between client and server

Certificate Policy and CPS

The company needs to issue digital certificates to its distributors. To ensure compliance to its policies, the company implements the following processes:

♦ The company creates a certification policy that is available to all its distributors. The certification policy has all the necessary rules and regulations that a distributor needs to know. The company has also published these rules on its promotional and official Web sites so that these are easily accessible.

♦ The certification policy also has a section on when a distributor certificate is revoked. It also states that the Certification Revocation List (CRL) will be updated each time a certificate is revoked.

The corporate office in the United States will issue all certificates. Therefore, the Certification Authority (CA) needs to be established at the corporate office. However, considering the vast geographical spread of the company, the CA will not be able to handle certification requests. Therefore, it is decided that the CA will not accept any certification request directly and each request needs to be routed through a Registration Authority (RA). The RAs will operate at the regional office level. Below the RA, the regional offices will have the distribution office manager (DM) who will forward all requests to the RA for validation. Thus, the same corporate structure that was depicted in Figure 12-1 previously now has roles assigned to each level in the hierarchy. The structure is shown in Figure 12-6.

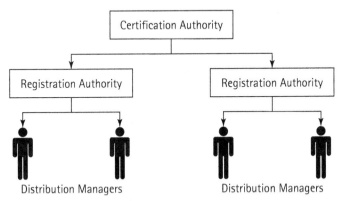

Figure 12-6: Roles in AllSolv, Inc.

Certificate servers are installed at the CA. The certificate server is used for storing public keys for all distributors. The Certification Practice Statement (CPS) that has the certification policy and the CRL are also published on the certificate server.

 To read the CPS of AllSolv, Inc., refer to Chapter 4.

Business Enhancement by the Solution

AllSolv, Inc. has been able to obtain many advantages by deploying a PKI solution. The solution has enabled the company to meet its business requirements effectively. Let us examine how the company has benefited from the PKI solution.

◆ When a distributor enrolls as a member of the company, the two levels of security validations at the DM and the RA levels enable the company to assure itself that the request is genuine. This has ensured that the company is able to provide quality service to its indirect customers.

◆ The company is able to ensure the identity of the distributor each time the distributor transacts on the Web site. Even the distributor cannot deny having made the transaction. Thus, transactions are non-repudiated.

◆ When the distributor shops on the Web site, the geographical location of the distributor is determined on the basis of the information obtained when the distributor was issued the certificate. The catalog of products available for the user is filtered accordingly. Therefore, the problem of filtering inventory for different destinations is automatically taken care of.

◆ Employees, at the end of every day's transactions, update the revenue generated from distributors in the databases at corporate office. The employees are also issued digital certificates for this. Therefore, the transactions across the company network are absolutely secure.

◆ If a distributor does not abide by the company norms or abdicates his or her membership, the certificate issued to the distributor is revoked. Each time the certificate is revoked, the CRL is updated. Therefore, the next time a former distributor attempts to make a transaction, the server checks the CRL and the transaction is canceled.

◆ The above-mentioned point is also applicable for the company employees. Therefore, company employees are also not able to misuse their privileges.

◆ Certificates of distributors are renewed every year. Each time a certificate is renewed, the company has a chance to audit the distributors for compliance to company regulations. Thus, the company is able to maintain a high standard of service to its customers.

Central to all transactions that take place in the company is the Web site. The infrastructure of the Web site is shown in Figure 12-7.

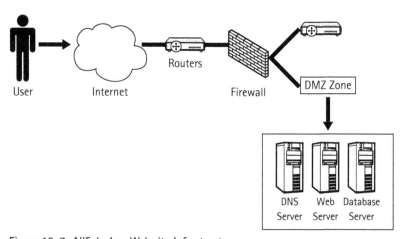

Figure 12-7: AllSolv, Inc. Web site Infrastructure

In the infrastructure depicted above, the company uses a demilitarized zone (DMZ) for its transactions. The Web server, through a firewall, receives the request from distributors. These requests are processed based upon data that is retrieved from the Database server and the business rules that are stored on the Web server and the DMS server.

Let us now examine the security requirement of AllSolv, Inc. during communication, especially when the communication happens at the upper echelon of the company. We will deploy a Pretty Good Privacy (PGP) solution to ensure the confidentiality and integrity of mails being exchanged by the top managers of the company.

The regional heads of all the regions need to be in constant touch with each other. This is highly important, because:

♦ They always must have an up-to-date knowledge of the inventory levels in each other's region. This is important because if a region requires a product or some products urgently, time must not be wasted in search and subsequent relocation of the product.

♦ They also must have an up-to-date knowledge of inter-region resource allocation. This helps the regional heads to accommodate movement of resources, infrastructure, and employees.

Apart from the day-to-day transactions, extremely confidential company data must also be exchanged between regions. Also, the senior management at the corporate headquarters must be kept informed about the latest happenings including the confidential data.

Because of the vast expanse of the company globally, e-mail has emerged as the most suitable communication medium. It is actually the cheapest and the fastest way of exchanging data between two entities – be it two regional heads or between the region and the corporate head office.

However, the data being transacted on a daily basis can be extremely confidential and critical for a company's growth. If the data is tampered with or even merely sniffed and happens to fall in the hands of competitors, the company stands to lose huge amounts of money.

In fact, last month they lost a bid to a rival company in Indonesia that they were very sure to win in spite of the reasonable prices they had quoted. They suspect that somehow the data sent by the corporate office to the Indonesian head office was intercepted and used by the rival company.

Learning from this experience, they have decided on two things:

♦ They'll still continue to use e-mails as the primary method of communication. This was a difficult decision for the management, who are wary of the medium now. However, on considering other methods, such as satellite communication that offer relative security, they realized that it would increase the cost of daily operations of the company two-fold, as satellite communication is a very expensive medium. After a lot of analysis, they've decided to use e-mail.

◆ Though they have decided to continue using e-mail, they want the method to offer a high degree of security. There would be no compromise on this score. However, they are also adamant that no extra budget would be allocated for the solution.

The Solution

After a lot of research, the technical support team at the corporate headquarters has arrived at the conclusion that Pretty Good Privacy (PGP) is the best solution in the given situation.

PGP is one of the well-known public key crypto-systems that provides services like authentication and confidentiality and is typically used in securing e-mail messages over the Internet. PGP is one of the most powerful encryption techniques being used today as it makes use of some of the best-known cryptographic algorithms used in PKI. Therefore, PGP has gained huge popularity in little time and is now being used by masses worldwide.

The company directors have decided to implement PGP for encrypting their e-mail messages. By deploying this solution, the directors are able to communicate securely. For example, if the director of the UK region needs to send a secure message to the director of the Malaysian region, she can install the PGP client and encrypt it with her private key. For encrypting the message, she can use the PGP menu while composing the mail message. The relevant menu options are displayed in Figure 12-8.

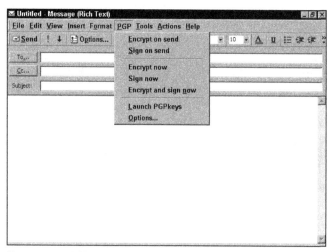

Figure 12-8: PGP menu options

When the user clicks Encrypt and Sign Now command from the PGP menu, the Recipient Selection dialog box appears. In this dialog box, the user is able to select the list of directors to which the encrypted message needs to be sent. The list of directors for which the director of UK has added the public key appears in the Drag users from this list to the Recipients list column in the Recipient Selection dialog box. This dialog box is shown in Figure 12-9.

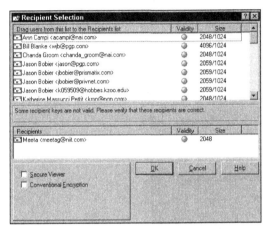

Figure 12-9: Recipient Selection dialog box

When the user has selected the required recipients, the PGP Enter Passphrase for Selected Key dialog box appears. This dialog box is shown in Figure 12-10. In this dialog box, the user needs to specify the passphrase for her private key.

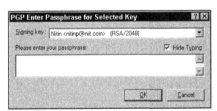

Figure 12-10: PGP Enter Passphrase for Selected Key dialog box

After specifying the passphrase, the message is encrypted, as shown in Figure 12-11.

When the encrypted message reaches the director of Malaysia, the director is able to decrypt the message by selecting the Decrypt/Verify option in the PGP menu. This option is displayed in Figure 12-12.

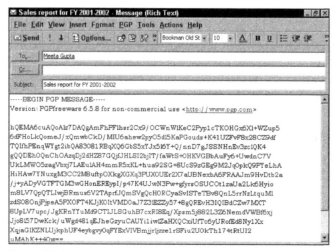

Figure 12-11: An encrypted message

Figure 12-12: Decrypt/Verify option in the PGP menu

The PGP Enter Passphrase for a Listed Key dialog box appears, as shown in Figure 12-13. In this dialog box, you specify the passphrase for the private key.

While implementing PKI, Chris, the project manager, warrants that every employee of AllSolv, Inc. familiarize himself/herself with the Utah Digital Signatures Act, which lays down the directives for digital signatures.

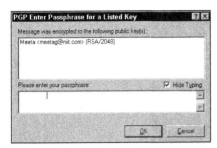

Figure 12-13: PGP Enter Passphrase for a
Listed Key dialog box

To learn more about the Utah Digital Signatures Act, refer to the Web at
`http://www.le.state.ut.us/~code/TITLE46/46_03.htm`.

Summary

In this chapter, we used the example of how a company might implement a PKI
solution to meet its business requirements. We explained and illustrated the role of
PKI in enabling secure transactions. As a result, we attempted to offer some
insights into how you might deploy the PKI solution in your company.

Appendix A

IDNSSE and SDSI

IN THIS APPENDIX

- ◆ Internet Domain Name System Security Extension (IDNSSE)
- ◆ Simple Distributed Security Infrastructure (SDSI)

Domain Name System (DNS) is a very important component of the Internet. It is used for resolving user-friendly names into their corresponding IP addresses. DNS lacks the security in authenticating the *resolver*. A resolver is an entity that issues a query to the DNS server to obtain the IP address of the requested name. This means that any resolver without going through any authentication can obtain the IP address of the hosts from the DNS server.

Internet Domain Name System Security Extension

To address this issue of authentication, security extensions are included in DNS forming the Internet Domain Name System Security Extensions. Let's first look at how DNS functions, and then we will move on to security extension.

DNS

DNS was designed by Paul Mockapetris in 1984 with the intention of solving the ever-increasing problems of mapping the host name to the IP address. Initially, the Stanford Research Institute's Network Information Center (SRI-NIC) maintained a single file, referred to as the host table, which stored all the host names. SRI-NIC would update this host table twice a week to keep up with any new host names that were added. After the host table was updated, the system administrators would download the latest version via the FTP and would subsequently update their domain name servers. However, as the Internet gained popularity, it became quite impractical for a single organization, SRI-NIC, to distribute and update all the information related to host name mapping. Hence, to solve this problem Paul Mockapetris and a few others came out with a better solution, known as the Domain Name System (DNS). DNS did away with the concept of a single organization updating the information and introduced a distributed database. DNS works with the help of many servers all around the world, rather than just one server at SRI-NIC.

DNS is a hierarchy of *domains*, arranged in an inverted tree-like structure. A domain is a collection of hosts that belong to an organization or are related to each other. The top of the DNS hierarchy is called the root domain and is denoted by a single dot. Under root domain are the top-level domains. Some of the top-level domains are com, edu, mil, org, net, gov, and the two-letter country codes, for example, AU for Australia, HK for Hong Kong. The top-level domain further contains sub-domains and these sub-domains contain hosts or another sub-domain.

These sub-domains are specific to the organizations. For example, the top-level domain .com can contain the domain .au, which can further contain the sub-domain "allsolv," where AllSolv is the name of an organization. Thus, the allsolv domain is a part of both the .au domain and the .com domain.

Each domain has one or more domain name servers. A domain name server is just a server or a computer on which the DNS software is installed. The DNS server is comprised of two components: the name server itself and a resolver. All name resolution, that is, the name-to-address-conversion is done by the name server, while the resolver obtains the IP address information of the requested host by querying another DNS if the current DNS is unable to resolve the name. The information in the name servers is contained inside innumerable files known as *zones*. A zone is an authority for a domain and thereby manages all the information of the domain.

Let us take the following example for understanding the DNS hierarchical structure as shown in Figure A-1. AllSolv, Inc., a software solution provider, is assigned a domain name allsolv.com under the top-level domain com. All hosts in AllSolv, Inc. can become part of domain allsolv.com or can become members of sub-domains inside allsolv.com.

Sub-domains can be defined on the basis of departments such as research, marketing, etc. For example, Alice's computer, a client of the research department in AllSolv, Inc., will have a *Fully Qualified Domain Name* (FQDN), Alice.research.allsolv.com. FQDN is the complete reference of a host including its domain name and all sub-domains, if any. All the hosts directly under allsolv.com domain can be inside the allsolv.com zone, whereas the research sub-domain can have their own zone containing the hosts under the research department.

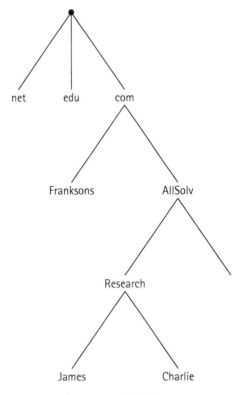

James.research.allsolv.com

Figure A-1: DNS hierarchy

Now let us examine the name resolution process:

1. Frank, a host in suresolv.com domain, contacts his local name server for obtaining the IP address of another host, Alice in the research department of allsolv.com domain.

2. Local name server searches for the queried record in its database. If the record is not found in the database, it contacts one of the root name servers.

3. The root name server does not have authority for the queried record. But it returns the name server address for com domain to the local name server.

4. The local name server then queries the com name server for allsolv.com domain. On receiving the request, the com name server returns the name server address of the allsolv.com domain.

5. Now, the local name server contacts allsolv.com name server, which returns the name server address of research.allsolv.com.

6. Finally, the local name server queries the research.allsolv.com name server, which returns the IP address of Alice.research.allsolv.com.

7. On receipt of the IP address of the queried host, local name server returns the address to the resolver.

All addresses known during the name resolution process are stored in the local cache of the local name server. This is useful in case the same host requests the server repeatedly. For example, coming back to AllSolv when another request comes for some other host in research.allsolv.com, the local DNS server directly contacts the research.allsolv.com name server without going to the intermediary name servers again. These entries are maintained in the local cache for a specified period known as time-to-live (TTL), which is determined by the name server returning the host address. In our example, TTL is determined by the name server of research.allsolv.com.

Security Extensions in DNS

DNS is a global name resolution service used mainly for an Internet environment. In addition to the name resolution function performed by DNS, the inclusion of server extensions further enhances the functionality of DNS. The server extensions facilitate the distribution of the public key through DNS and also provide host and data authentication.

The data in a DNS is organized into zones. DNS might consist of one or many zones. Inside a zone the data is stored as records referred to as Resource Records (RR). Every RR has a *key RR* associated with it. The key RR, in addition to containing the information about the entity of the RR, also contains the public key associated with the entity of the corresponding RR.

Each zone in a DNS has a key pair associated with it. While the private key of this key pair signs the *SIG RR* of the entire zone, the public key is distributed across DNS servers and entities. SIG RR is the record that contains the signature information used to verify the corresponding RR. SIG RR is the most basic way of authenticating data in a DNS. It forms the very core of DNS security.

Since the public key of the zone is distributed across the DNS server and entities, the entities can query the DNS server for the required information. If the DNS server contains the required information it sends back the RR along with the associated key RR. The entity then decrypts the information of RR with the help of key RR's public key. In case the information is not available with DNS, it transacts with other DNS and returns the public key of that DNS. On receiving the public key of other DNS, the entity then queries this DNS, and the same process continues until finally the requested information is received.

DNS security extensions for e-mail and secure-IP are already defined and can provide a general public key distribution system for other protocols. Let us look at the role of DNS security extensions in an example where Alice@allsolv.com wants to send a secured message to Bob@webeyes.com. Alice requires Bob's public key to encrypt the message.

Alice contacts her local DNS server (allsolv.com) with a request for all the KEY RR of Bob.webeyes.com.

The local DNS server contacts the root name server if it has the key for root or contacts the com name server for the KEY record of com's super-zone that is root.

Once the KEY record of the root name server is obtained, the root name server is queried for the KEY and SIG record of the com name server, and the root name server will return the IP address of com name server along with the KEY and SIG record.

Now the com name server will be queried for the address of the webeyes.com name server, which returns the address for webeyes.com server along with the KEY and SIG record for webeyes.com zone.

Upon receipt of the address of webeyes.com, the DNS server of webeyes.com is queried, which returns the KEY record as there is no IP address associated with Bob.webeyes.com.

Now the local name server has the KEY record for Bob@webeyes.com. Bob's e-mail key can be determined by looking into the appropriate flag in the KEY record.

Alice, after selecting the right key, encrypts the message and sends it to Bob. Bob, upon receipt of Alice's e-mail, can verify Alice's signature by obtaining his public key in the same manner.

Security extensions in DNS not only provide a method of verifying the servers that claim to be DNS servers but are also used for verifying the records that are handled by DNS. In addition, security extensions in DNS allow DNS to be used as a central distribution service for public keys.

Simple Distributed Security Infrastructure (SDSI)

The PKI certificate systems issues certificates on the basis of the identity of an individual. In order to simplify the process of certificate management, SDSI system was introduced by Ron Rivest and Butler Lampson. In contrast to PKI-based system, SDSI issues certificates on the basis of user credentials and attributes.

SDSI allows you to digitally sign certificates by using public key cryptography. In addition, it allows you to define user access rights by creating Access Control Lists (ACLs). The use of ACLs not only enhances the security of your network but also helps you in managing the network resources in a more efficient manner. To modify user access rights you can issue certificates that are based on security groups defined in the ACL. SDSI also provides you with a graphical user interface (GUI) through which you can not only request a certificate but also issue and view certificates.

The entities in SDSI are known as *principals*. These principals apply digital signatures to the certificates issued by them. These entities or principals can issue different types of certificates as per the requirements. In other words, in SDSI certificates can be issued and signed by any principal and thus each principal in SDSI can act as a CA. While issuing certificates the policies and procedures that are followed are determined by the principals themselves. Principals can also define their own local names and can use these names for referring to other principals.

Types of certificates used in SDSI system are

- ◆ Identification certificate
- ◆ Name binding certificate
- ◆ Group binding certificate

Identification Certificate

You can identify the name of the person associated with a principal with the help of the Identification certificate. This certificate binds the entity information such as entity's name to a principal. Such information when available on the certificate would help in identifying the entity.

Name-Binding Certificates

Name-binding certificates bind a name to the principal to whom the certificate is issued. After being bound, this name becomes a part of the local names of the principal that is issuing the certificate.

Any remote principal can link to this name through the principal containing this name in his list of local names. The following example will make the process of name-binding certificate clearer. Bob, a principal, binds a name David to another principal, Frank. Alice, a remote principal, can refer to the principal Frank as Bob's David. In the same manner Bob can also refer to the principal of Alice.

Group Membership Certificates

Group membership certificates resemble identity certificates in functionality. But as the name suggests, they are issued for a group rather then individual entities. The name of the group becomes a part of the local name list. A group can contain principals as well as other groups.

SDSI groups can be used to implement security policy for accessing resources. You can create a group and include it in the Access Control List (ACL). This ensures that only group members defined in the ACL can access the resources.

Let's say there is some confidential data on the finance server. Alice, the administrator, is asked to give access privilege to only employees of the Finance department. For this purpose, Alice creates a group Fin-access on SDSI server. She then makes Bob, Frank, and Kenneth members of Fin-access. These are the principal employees in the Finance department.

Now let's see how a Finance department employee gains access to the Finance server:

1. Bob, an employee in the Finance department, sends a request for the membership certificate of the Fin-access group to the SDSI server. He also sends his principal and group name along with the request.

2. SDSI server checks the group membership of Bob. SDSI server sends a membership certificate to Bob once the membership of Bob has been established.

3. Bob can now access the data on the Finance server by presenting the membership certificate.

Figure A-2 illustrates how SDSI works.

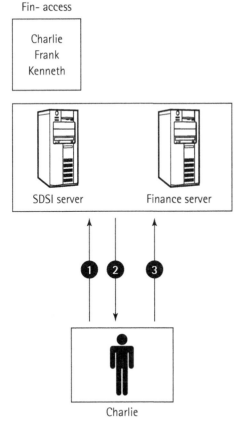

Figure A-2: The way SDSI works

SDSI does not follow any hierarchical global infrastructure. However, there might be situations when some principals are given a higher priority than others. In such situations, SDSI provides a special status referred to as "special roots" to these principals.

You can obtain more information on SDSI on the Web at `http://theory.lcs.mit.edu/~rivest/sdsi11.html`.

Appendix B

VPN Basics

IN THIS APPENDIX

- ◆ Introduction to VPNs
- ◆ Need for VPNs
- ◆ Working of VPNs
- ◆ Types of VPNs
- ◆ Tunneling protocols

IN THE PAST FEW years, there has been a significant change in the way organizations conduct their business. Earlier, organizations were localized and had a limited area of operation. Today, most organizations are global. Also, there has been a significant increase in mergers and acquisitions of organizations. As a result, most organizations have their branch offices and clients in various geographic locations. Hence, there is a need for fast and secure transmission of information to employees, business associates, and clients. Most organizations are implementing Virtual Private Networks (VPNs) to ensure secure and reliable information transmission.

You can use PKI for implementing security in VPNs. PKI provides VPNs with the ability to use strong authentication techniques, certificate management, and support certificate life time by using Certificate Revocation Lists (CRLs). The policy management feature of PKI allows the VPN to enforce policy control throughout a network.

In a VPN solution, the network device generates its public key and private key. These keys are then sent to a CA for certification. A network device (which is a part of VPN solution) can either generate two key pairs, one for signing and the other for authentication, or can use a single pair of keys for signing and authentication. The process is the same as any PKI-based client authentication or trust relationship. However, in this case the end devices are network devices, such as firewalls and routers. The following sections discuss the basics of a VPN.

Introduction

In today's world, competition has given rise to partnerships and alliances among organizations located across the globe. Employees of these organizations might need to access information from multiple locations, their homes, or from remote locations. To ensure an effective transfer of information over the corporate network, organizations can use VPNs. As VPNs allow network connectivity over a large geographical area, they are at times referred to as WANs that use public networks, such as the Internet.

VPNs are IP-based networks that use dedicated channels called *tunnels* to transfer data. VPNs provide a secure connection between distributed units of a corporate network over the public networks, such as the Internet, without being dependent on the expensive leased lines.

A VPN allows remote employees working in branch offices to communicate securely with the network at the corporate headquarter. These remote employees use the same network and addressing scheme as the employees on the corporate network. Although remote users connect to the corporate VPN by using a public network, such as the Internet, they are validated at the corporate VPN. The data that is transmitted between the remote locations and the corporate VPN is secure because it is transmitted using a tunneling protocol through the Internet.

In other words, a VPN is a shared infrastructure that provides security benefits that are similar to a private network at a reduced cost. However, in contrast to private networks that use leased lines, VPNs utilize IP networks including the Internet. VPNs are more flexible and cost-effective as they can use different technologies such as the Internet, ISPs, and Asynchronous Transfer Mode (ATM) and do not need dedicated leased lines. ATM is a connection-oriented, high-speed switching and multiplexing technology that uses 53-octet fixed-length cells to transmit network traffic. It is known as asynchronous because the cells that transmit data might not be periodic.

A typical VPN is shown in Figure B-1.

You can use VPNs to connect all or specific branch offices to a corporate network. For example, only certain branch offices might require secure access to the central network at the corporate office. Therefore, you might set up a VPN connection with these offices and provide the remaining branch offices with access through the Internet. The requirement for VPN also depends on the applications that are used on the network. For example, if all the branch offices and mobile users connect to corporate headquarters for e-mail services only, you can set up a single VPN, which will consist of e-mail servers and the clients of the branch office. Other points that need to be considered while deciding on the use of a VPN are

- The amount of data that needs to be shared on the network
- The type of application that will run
- The security policy that will be applied
- The type of business models that will be implemented
- The level of user access required for the Application server
- The level of user access required for the Internet server

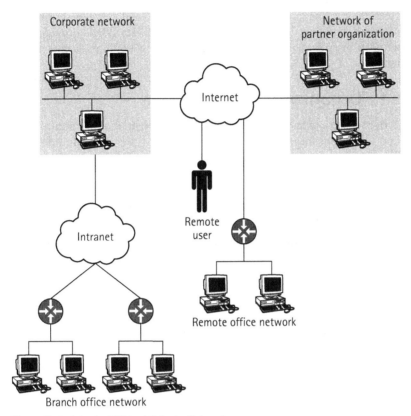

Figure B-1: A typical Virtual Private Network

VPN is basically platform-independent, and therefore any existing IP-based network can be converted to a VPN by installing the software required to enable remote access. You can also set up a VPN between two corporate networks. In case of a VPN setup within a company or in an intranet, all resources are managed internally by the organization. Whereas in the case of a VPN that has been set up between two companies, each company handles its own port of VPN at its own end. In this way, the responsibility is shared.

The Need for VPNs

Now that you know what VPNs are, the next obvious question is why should organizations use VPNs. With the advent of the Internet, the way business is handled has changed. While business organizations harnessed the Internet to carry out business effectively, computer professionals came out with various technologies that utilized the features of the Internet to provide effective sharing of information. VPN is one such technology that provides economical, faster, and reliable sharing of information. Besides enabling fast and reliable transfer of data, VPNs provide significant benefits to organizations and ISPs. The following sections discuss these benefits in detail.

Benefits to Organizations

Most organizations are considering VPNs to solve the problem of a fast, secure, and reliable method of sharing information. However, besides providing safe information transmission, VPNs offer the following benefits to organizations:

- VPNs are flexible and scalable networks. Therefore, organizations can conveniently extend their networks to provide connectivity to remote offices, business partners, and clients, based on their business requirements.

- VPNs utilize the IP backbone for connectivity purposes. This situation helps to simplify the network topologies considerably, and leads to reducing the burden on management. Since the IP backbone is owned by either an ISP or an Application Service Provider (ASP), each one is responsible for its respective administration.

- VPNs are cost-effective as compared to private networks. This is because VPNs do not require dedicated leased lines. The total cost of operation for VPNs is also less as they use low-cost transport bandwidth and backbone devices.

Benefit to ISPs

Today, most ISPs aim toward providing services to small corporations that provide higher margins. However, this requires expanding capacity and coverage of large geographical areas. VPNs can be used to add these new services without major capital investments. To add VPNs to an existing network, you need software or broadlevel upgrade VPNs. A software-based VPN requires installation and configuration of a server OS such as Windows NT/2000 or Netware on the server hardware. These can be used for multiple VPN applications, which offer substantial benefits in terms of their costs, as they do not require any additional infrastructure to support them. Besides these benefits, VPNs have the following advantages:

- VPNs not only provide Internet access but also provide remote-access outsourcing and branch-office connectivity. Using VPN technologies, ISPs can also capture information related to tunnel users for itemized billings.

- VPNs enable coverage of large geographical areas with low capital investments. ISPs and the Network Service Providers (NSPs) can provide value-added services and geographic expansion by using any of the three applications of VPNs:

- Dial access outsourcing: In this system, the organization has complete control over user-authentication and network access because the tunnel carries with it the information about end users.

- Virtual leased line: VPNs are useful for the NSPs that provide connectivity over the value-added IP networks. This makes the network management simpler and reduces the cost of providing these services to the enterprise customers. VPNs are useful as all the traffic from the enterprise customers can pass through the same network but in different tunnels. This balances the load on the network.

- Virtual Point of Presence (VPOP): This system is useful for those ISPs who do not want to spend money on the infrastructure. In this system, a user connects to the ISP through a point, referred to as the VPOP. This point is not operated by the ISP, and when the user calls to the VPOP the call is relayed to the intended ISP through a third party.

If an organization is using a VPN-enabled router to connect to the ISP, the tunnel can be extended to the network of the enterprise.

Working with a VPN

Let us consider a situation to understand the working of a VPN. A global organization has implemented a VPN to enable a faster and secure way of sharing information with the sales representatives based at remote locations. To gain access to the organization's network, a sales representative dials in the local ISP and logs on to the ISP network, as shown in Figure B-2.

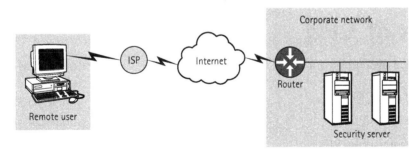

Figure B-2: Dialing into the ISP

To establish connectivity with the corporate network, a request to create a tunnel is sent to the security server on the corporate network.

When the tunnel is established, the data is sent through the tunnel over the ISP connection, shown in Figure B-3. The VPN software encrypts this data before it is introduced into the tunnel.

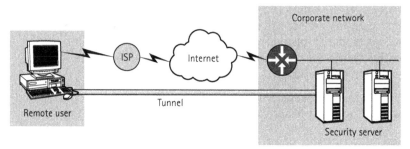

Figure B-3: Sending data through the tunnel

When the security server receives the encrypted data, it decrypts the data. The security server then sends the decrypted data to the corporate network, as shown in Figure B-4. Any information that is sent back to the remote user is also encrypted.

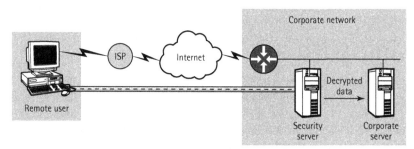

Figure B-4: Sending decrypted data to the corporate network

Types of VPN

Depending on the purpose for which they are deployed, VPNs can be categorized as

- ◆ Intranet VPNs
- ◆ Extranet VPNs
- ◆ Remote-access VPNs

Intranet VPNs

Intranet VPNs are used to connect branch offices and corporate departments. Intranet VPNs can improve or replace private lines by utilizing the shared infrastructure provided by service providers. They ensure secure information transmission between various departments of an organization and the branch offices. As sensitive information is transmitted between different departments, intranet VPNs provide strong encryption services. You can create intranet VPNs by using the Internet, ATM network, or Frame Relay. Figure B-5 shows an intranet VPN.

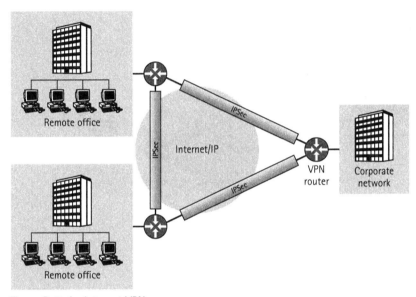

Figure B-5: An intranet VPN

The advantages of an intranet VPN are:

◆ Convenient and quick connectivity to new sites: Since intranet VPNs are based on the IP, Frame Relay, and ATM networks of the ISP or the Internet, they provide quick and easy connectivity.

◆ Reduction in the bandwidth cost.

◆ Increased network uptime: Intranet VPNs help to provide an increased network uptime by allowing redundancy of wide area network (WAN) links across ISPs.

Extranet VPNs

In a private network environment, it is very difficult to extend the connectivity to corporate suppliers and partners. Hence, extranet VPNs are used to connect an organization with its business associates, suppliers, and customers. These VPNs are based on open, standard-based solutions to ensure interoperability with different networks at business partners and customer ends. To organize extranet connectivity, you utilize the same architecture and protocols that are used to implement an intranet and a remote-access VPN. An extranet VPN is shown in Figure B-6.

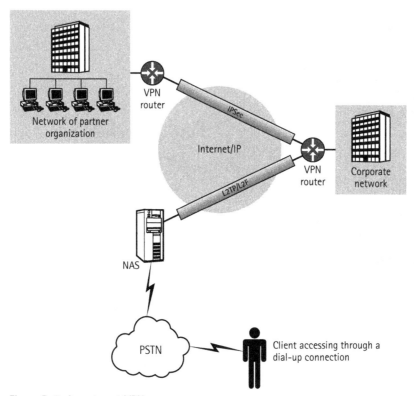

Figure B-6: An extranet VPN

Remote-Access [CS1]VPNs

Remote-access VPNs connect a remote location and the corporate network. They extend the corporate network to mobile users, remote offices, and telecommuters with a minimum amount of WAN traffic as they allow users to connect to their intranet or extranets over the shared infrastructure as they would connect to the private network. A remote-access VPN helps to reduce communication expenses by using the dial-up infrastructures of the ISP for establishing the connection.

Centralized management and scalability is required by a remote-access VPN. Figure B-7 shows a typical remote-access VPN.

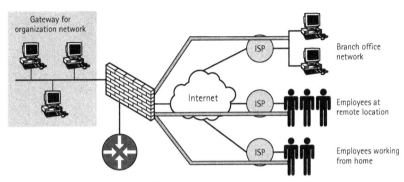

Figure B-7: A remote-access VPN

The advantages of remote-access VPNs over the private dial-up network are:

◆ Cost reduction.

◆ Increase in scalability as they allow more users to be added to the network and also provide flexible methods of accessing the network, such as ATM, Integrated Services Digital Network (ISDN), Digital Subscriber Line (DSL), and wireless IP technologies.

As the organizations that use remote access VPNs do not need to manage the dial-up network, they can concentrate more on their business objectives. When implementing a remote-access VPN, you need to decide whether tunneling and encryption should be initiated from the client side or from the Network Access Server (NAS). NAS is a server on the network that manages the network resources. Access to the network of an organization is generally gained through this server.

In a client-initiated model, an encrypted tunnel is initiated at the client end by using PPTP, L2TP, or IPSec. Thus, in this case the service provider's network acts just as a transport medium to the corporate network. In a client-initiated model, the service provider's network, which is used for dialing to Point of Presence (POP), is secured. In this type of model, each client end that accesses VPN needs to have tunneling and encryption software.

In a NAS-initiated model, the remote user dials in a service provider POP by using the Point-to-Point Protocol/Serial Line Internet Protocol (PPP/SLIP) connection. The service provider authenticates the user and then starts a secure tunnel from POP to the corporate network. The benefit of using a NAS-initiated model is that the organization does not need to maintain any end-user client software. Figure B-8 shows NAS remote-access VPN.

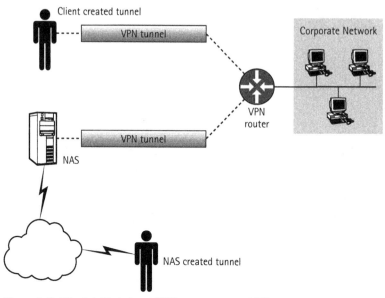

Figure B-8: Client-initiated and NAS remote-access VPNs

Tunneling Protocols

VPNs use the tunneling technology to transfer data. Tunneling is a method of transmitting data in a hidden form by encapsulating data packets into a tunneling protocol. A tunneling protocol is a standard that manages tunnels and encapsulates data. These encapsulated data packets are then transferred from one network to another by using dedicated tunnels. A tunnel is that part of the network connection which contains the data in encapsulated form.

The tunneling process involves three basic steps. In the first step, data packets are encapsulated within a tunneling protocol packet. Next, these encapsulated packets are transmitted across the network. When these encapsulated data packets reach the end of the tunnel, the final step is to extract the original data from the encapsulated packet and forward it to its final destination.

The most common tunneling method between a source and a destination router is Generic Routing Encapsulation (GRE). The source routers are referred to as ingress, and the destination routers are referred to as egress. In this method, the data packets that need to be transmitted are encapsulated again (after being encapsulated initially) within the new GRE tunnel, with the destination address of the GRE tunnel end point. At the tunnel end point, the GRE header is stripped away and the packet moves forward to the destination, which was assigned in the original IP packet header. GRE tunnels are typically point-to-point.

Although for each tunneling protocol there might be a slight variation in the way the process of tunneling takes place, these basic steps remain the same. The tunneling protocols can act at either Layer 2 or Layer 3 of the OSI model. The Layer 2 and Layer 3 protocols are implemented differently.

VPNs can be configured to use any or a combination of these tunneling protocols:

♦ **Point-to-Point Tunneling Protocol (PPTP):** Is an extension of PPP and hence inherits its features and limitations. PPP is a remote-access protocol that was developed to handle secure dial-up connections. PPTP supports multiprotocol networking over public networks, such as the Internet.

♦ **Layer 2 Forwarding (L2F):** Is a tunneling protocol that encapsulates the data packets into PPP before transmitting them to an L2F server. The L2F server then de-encapsulates these packets before forwarding them to the destination. It supports multiple tunnel connections from the same Virtual Private Dialup Network (VPDN) client.

♦ **Layer 2 Tunneling Protocol (L2TP):** Combines the best features of PPTP and L2F and incorporates them for use over PPP. L2TP supports a variety of routed protocols, such as IP, IPX, and AppleTalk. It also supports a variety of backbone technologies, such as Frame Relay, ATM, SONET, and X.25.

♦ **Internet Security Protocol (IPSec):** Is a layer 3 tunneling protocol that provides encryption security services to ensure integrity and authenticity of data packets that travel over the Internet.

Open Standards Interconnection Model

The Open Standards Interconnection (OSI) model is a model developed by the International Standards Organization for defining different networking protocols and distributed applications. This model consists of seven layers, namely:

♦ **Layer 1: Physical Layer.** Defines the mechanical, electrical, and procedural events that take place when the data is being physically transmitted as electronic signals on the wire.

♦ **Layer 2: Data Link Layer.** Defines data format (on the network and facilitates a reliable and error-free transfer of data (in the form of frames) across the physical layer.

♦ **Layer 3: Network Layer.** Transmits packets of information from the sender to the receiver. It provides establishment, maintenance, and termination of connections.

♦ **Layer 4: Transport Layer.** Provides reliable, transparent transfer of data between end points. The transport layer is considered at the top of the lower layers of the OSI model – physical, data link, network, and transport layer.

- ◆ Layer 5: Session Layer. Provides services such as data exchange, dialog control, synchronization, and error reporting for connections (sessions) between users.

- ◆ Layer 6: Presentation Layer. Provides services such as data compression, encryption/decryption, and protocol conversion. In this layer, data transmission is standardized such that the computers using different data structures can communicate.

- ◆ Layer 7: Application Layer. Provides services (such as network management, transaction server) and protocols (such as Telnet, FTP, and SMTP) to the different network applications.

Appendix C

Cryptographic Algorithms

IN THIS APPENDIX

- ◆ Symmetric cryptography
- ◆ Public key cryptography
- ◆ Hash functions

CRYPTOGRAPHY NOT ONLY PREVENTS data from modification, but also performs authentication. For accomplishing the security of data, three types of cryptography can be used:

- ◆ Symmetric cryptography, which uses a single key for both encryption and decryption.
- ◆ Public key cryptography, which uses two keys, one for encryption and the other for decryption.
- ◆ Hash functions, which use mathematical processes to encrypt data.

You have already learned about these cryptographic schemes in detail. In the process of encryption and decryption, a variety of communication protocols, cryptographic algorithms, and standards are used. Table C-1 describes some of the algorithms that are available.

TABLE **C-1** CRYPTOGRAPHIC SCHEMES AND DESCRIPTIONS

Cryptographic Schemes	Description
Blowfish	Blowfish is a secret-key, block-cipher cryptosystem, which was designed by Bruce Schneier. It has a varied key length and is used as an alternative to DES. For details on Blowfish refer to http://www.counterpane.com/blowfish.html.

Continued

Table C-1 CRYPTOGRAPHIC SCHEMES AND DESCRIPTIONS *(Continued)*

Cryptographic Schemes	Description
Capstone	It is a project developed by U.S. National Institute of Standards and Technology that is supported by a variety of computer chips. For details on Capstone, refer to http://csrc.nist.gov/keyrecovery/cap.txt.
CAST-128/ CAST-256	CAST-128, developed by Adams, is a secret key cryptosystem that uses 128-bit keys. CAST-256 is also a secret key cryptosystem but uses 256-bit keys. CAST-256 was developed by Stafford Tavares.
	For details on CAST-128, refer to ftp://ftp.isi.edu/in-notes/rfc2144.txt.
	For details on CAST-256, refer to http://www.entrust.com/resources/pdf/cast-256.pdf.
Cramer-Shoup	Cramer-Shoup is a public key cryptosystem that was developed by R. Cramer and V. Shoup.
Fortezza	Formally known as Tessera, this is a PCMCIA card that is used to implement capstone algorithms.
IDEA	International Data Encryption Algorithm is a secret key cryptosystem developed by Ascom.
KEA	Key Exchange Algorithm is a variation of Diffe-Hellman key exchange. It was proposed for the Capstone project.
MOSS	MIME Object Security Standard provides Privacy Enhanced Mail-based security services to the messages that comply to MIME standards.
PCT	Private Communication Technology was developed by Microsoft to provide security of data transmitted over the Internet. It supports Diffie-Hellman and RSA methods for key exchange. PCT also supports DES, RC2, and triple-DES methods for encryption.
Pegwit	Pegwit is software that provides public key encryption and authentication. It can be downloaded from the Internet free of cost.
PEM	Privacy Enhanced Mail ensures security of electronic mail. It supports encryption, authentication, and key management features. For details on PEM, refer to RFCs 1421,1422,1423, and 1424.

Cryptographic Schemes	Description
Scott	Scott is a cryptographic algorithm that uses a variable key size.
SGC	Server Gated Cryptography was developed as an extension of SSL. It uses RC2, RC4, DES, and triple-DES to provide strong encryption. It is usually used by online banking and financial applications.
Skipjack	Skipjack is a symmetric key encryption scheme developed for the Capstone project. For details on Skipjack, refer to `http://csrc.nist.gov/encryption/skipjack/skipjack.pdf`.

Appendix D

LDAP

IN THIS APPENDIX

- ◆ The LDAP open standard
- ◆ Similarities with X.500
- ◆ Differences Between LDAP and X.500

LIGHTWEIGHT DIRECTORY ACCESS PROTOCOL (**LDAP**) was developed in 1995 to address the shortcomings in its predecessor, X.500. The main intent of LDAP was to ease the burden of access from X.500 and to make the directory service available to a wide variety of applications and computers. Since LDAP is based on X.500, LDAP is used for accessing information directories. However, it is much simpler than X.500. Most importantly, it supports TCP/IP, which is necessary to access the Internet.

Lightweight Directory Access Protocol

LDAP was developed at the University of Michigan for accessing X.500-based directory services on the Internet and for querying and manipulating this information. This information is arranged in a hierarchical tree-like structure. As a client/server protocol, it allows browsing, reading, and searching information stored in the Internet-wide X.500 directory services and simple management tasks.

Not only an access protocol, LDAP represents a lightweight, fast, and scalable directory service. Lightweight implies that it is a simpler version of X.500, which simplifies the access to X.500 directories. Therefore, LDAP is sometimes also referred to as *X.500-lite*. Although only a subset of X.500 functions has been reused in LDAP, it is capable of complete X.500 DAP functionality. At the same time, it is completely compatible with X.500. Since it realizes lightweight and easy access to directory services, it is a better choice for the Internet environment. It has now been fully accepted as the Internet standard for directory services that run over TCP/IP.

The success of LDAP has been such that many directory service vendors use LDAP as the core technology. A few of these are Microsoft Active Directory Service (ADS), Banyan StreetTalk, and Netscape Directory Server.

Directory Service is a location in which all the information is stored in a systematic and defined format. Active Directory in Windows 2000 is the new directory service that allows integration of users, multiple domains, sites, and the Internet. Active Directory helps you to locate network resources, such as printers, applications, and users, and shares information about these network resources.

There are already three versions of LDAP available: LDAP, LDAP version2, and LDAP version3. LDAP was released in 1993. LDAP version2 came out in 1996 and was adopted commercially. LDAP version3 is the current version, which was ratified in 1997. Active Directory Service (ADS) and NDS support LDAP version3.

The LDAP Open Standard

LDAP is an open standard. Therefore, it allows any application running on any platform to access standalone LDAP directory services or the directory services that are back-ended by X.500 and retrieve information from them. To access these services, *ldap://* is prefixed in the URL of the LDAP server. This is very similar to using File Transfer Protocol (FTP) and HyperText Transfer Protocol (HTTP). Services supported by LDAP include e-mail address lookup facility in an e-mail client using LDAP, text, animations, audio, Uniform Resource Locator (URL), and authorized access to sensitive information, such as public keys.

Similarities of LDAP with the X.500 Protocol

Since it is based on X.500, LDAP shares many similarities with X.500. These include the same directory structure, data and namespace model, and similar way of accessing information. The various ways LDAP is similar to X.500 are listed below:

◆ It uses a global directory structure, whose information model is very similar to the one used in X.500. For example, information in an LDAP server is stored as entries. The type is defined by the object classes to which the entries might belong. Each entry is a set of attributes that contains the actual information.

◆ The data and namespace model of LDAP also resembles the X.500 model very closely. One or more LDAP servers contain the data that make up the LDAP Directory tree. LDAP uses the same hierarchy of entries as in X.500. The hierarchy starts from the root and ends at the individual names.

♦ The information is organized and accessed in the same way as per X.500 specifications. An LDAP client can send a request for information or submit information that has to be updated. On receiving a request, the LDAP server checks the client's rights for the information requested as well as supplied. If the client has the proper access rights, the server responds to the request or can refer the client to another LDAP server where the information is available.

♦ Access control can be imposed on privileges to read, write, search, or compare information available on the LDAP server(s). Access control can be implemented on the basis of individual as well as groups of individuals. Access control can be done on a portion of the tree, entry, or even an attribute.

♦ Replication of information is also allowed on LDAP servers.

Differences Between LDAP and the X.500 Protocol

Although there is a strong resemblance between LDAP and X.500, they are a few differences between them. The major differences between LDAP and X.500 are listed below:

♦ The biggest difference between LDAP and X.500 is that LDAP is designed to run over the TCP/IP protocol stack, which gives it capability to access the information available on the Internet as well. X.500 lacks this capability, since it doesn't support TCP/IP.

♦ LDAP is much simpler in concept and easier to implement. This is why it has gained vendor acceptance quickly.

There are many LDAP clients that can be used to browse through LDAP-compatible directories. The most famous LDAP clients are e-mail clients like Post Office Protocol 3 (POP3) and Internet Message Access Protocol (IMAP4). These clients when integrated with LDAP can access extensive information in the form of address books. Not only this, but any client that has appropriate access permissions can access any LDAP server.

Glossary

3DES Triple Data Encryption Standard. It operates on 64-bit data blocks. This algorithm uses the DES algorithm three times.

Access Code A series of numbers and/or characters that can be used to access a computer.

Access Control List (ACL) A list of users and groups and the permissions they have, to access the network resources.

Access Control Policy Is a set of rules, regulations, and criteria that specify how access can be granted to a user.

Administrator A trusted person who is responsible for a set of users.

Advanced Encryption Standard (AES) The replacement algorithm for DES.AES has key lengths of 128, 192, and 256 bits, as compared to the 56-bit key used by DES.

Adversary The person who attacks the system (network or communication) with either a malicious intent or just for fun.

Algorithm A series of steps that are used to complete a task.

Alternate name The X.509 version 3 certificate extension that contains a user-friendly name of the entity, such as e-mail address in addition to the subject name. The use of alternate names in X.509v3 certificates help to identify the entity without referring to the X.500 directory.

American National Standards Institute (ANSI) The organization that guides the development of communication and technology standards in the United States.

API Application Programming Interface. API is a set of tools, protocols, and procedures that is used for developing applications, which are consistent with the operating system. Each operating system provides an API that can be used to create applications on that operating system.

Archiving The process of maintaining records of the certificates that are issued, need to be revoked, or have expired. These records are essential for future references, such as determining the reason for certificate revocation.

ASCII American Standard Code for Information Interchange. It is the most popular encoding method. This is a coding system that assigns numeric values to characters such as letters, numbers, punctuation, and other symbols.

Asymmetric key encryption A method of encryption that uses two –keys: one key, known as the public key, is distributed to multiple users, and the other key, known as the private key, is held by the owner. The public key is used to encrypt messages; only the corresponding private key can decrypt the messages. Also see public key encryption.

Attack An attempt at breaking a cryptosystem. Brute force attack, differential cryptanalysis, and linear cryptanalysis are a few examples of security attacks.

Attribute certificates Certificates that contain attribute information of the entity.

Authentication The process of verifying the identity of an entity by means of some proof, such as used ID, and password. It is the method by which the claimed identity of an individual is verified.

Authority Revocation List (ARL) A CRL that contains revocation information about CA certificates. ARL is issued by the CA that issues CA certificates.

Authorization Refers to the process of granting permissions to a user.

Authorization Policy It is the set of standards and conditions that govern who has access to systems; it also identifies the level of access that can be granted.

Availability It is the readiness to provide a service or some information when needed by an approved user.

Avalanche effect A shift of one bit in the input string, which will cause a shift of about half of the total bits in the resulting string.

Backdoor It is a loophole in the system that allows a way of gaining access to a program, an online service, or an entire computer system. This is a potential security risk to the system.

Backup A duplicate copy of data that is maintained for archival purposes and for protecting the data against any damage or loss.

Base A content type class that comprises non-cryptographic data.

Basic certificate request When the subject of a certificate from the same CA makes a certificate request, it is known as a basic certificate request.

Basic revocation request A certificate revocation request made to the CA by the subject of the certificate.

Biometrics Using biological properties to identify individuals; for example, fingerprints, a retina scan, and voice recognition.

Bit A binary digit. This is either 1 or 0.

Block A sequence of bits of fixed length.

Block cipher A symmetric cipher that decrypts data in blocks.

Boolean expression A mathematical expression that operates on two values – 0 and 1.

Bridge CA architecture Links PKIs that implement different architectures. Users are not directly issued certificates in this architecture.

Brute Force Attack An attack in which every possible key is tried until a correct key is found.

Byte The basic unit of computing that consists of a set of 8 bits.

CA certificate Certificate issued to a CA. It is the certificate for the public key of a CA.

CA certificate request A certificate request made by one CA to another CA.

CA Domain It is the list of people and processes that belong to the same Certification Authority (CA).

CA hierarchy An inverted tree-like structure that depicts the arrangement of CAs in the PKI system. This is a trust model for certificates where parent-child relationships are established between CAs.

CA policy management It is the process which defines the location of storage of the CA key, the algorithm used to encrypt the CA signing key, and the frequency of updation of the certificate revocation details.

CA Signature Algorithm An algorithm used by the CA to sign the certificate.

CAST-128 This algorithm uses a variable key length and uses block sizes of 64 bits. CAST-128 has shown very good encryption/decryption performance.

Certificate A digital document that contains identity information and a public key to be used in a PKI. It is an attachment to an electronic message and is used for security purposes. The most common use of a certificate is to verify that a user sending a message is who he or she claims to be.

Certificate and CRL distribution message A message type that is used as an indication of certificate or CRL issuance.

Certificate Distribution System (CDS) A system to distribute certificates to users and organizations based on PKI implementation.

Certificate enrollment The process by which a user obtains a certificate.

Certificate expiry It is the date after which a user's certificate can no longer be trusted. The certificate expiry date is contained within the certificate.

Certificate issuer The CA that issues the certificate.

Certificate Management Protocol (CMP) Protocols required for online interactions between different PKI entities.

Certificate policy A set of rules and guidelines followed by the CA to use the certificate. This also defines the requirements for certificates, such as certificate lifetime and public key lengths.

Certificate Practice Statement (CPS) Specifies practices followed by the CA to create, issue, and manage certificates. This also defines the policies under which the CA operates.

Certificate renewal It is the process of issuing a new certificate to a user using the existing public key from the previous certificate.

Certificate request A request made to a CA by an entity to issue a certificate.

Certificate request and response message A message type that is required for the purpose of request and delivery of certificates to users.

Certificate revocation The process of revoking a certificate when it is no longer valid due to reasons such as key compromise and affiliation change.

Certificate Serial number A unique integer value associated with each certificate.

Certificate validation The process of validating a certificate to ensure that the information in the certificate is authentic and that the certificate is used for its intended purpose.

Certificate version The version of the certificate.

Certification Authority (CA) An entity, service, or server that creates, issues, and manages certificates. The CA issues a digital certificate containing the applicant's public key and some other identification information. The CA makes its own public key available through a public domain.

Certification path constraint An extension that is used to restrict the certification path in a trust model.

Certification Revocation List (CRL) A signed list of certificates that are not valid and have been revoked by a CA. This also contains the reason for revoking a certificate.

Challenge password enrollment An enrollment process where the entity provides a password to the CA. Based on this password the CA authenticates the request.

Checksum A computation done on the message algorithm to detect errors during data transmission.

Cipher An algorithm used for encrypting and decrypting data.

Ciphertext The data in encrypted form.

Cleartext It is the unencrypted form of data and is also referred as plaintext.

Client/Server A method of organizing a computer network, in which many users, called "clients," are connected to computer systems, called "servers." The server acts as a central information repository and provides the clients with the required software applications or data or access to the required network resource as the case may be.

Code signing The process of encrypting a normal code or file by signing it.

Complete CRL A certificate that stores the complete certificate revocation information about a CA.

Compression The process of compressing plain text by using a compression algorithm. This process usually takes place after fragmentation but before encryption.

Compression algorithm An algorithm used to compress plaintext.

Compromise The inadvertent disclosure of a key or a secret.

Confidentiality The property to keep information secure from unauthorized users so that only the intended recipient can use the information.

Content type A field that outlines the specifications for the format of the content of message. This is also referred to as an object identifier.

Cookie It is the information that is transmitted from a Web site to a user's computer. It is a text file and contains information about a user's preferences.

Corporate Security Policy It is the policy that governs the extent of availability of information to end users of an organization network. This policy forms the basis for implementing a security framework that provides confidentiality and integrity to company data.

Credentials It is the information that proves that the person is who he or she claims to be.

CRL caching The process of caching or storing CRLs by users on their local machines. This process helps to speed up the certificate verification process.

CRL distribution point The location where a CRL is stored.

Cross-certification The process of establishing a trust relationship between two CAs by issuing CA certificates. It is the process which users in separate PKIs can interoperate with each other. This process involves the comparison of the policies and procedures of both the domains, and if they are equivalent, then the CAs in each domain issue certificates for each other. Cross-certification certifies that the other CAs have equivalent security policies and practices and is as trustworthy as a certifying CA.

Cross-certification request and response message A message type that is required for the purpose of request and delivery of certificates to CAs.

Cross-certified enterprise PKIs In this PKI architecture, the root or a subordinate CA of a particular PKI establishes a relationship with the corresponding root or subordinate CA.

Cryptanalysis Is the science which involves decrypting the encrypted information or creating a new encryption technique.

Cryptography The technique of protecting data by changing it into an unreadable form for secure transit. This is done using a key.

Cryptographic keys It is a set of values that are applied using a wide range of algorithms to translate encrypted text also called ciphertext into plaintext.

Cryptology It is the science of encrypting and decrypting data.

Cryptosystem The infrastructure for cryptography, which comprises an encryption/decryption algorithm, plaintexts, ciphertexts, and keys.

Cycle attack In this attack, the ciphertext is decrypted repeatedly, counting the iterations, until the original text appears. A large number of re-cycles will decrypt any ciphertext. This method is very slow and for a large key is not considered to be a practical attack.

Data Encryption Standard (DES) A cryptographic algorithm approved by the National Bureau of Standards and Technology (NIST), published in Federal Information Processing Standards (FIPS) 46, mainly for government and public use. See also AES.

DEA Data Encryption Algorithm

Decryption The process of retrieving the original message from its encrypted form.

Delta CRL Updates or partial CRLs that help to keep the size of a CRL under control and ease the process of CRL distribution.

Denial Of Service (DoS) An attack designed to prevent the normal functioning of a system and thereby to prevent lawful access to the system by authorized users. An unauthorized user can cause denial of service attacks by destroying or modifying data or by inserting spurious messages into the system's servers until service to authorized usersis prevented.

DES Cracker A machine especially designed to break DES. This machine was used by the Distributed Net group to break DES.

Differential cryptanalysis attack The Differential cryptanalysis attack looks specifically at pairs of ciphertexts whose plaintext have particular differences. It analyzes the evolution of these differences as the plaintext propagates through the various rounds of DES when they are encrypted with the same key.

Diffie–Hellman algorithm One of the most commonly used algorithms for key exchange. This does not involve the actual transfer of keys, but once the key information has been exchanged the entities can generate identical keys based on the key information.

Digest The output obtained after applying a hash algorithm over some data.

Digested data A content type field as defined by PKCS#7.

Digital certificate A certificate of identity like an ID card that binds the identity information with the public key.

Digital envelope A security method that uses two types of encryption to secure a message. First, the message is encrypted using symmetric encryption, and then the key to decode the message is encrypted using asymmetric encryption. This technique overcomes one of the major drawbacks of the public key encryption, which is that it is slower than symmetric encryption. Since it is only the key that is protected with public key encryption, there is very little overhead.

Digital Signature Standard (DSS) A standard algorithm developed by U.S. National Security Agency (NSA) in 1994 for creating digital signatures.

Digital signatures The result of encrypting a message hash by using the private key of the sender. This is a proof of integrity and authenticity of message.

Digital timestamp The process of signing a document to specify the time of its creation.

Direct digital signatures A digital signature that can be formed by encrypting the entire message with the sender's private key or by encrypting a hash value of the message with the sender's private key.

Directory Information Tree (DIT) A hierarchical tree structure that consists of entities that represent a global directory. The entity at the top of the hierarchy is referred to as "root," followed by the "countries" and so on.

Directory Service Agents (DSA) Databases that maintain and store information of an organization as per the X.500 directory standard. They can also contain information about multiple organizations.

Directory Service server A X.500 compliant directory service server where all certificates are published.

Directory User Agent (DUA) An intermediary between the user and the directory database to retrieve information from the directory.

Distinguished Name (DN) A unique name assigned to each entity in the directory. It identifies an entity in a particular system. This name is bound to the individual's public key that is represented by the DN using a digital signature from a trusted third party.

Distributed key A key that is split up into many parts and shared (distributed) among different participants. See also Secret Key.

Distributed Net A coalition of computer enthusiasts from all over the world formed to decipher a DES-encrypted ciphertext and who recovered the key in a record-breaking time of 22 hours and 15 minutes.

Domain A collection of hosts that belong to an organization or are related to each other.

Domain Name Service (DNS) A service used on the Internet to resolve user-friendly names into their corresponding IP addresses.

DSA Directory Service Agents. Databases used in X.500 that store the information of one or more organization(s).

DUA Directory User Agent. The intermediary between a user and an X.500 directory.

Dual Key pair model A method in which two pairs of keys are used, one for signing and signature verification and the other for encryption and decryption.

E-commerce Business transactions conducted over the Internet.

E-mail Messages sent electronically from one person to another via the Internet.

Encryption The process of converting plaintext to ciphertext. See also Ciphertext.

Enterprise CA A type of Windows CA that issues certificates to users and computers that is a part of an organization.

Enterprise CA architecture PKI architecture where various CAs are responsible for issuing certificates and CRLs to entities.

Enveloped data A content type field as defined by PKCS#7.

Expiration date The date on which a certificate will expire.

Extended trust list architecture Single CA, hierarchical PKI, or mesh PKI Architecture where all the end entities maintain the list of multiple trust points.

Extensions Additional attributes stored in a certificate or a CRL. These were introduced in X.509 v3 certificates and v2 CRL.

External revocation request A certificate revocation request made to a CA by an entity other than the subject of the certificate.

Fabrication An attack where a third party inserts spurious messages into the organization network.

Factoring Breaking down of an integer into the smallest prime number.

Federal Digital Signature bill A bill passed by the U.S. government stating that digitally signed electronic transactions have the same legal weight as transactions signed in ink.

FIPS Federal Information Processing Standards (FIPS): These are standards published by the NIST. All U.S. government computers need to comply with this standard.

FIPS 140-1 A FIPS standard that defines the minimum requirements that cryptographic systems that perform signing must meet.

Firewall A network security device that applies rules and filters to control the type of network traffic that enters an organization's network.

Fragmentation The process in which the block of data received by record protocol is fragmented into records of size 16,384 bytes or less.

Fully Qualified Domain Name (FQDN) The complete reference of a host including its domain name and all subdomains, if any.

Group-membership certificate A certificate that is issued for a group rather than individual entities. The name of the group becomes a part of the local name list. A group can contain principals as well as other groups.

Hacker A person who tries (and might succeed) to attack a computer security system for mere fun or other spurious reasons.

Handshake protocol A protocol that allows two entities to agree upon the session information during a session establishment.

Hash-based MAC MAC that uses a hash function to reduce the size of the data it processes.

Hash function A function that takes a variable-sized input and returns an output of fixed size.

Header A CMP component that contains the sender and recipient name, time of message, cryptographic algorithm used to encrypt the message.

Hierarchical PKI Architecture Also known as superior-subordinate architecture, PKI services in this model are provided by multiple CAs. All the CAs in this model share a trust relationship amongst themselves.

Hybrid PKI Architecture A combination of CA trust list, hierarchical PKI, and mesh PKI Architectures.

HyperText Transfer Protocol (HTTP) Is a standard protocol that is used to transfer content over the Internet.

HyperText Transfer Protocol Secure (HTTPS) It is a protocol that provides security to the information transmitted over the Internet.

IDEA International Data Encryption Algorithm. It is a symmetric block cipher, which uses a 128-bit key to encrypt data in blocks of 64 bits. This is why it is referred to as a block cipher method.

Identification certificate A certificate that contains the identification information of the entity to which the certificate is issued.

IETF Internet Engineers Task Force.

IKE Internet Key Exchange. This protocol is generally used in conjunction with the IPSec standard, where it enables IPSec communication.

Impersonation A security threat where an entity pretends to be someone it is not.

Indirect CRL A method that proposes the consolidation of CRLs, where a group of CAs makes one single authority responsible for issuing CRLs. This authority contains the revocation information of multiple CAs and thereby shares the load of other CAs.

Indirect CRL Authority (ICRLA) The authority trusted by a group of CAs to issue CRLs.

Initial certificate request A certificate request made by an entity other than the subject of the certificate already issued by the CA.

Initiator It is a computer or individual that starts the communication process with another computer or individual.

Institute of Electrical and Electronics Engineers (IEEE) A body that specifies various national and international standards.

Integrity A property that ensures that the message content is not altered during transit.

Interception An unauthorized individual intercepts the message and changes its content or uses it for unfair purposes. This attack affects the confidentiality of a message.

International Telecommunications Union - Telecommunications (ITU-T) An organization that recommends worldwide technology standards.

Internet A network of computers from all over the world that forms a worldwide network.

Internet Domain Name System Security Extensions (IDNSSE) Security extensions included in DNS to provide host and data authentication.

Internet Engineering Task Force (IETF) An organization that defines standards for Internet communication.

Internet Protocol Security (IPSec) A standard for secure transmission of TCP/IP traffic over the Internet. This is one of the primary protocols used in Virtual Private Network (VPN).

Internet Service Provider (ISP) Is a server that connects individual computers to the Internet.

Interruption The systems of the organization become unusable due to attacks by unauthorized users. This leads to systems being unavailable for use.

Intranet A TCP/IP based network that uses standard Internet services and applications within the confines of a particular organization.

Invalidity date The date on which a certificate becomes invalid.

Issuer name The name of the CA that has signed and issued the certificate.

Issuer unique identifier A unique ID of the certificate issuer.

Kerberos An authentication service developed by the Project Athena team at MIT.

Key A string of bits used widely in cryptography to encrypt and decrypt data. Given a cipher, a key determines the mapping of the plaintext to the ciphertext.

Key and certificate management It is the process of generating keys for encryption and signing, storing these keys in certificates, and administering these keys so that they are available to users when they are required.

Key backup The process of keeping a backup copy of the original key. Backing up the keys is an important process in certificate management. The key can be restored from the backup copy in case the user looses his/her private key.

Key compromise An unintentional disclosure of the keys to an entity other than the owner of the key. Key compromise results in a certificate becoming invalid.

Key generation A process of creating keys.

Key length The length of a key in bits. Data encrypted by using a 128-bit key is considered to be safer than the one encrypted by using a 64-bit key.

Key lifetime Is the time period for which a key is valid. Each company should have a policy that determines the key lifetime and considers the risks and threats of key disclosure due to brute force attacks.

Key management Processes involved in the creation, distribution, authentication, and storage of keys.

Key pair Combination of a private key and its corresponding public key, which is used in public key cryptography.

Key recovery A special feature of a key management scheme that allows messages to be decrypted even if the original key is lost.

Key recovery request and response message A message type that is required for transferring the private key for backup purpose.

Key rolling A process in which the older keys are replaced by new keys and the older keys are discarded. This is done on a periodic basis or as per the need or policy of the providing authority.

Key RR The resource records (RR) that contain the public key of an entity along with other information about an entity.

Key update It is the process of creating a new key pair and generating a corresponding public key certificate.

LAN (Local Area Network) A network that is used to connect computers in a single building, business, or campus environment.

Least significant bit The right-most bit of a byte.

Lightweight Directory Access Protocol (LDAP) A protocol used to query the information stored in an X.500 compliant database. LDAP is a standard protocol used to access data from the directory.

Linear cryptanalysis attack This method of attack is based on the concept that if you XOR some of the plaintext bits together, XOR some ciphertext bits together, and then XOR the results, you will get a single bit that is the XOR of some of the key bits.

Local cache A place in the local name server where all addresses known by a local DNS server during the name resolution process are stored.

Manual enrollment An enrollment process where the entity has to wait for CA request until the time the CA manually authenticates the identity of the entity.

MARS An algorithm developed by IBM as a part of the competition organized by NIST to develop a substitute of existing DES.

MD2, MD4, and MD5 These algorithms were released by RSA Data Security Inc. These algorithm can produce an output of a 128-bit hash value. MD5 was designed for an 8-bit processor, while MD4 and MD5 were developed for 32-bit processors.

MD5 (Message Digest Algorithm 5) A message digest algorithm released by RSA Laboratories. This algorithm is used for digitally signed messages and outputs a 128-bit message digest.

Mesh PKI Architecture In this PKI model, CAs share peer-to-peer relationships with each other. All CAs can act as a trust point in the model.

Message Authentication Code (MAC) A function that takes a variable length input and a key to produce a fixed-length output. An integrity check value is computed after the data has been compressed, and it is recomputed at the receiving end to verify data integrity.

Message digest The result of applying a hash function to a message.

Middle-person attack Person who intercepts a key during transit.

Modification The attack where the content of a message is modified by a third party, thus affecting the integrity of the message.

Most significant bit The left-most bit of a byte.

Multipurpose Internet Mail Extensions (MIME) An Internet standard that allows for transmissions of text, images, audio, or video in e-mail messages.

Name-binding certificate A certificate that binds a name to the principal to whom the certificate is issued. After being bound, this name becomes a part of the local names of the principal that is issuing the certificate.

Name server A DNS server is a server for querying IP addresses based on computer host names.

Next update A field in the CRL that contains the date on which the next CRL will be issued or the current CRL will expire.

NIST National Institute of Standards and Technology.

Non-repudiation A property of a cryptosystem, which ensures that the users cannot deny actions performed by them.

OCSP responder OCSP responder is a trusted entity, which on receiving the online requests for the revocation information processes the request and replies back with the status information of the certificates.

OID Also called an Object ID, it identifies an object uniquely in the X.500 directory.

One-way hash function A function that takes a variable-sized input and creates a fixed-size output. It converts a variable-length string into a fixed-length binary character sequence set. The original string cannot be retrieved from the fixed-length string.

Online Certificate Status Protocol (OCSP) A protocol used to obtain the online information about the revoked certificates.

Padding Extra bits added to a byte, key, plaintext, or even a password.

Password integrity mode Exchange mode of PKCS#12, where integrity is ensured by the use of a digital signature obtained from source platform's private signature key.

Password privacy mode Exchange mode of PKCS#12, where personal information is encrypted with a digital key derived from a user name and password.

Periodic rolling Key rolling done on a periodic basis.

PGP (Pretty Good Privacy) Developed in the year 1991 by Phil R. Zimmerman, PGP has gained huge popularity and is now being used by masses worldwide. PGP is one of the most powerful encryption techniques being used today as it makes use of some of the best-known cryptographic algorithms used in PKI.

PGP key ring Collection of public keys of entities with whom the owner intends to communicate. PGP key rings are of two types – private and public.

Piggyback Is the process of gaining unauthorized access to a system using a legitimate user's connection.

PKCS#7 A cryptographic standard that defines the syntax for cryptographic data such as digital signatures.

PKCS#10 A standard that defines the syntax for certificate requests.

PKI client Client applications, such as e-mail and Web browser, that request for resources and services for the server.

PKI management protocol A protocol that enables CAs to collect information required for issuing and revoking certificates.

Plaintext A message in an unencrypted form. This is also known as cleartext.

Policy mapping An extension that facilitates the inclusion of policy mapping information. For the policy of one CA be recognized by the entity of another CA, the policy of the first CA should be mapped with the policy of the second CA.

Principals The entities in SDSI. These principals can issue different types of certificates as per requirements.

Private key A part of a key pair that is used to decrypt the data. Private key is always kept with the owner. In public key cryptography, this key is the secret key. It is primarily used for decryption but is also used for encryption with digital signatures.

Proof of possession challenge and response message A message type that is required as a proof of owning the private key during key negotiation.

Protocol A series of steps that two or more parties agree upon to complete a task.

Public key A part of a key pair that is used to encrypt the data. Public key is transferred to the users and is typically stored in a public directory. In public key cryptography this key is made public to all; it is primarily used for encryption but can be used for verifying signatures.

Public key cryptography A cryptography technique based on a combination of two keys. This is also called asymmetric cryptography.

Public Key Cryptography Standards (PKCS) A series of cryptographic standards dealing with public key issues, published by RSA Laboratories.

Public key integrity mode Exchange mode of PKCS#12, in which personal information is encrypted with a symmetric key. This key is derived from the name of a user and the privacy password.

Public key privacy mode Exchange mode of PKCS#12, in which personal information is enveloped on the source platform by using a trusted public key of a known destination platform.

RA (Registration Authority) Falls under the jurisdiction of a Certificate Authority (CA) and validates users that apply for a certificate.

RC2 Designed to replace DES, this is a 64-bit block cipher algorithm that uses variable-sized keys. It is a variable key-size block cipher. It is faster than DES and is designed as a replacement for DES.

RC4 An advanced version of RC2, it is used in a number of commercial systems like Lotus Notes and Secure Netscape. RC4 is a stream symmetric cipher rather than a block symmetric cipher.

RC5 RC5 is another block cipher designed by Ron Rivest for RSA Security in 1994. Along with a variable key size, and a variable number of rounds, the size of RC5 data blocks is variable. The block size can range from 32 bits, 64 bits, to 128 bits. Similarly, the number of rounds can range from 0 to 255, while the key can range from 0 bits to 2040 bits in size.

RC6 An algorithm developed by Ron Rivest of RSA Labs, the creator of the widely used RC4 algorithm as part of the competition organized by NIST to develop a replacement of existing DES.

Record protocol A protocol that works below the handshake protocol and ensures a secure handshake process. The record protocol uses the session key negotiated during the handshake process.

Redirect CRLs The CRLs that point to multiple CRL distribution points where the CRLs are located. Using this, the location of CRL information can be changed without affecting the status of the certificate.

Registration Authority (RA) An authority that acts as an interface between a user and a CA. This receives the certificate request from the user, authenticates the identity of the user, and submits the certificate request to CA.

Registration authority console This is a server, which receives registration requests from users. On receiving the requests, this server communicates with the CAs.

Replay protection The protection against one transaction being recorded and replayed multiple times by a hacker.

Repository A publicly accessible database that contains the user's public key certificates and the Certificate Revocation Lists. This database is based on the X.500 recommendations.

Resolver An entity that issues a query to the DNS server to obtain the IP address of the requested name.

Resource Record (RR) The data in the form of records stored inside a zone.

Revocation delay The time difference between when the certificate is revoked and when the revocation information is posted in the CRL.

Revocation request and response message A message type that is required for requesting the revocation of a certificate and its response.

RFC Request For Comments. It is a series of specifications about the Internet that contain information about different protocols, procedures, and networking concepts.

Rijndael An algorithm designed by Daemen and Rijmen. This algorithm was one of the entries in the competition organized by NIST in an endeavor to find the replacement for DES.

RIPEMD-160 This hash algorithm was designed to replace MD4 and MD5 to provide better and safer hashing methodology. It can produce a 160-bit message digest.

Root It is the most trusted individual in a PKI system. It forms the basis of trust for the system.

Root CA The CA at the top of the CA hierarchy. The public key of a root CA is the most trusted one.

Root domain The root of the DNS hierarchy. It is denoted by a single dot.

RSA Stands for Rivest, Shamir, and Adelman, who developed the RSA algorithm. This public key encryption system is based on the factoring problem.

S-HTTP Secure HyperText Transfer Protocol. Provides security for transactions over WWW.

SCEP Simple Certificate Enrollment Protocol. Developed by Cisco Systems Inc., this is the communication protocol used by PKI.

SDSI Simple Distributed Security Infrastructure. Issues certificates on the basis of user credentials and attributes.

S-MIME Secure Multipurpose Internet Mail Extensions.

Secret Key A key used for both encryption and decryption.

Secure channel A communication medium that is safe from the threat of eavesdroppers.

Secure Electronic Transactions (SET) A set of specifications developed by Visa and MasterCard that define a protocol for secure credit card transactions.

Secure Hash Algorithm (SHA-1) A hash algorithm published by the U.S. government. This algorithm can output a 160-bit hash value.

Secure Multipurpose Internet Mail Extension (S/MIME) A standard proposed by Internet Engineering Task Force (IETF) for e-mail applications and secure transfer of electronic messages.

Secure Sockets Layer (SSL) The most widely used standard for providing secure access to Web sites. The server that uses SSL authenticates itself to the client by using a digital certificate and also encrypts transactions.

Security It is a set of techniques that are applied in an organization to ensure that the data in the organization is not compromised. Most security measures that are available today either make use of encryption technologies or make use of passwords to protect the system.

Security policy Policies defined by an organization for the use of cryptography. It also defines how the organization manages public and private keys.

Segmentation Mechanism of breaking large message into smaller blocks, so that these blocks can successfully be transmitted over the network.

Serpent An algorithm designed by Ross Anderson, Eli Biham, and Lars Knudsen, which was one of the entries in the competition organized by NIST to find a replacement of existing DES.

Server A system entity that provides a service in response to requests from clients. It manages network resources. Each server on the network performs specific tasks for the network, such as the file server, which manages files on the network, and the print server that maintains files to be sent to the printer.

Server certificate Certificate that is issued to servers to enable secure communication between clients and the server. Server certificates are typically used by a Web server or a specific URL of the Web server for securing the user name and password during the login process.

Session key A key for symmetric key cryptosystems, which is used for the one message or communication session.

Shared key The secret key shared by two (or more) users in a symmetric key cryptosystem.

SHA-1 Secure Hash Algorithm –1. Published by the U.S. government, this algorithm can produce an output of a 160-bit hash value.

SHS Secure Hash Standard. See SHA-1.

Signature certificate A certificate that is used to verify digital signatures. This is not used for encrypting data or for any other cryptographic function.

Signed data A content type field as defined by PKCS#7.

SIG RR A resource record that contains the signature information for verifying the corresponding RR.

Simple Certificate Enrollment Protocol (SCEP) A communication protocol developed by Cisco Systems. This protocol was designed for issuing certificates to the various network devices (by using whatever technologies were available) in a secure and scalable environment.

Simple Distributed Security Infrastructure (SDSI) A credential-based system that issues certificates on the basis of user credentials and attributes. This was introduced by Ron Rivest and Butler Lampson.

Simple Mail Transfer Protocol (SMTP) It is a protocol that enables transmitting e-mail messages from one computer to another.

Single CA Architecture Basic CA architecture, where just one CA issues and distributes certificates and CRLs to the requesting entities.

Single key cryptography A cryptography technique that is based on a secret key. It uses the same key for encrypting and decrypting data and is therefore not a very secure mechanism for encrypting the data. This is also called symmetric cryptography.

S/MIME It is a secure version of MIME. It provides support for many common cryptographic security methods, such as digital signatures and encryption. It allows users to transfer and accept information in a secure way.

Snail mail The traditional method of sending letters to an addressee. This is a slow method of communication.

Spam Unwanted e-mail.

SSH Secure Shell. It is used to secure communications between a client and the server.

Standalone CA A type of Windows 2000 CA that issues certificates to users and computers that are not a part of an organization.

Stream cipher Bit-wise secret key encryption algorithm.

Subject directory attributes An extension that contains the attribute values of an entity in addition to the subject's name.

Sub key The resultant value of scheduling a key during a round of block cipher.

Subject name The name of the certificate owner.

Subject public key information A public key with an algorithm identifier with which the key is used.

Subject unique identifier A unique ID of the subject of the certificate.

Subordinate CA A CA under the root CA in a PKI hierarchy. The certificate signature key of a subordinate CA is certified by another CA.

Subscriber An entity that is the subject of a certificate and possesses a private key that corresponds to the public key listed in the certificate.

Superior CA A CA who certifies the certificate signature key of another CA.

Suspended certificates Certificates that have not been revoked and cannot be used until they are activated again.

Symmetric cipher Encryption algorithm that uses the same key for encryption as well as decryption.

Symmetric key cryptography See Single key cryptography.

This update A field in the CRL that contains the date on which the CRL is issued.

Threat A condition that is likely to adversely affect the working of a system. Such a condition can completely destroy a system, disclose confidential information to unauthorized users, or modify essential data.

Time-to-live (TTL) The time for which the entries in the local cache are stored.

Timestamp A record that links a document to a key.

Transport Layer Security (TLS) A protocol that is used to encrypt all Web communications, thereby providing a secure channel of communication. TLS is an extended version of the SSL protocol.

Triple-DES A cryptographic algorithm that encrypts data three times. See also 3DES.

Trust List A compilation of trusted certificates that are used to authenticate other certificates.

Trusted certificate A certificate that is trusted by the users. This certificate consists of public keys, which initiate certification paths.

Trusted Third Parties (TTP) PKI systems operated by commercial CA outside an organization. It is an organization that is approved and trusted by the parties involved in the exchange to provide security services, such as a Certification Authority.

Twofish An algorithm from Counterpane Internet Security, Inc.; it was one of the entries in the competition organized by NIST to develop a replacement of existing DES. This design was highly suited for large microprocessors and smart card microprocessors.

User certificate Certificates that are issued to individual entities or organizations for authentication.

User Datagram Protocol (UDP) A connectionless, unreliable data transmission protocol. This protocol works at the transport layer.

VA Validation Authority. Verifies the status of a certificate.

Validity A field that contains two dates. These two dates indicate the beginning and end of the certificate validity period.

Verification The act of finding out the right identity of an entity.

Virus A computer program created with malicious intent and is capable of replicating itself repeatedly without user knowledge or permission. One category of viruses attaches itself to files so when the infected file is executed, the virus also is executed. The other category of virus resides in a computer's memory and infects files.

Virtual Private Network (VPN) VPN is an acronym for virtual private network. It is a network that is constructed by using public medium such as the Internet. These systems use a variety of security mechanisms to ensure that only authorized users access the network and that the data cannot be intercepted.

Whois model A model used by Yellow Pages directory comprising a single database.

Whois++ model A model based on Whois model followed by Yellow Pages directory service to enable easy search. Whois++ uses interconnected index servers that contain pointers to the Whois++ servers.

World Wide Web It is part of the Internet system that contains Web pages. A user can access a Web page using a Web browser.

Worms Parasitic computer programs that replicate. They can create copies of themselves on the same computer or can send the copies to other computers via a network.

X.500 A standard proposed by International Organization for Standardization (ISO) and International Telecommunication Union (ITU) for distributed global directory service. This directory service is used for the storage of certificates and CRLs.

X.509 A standard proposed by (ISO) and (ITU) for certificates and CRLs. X.509 defines the authentication framework for global directory services and is globally accepted by companies involved in producing PKI products.

XML Refers to EXtensible Markup Language. It is a standard for formatting Web pages developed by W3C. The formatting instructions along with the information being formatted are saved in a standard text format that is readable by any ASCII text editor.

XOR eXclusive OR. A Boolean operator that results in a zero if the two values that it operates on are the same. If the two values are different, the resultant of the operation is one.

Zone A zone is an authority for a domain and manages all the information of the domain. A domain can have multiple zones, depending upon how the domain structure is designed.

Index

Numbers & Symbols